GOING TO THE GRADIES

Jon Traer, M.D.

Published by Jon Traer, M.D.
2383 Julienton Drive, N.E.
Townsend, GA 31331-5021
USA
(912) 832-5150

Publisher's Note
Going to the Gradies is a work of fiction. Characters, names, places, and incidents mentioned are a product of the author's imagination, or are used fictitiously. Any resemblance to persons living or dead, or to businesses, establishments, and locals is entirely coincidental.

Cover Design
The cover design is by the author. However, the artwork on the back cover depicting Grady Memorial Hospital is derived from a lithograph of an original watercolor done by Ben Shute (1905-1986). This art was apparently commissioned as one of a dozen "Atlanta Scenes" done by Shute as a promotional calendar for the First National Bank of Atlanta. That Atlanta bank no longer exists. Should Ben Shute still be alive today, the author would thank him for capturing the "essence of the Gradies."

ISBN 1-4392-0861-1

Limited First Edition (2007)
Printed in the United States of America
by Darien Printing & Graphics
Darien, Georgia

Subsequent Editions
Available Through Amazon.com

ACKNOWLEDGMENTS

A work of fiction is almost never written in isolation. This is especially true regarding novice fiction authors, such as myself.

To my readers and proofreaders: Joan and Ed Stelle, Virginia and Harold Hicks, Karen Eckley, Pamela Pollack, and Trip Giudici, I give a very special thanks for their patience, suggestions, and expertise.

To an experienced author, Pamela Bauer Mueller, many thanks for your encouragement, advice, and information regarding the self-publication process.

To the Atlanta-based businesses and various institutions mentioned in this book: Indisputably, your dedication to excellence is not questioned. A special thanks goes to Atlanta's Grady Memorial Hospital, its patients, and devoted staff. The author's training at Grady provided most of the inspiration needed to create the fictional characters and events portrayed in this book.

And last but not least, a thanks to Kaye, my supportive nurse-wife. You're still my hazel-eyed sweetheart.

AUTHOR'S NOTE

This is a work of fiction about Dr. Mark Telfair. His surgical training occurs in the racially tense 1960s and largely takes place at Atlanta's Grady Memorial Hospital. The relatively naive young doctor finds Grady's inner-city environment a crisp contrast to the neighborhood where he grew up: Atlanta's Buckhead. Before experiencing Grady, he'd erroneously thought all of Atlanta was similar to Buckhead. What a colossal mistake!

Warning: Much to editorial chagrin, political correctness is here largely cast aside. If you have a view of reality that borders on innocent, this book is not for you. If you're a hyphenated-American, a staunch feminist, sensitive about your national origin, tender about your faith, a homophile of either flavor, or you simply find yourself easily offended by four-letter words—stop reading now!

Non-prudish adult Southern Bubbas and Bubbets, please read on. I think you'll find the reading humorous at times, sad at others. Either way, it's about as authentic as fiction gets. I can only promise Dr. Mark Telfair will present a view of a surgeon's training not often revealed to a layman ... which brings to mind an important question: Where did *your* surgeon train?

CONTENTS

ACKNOWLEDGMENTS...i

AUTHOR'S NOTE ii

INTRODUCTION iv

1. MR. NEW DOCTOR...1
2. CLINITEST TABLETS..10
3. THE SUPPOSITORY..15
4. TROUBLE MAKING HIS WATER 19
5. ONE FOOT IN THE TOILET.....................................23
6. MISTER CLEAN 33
7. I EATS BROOMS 40
8. THE CUE BALL..51
9. ICE WATER, PUS, AND GOLDFISH.............................62
10. FISH AND SPIDERS 74
11. HOT BODY, BONES, AND DNA 80
12. COWBOY...92
13. THE BUSH HOOK...104
14. WHERE THE SUN DON'T SHINE...............................118
15. MISS FRANCES 131
16. A STRANGE SOUND AND DOIN' THINGS RIGHT..............141
17. A STAR IN THE EAST..151
18. ZACK GOES TO MEDICINE 160
19. A COP AND DOCS MAKE A ROOTER'S DAY....................169
20. ANOTHER AMA AND A NEW ROOF 181
21. UNDER HOUSE ARREST 190
22. GOING TO THE DOGS...206
23. GOING TO POSSUM TROT 222
24. TUFFSTUFF..241
25. SAFE HARBOR...247
26. OFF TO THE WILD BLUE YONDER.............................250
27. COMMITMENT AND CONFINEMENT............................262

INTRODUCTION

To be, or not to be, that is the question ...
—from Shakespeare's *Hamlet*

To be a surgeon, or to be a mechanical engineer? The troubling question was one faced by pampered Atlanta teenager, Mark Telfair. He'd lived all his life in Buckhead, a moderately affluent neighborhood in Northeast Atlanta. During the entire summer of 1956, he approached his quandary with the same sheer desperation portrayed by the young Prince of Denmark in Shakespeare's *Hamlet*. In actuality, the problem wasn't larger than life itself; it just seemed that way to the frustrated teen, who'd been unable to make up his mind about what to be, or not to be, following his high school graduation. Mark Telfair even secretly hoped one of his two college applications would be rejected, and thus settle the issue for him. No such luck. He'd been promptly accepted at both Emory and Georgia Tech. Suddenly, he'd realized his summer vacation—his precious decision-making time—had rapidly grown short. In mid-August, mere days before his 18th birthday, he finally decided: *premed at Emory.*

For young Telfair, that very decision had been the starting point of an extended journey. His trip would not be charted in miles; instead, it would be measured in years. Four premed college years, then four postgraduate years at Emory's med school, all passed with deceptive calm and amazing ease. The smooth academic sailing he'd experienced upon seas sheltered by Emory's ivory towers had given him a very false sense of security, one soon to be ripped away. The final five-year leg of his educational adventure would suddenly grow turbulent. Storm clouds would soon form; they began to gather the instant he began his surgical internship at Atlanta's Grady Memorial Hospital. The 1,400-bed inner-city hospital would quickly snatch off his security blanket, his Buckhead-cocoon would split widely open, and he'd soon get his first glimpses of life in the real world—the one that existed outside the shelters afforded by his Buckhead neighborhood and the Emory campus. His previously calm life would soon begin breaking into clearly definable chunks of emotion: pride, fear, sorrow, joy, love, humor, and utter embarrassment. Those feelings would soon become guiding waypoints during his stormy voyage to the real world. All those elements would soon be absorbed into his new life's chaotic norm ... a norm that would diligently attempt to hammer out yet another qualified general surgeon. Once the assault was squarely upon him, he knew one thing for certain: *Humor* was essential to his survival—without it, he'd never make it through the five-year storm he'd just entered.

1

MR. NEW DOCTOR

As a third- and fourth-year Emory medical student, Mark Telfair had been inside the intimidating hulk of Atlanta's Grady Memorial Hospital. His visits there as a med student had centered largely around obstetrics. Most of the Emory medical students actually enjoyed obstetrics, even the ones who had no intention of someday becoming an obstetrician. They liked it simply because it gave them some of their first real hands-on clinical experience. Mark Telfair had attended many lectures at Grady, and had experienced highly supervised introductions to several other areas of clinical medicine. Those introductions included brief visits to Grady's two ERs; he was told over 300 emergency patients were seen daily. It didn't matter a bit to him that many of Grady's patients, for some strange reason, improperly called Grady Hospital "The *Gradies.*" Mark Telfair would soon discover all of his med school visits to Grady had been just that: *merely visits.* He'd soon learn he would have to be there continually—day in, and day out—before he became a true insider, and really understood life on the other side of Atlanta's tracks.

On the 1st of July, 1964, Dr. Mark Telfair anticipated his presence at Grady this sticky-hot morning would be somewhat different, especially in contrast to all his previous visits there as a medical student. A few weeks earlier he'd graduated from Emory Medical School, recently passed the licensing examination given by the Georgia State Board of Medical Examiners, and had been accepted as a straight surgical intern by Atlanta's Grady Memorial Hospital. It was the first day his crisp white uniform's name patch indicated he was a *real doctor;* a similar patch had recently identified him as Mark M. Telfair - Emory Medical Student. Carla Lay, his girlfriend of several years, had gotten up early and had sewn his new name patch on his new white jacket. She'd warmly kissed him goodbye before he left the apartment they shared in Northeast Atlanta near Buckhead. The 15-mile drive to Grady took longer than he'd expected. *Damn traffic,* he thought, fearing the embarrassment of being late on his first day of internship. Briskly, he walked from the Grady parking lot to the hospital. His scalp beneath short dark brown hair became damp, possibly a combination of both anxiety and heat. He adjusted his wire-rimmed Ray-Bans while walking and felt they really looked cool, while protecting his dark brown eyes from Atlanta's glaring morning sunlight. As he neared the hospital, his spotless new white Hush Puppy shoes were soundless on the sidewalk. His muscular body—all 145 pounds of it—tried to stand tall, but at five foot six that was virtually impossible. He settled for trying to appear relaxed and casual, and whistled a pop tune as he entered Grady's front door for the first day of his surgical internship. With the confidence of a bantam rooster, he strutted to the reception desk inside Grady's cavernous marble-clad lobby. He checked his watch. *Made it on time ... actually a little early,* his relieved mind told him.

"Hi," he said to the ancient hospital receptionist, whose stark wrinkled face seemed frozen in a permanent scour. "I'm Mark Telfair. *Doctor* Mark Telfair ... just reporting for my straight surgical internship," he said confidently.

"I know exactly who you are," replied the elderly receptionist. "I may be old but I can still read you know ... and I should tell you, your name tag's sewn to the *wrong* side of your jacket!" With a crooked arthritic finger she quickly scanned a printed personnel list on her desk. "Better get your young little doctor-butt over to the GAC by eight sharp!"

Taking a half-step back, Mark spoke. "Ma'am, I really can't believe that! That just can't be right! GAC? G-A-C ... are you absolutely sure?"

"Yeah I'm sure. GAC! As in General Admissions Clinic, *Doctor!* You'll be there the first two months of your internship, *Doctor.* Know where it is?" she responded, with a totally irritated tone, and a sour face that reminded him of an albino prune.

He nodded a quick "Yes," then stepped back from her desk and turned, hoping she wouldn't notice his intensely flushed face. He was confident his dark Ray-Bans hid the disappointment he knew was certainly present in his eyes. This long-awaited day was so special to him, and the first 30 seconds of it ...*Well, it just isn't going worth a damn!* he thought.

As a medical student he'd gained basic familiarity with the hospital's confusing layout. He had little trouble finding the GAC. Mark Telfair also knew the GAC had virtually nothing to do with surgery, and since he'd signed up for a straight surgical internship, he still felt some grave mistake had been made regarding his first intern assignment. Unfamiliar dressed-in-white peers soon began to show up at the GAC, also there for their own first day of internship. As they talked among themselves, Dr. Mark Telfair soon learned the three types of Grady internships—straight surgical, rotating, or straight medical—required a two-month period where *all* interns did time in the GAC. Though not at all happy with the situation, Mark felt at least some comfort knowing that he'd be getting the undesirable GAC tour out of the way at the very outset. He also felt some consolation knowing that he alone had not been selected for a special "punitive tour" in the GAC.

Precisely at 8:00 a.m., she appeared at the GAC to orient her dozen rookie intern recruits. "She" was one Ms. Rosa Costellanos, RN—Supervisor GAC, or so her highly polished name tag stated. She was a large woman, all muscle, in her mid-40s, just under six feet tall, and carried about 170 pounds of aesthetically distributed weight. She had pretty dark eyes, and shining short black hair that complemented her olive complexion. Though obviously part Hispanic, she would subsequently speak to them in completely unaccented English. Impeccably dressed in a crisply starched white uniform, complete with a white cap bearing a Grady logo pin, she radiated total professional perfection. Mark could not help but note her white shoes were absolutely spotless. He even felt she was attractive, though not in a soft feminine way. She cleared her throat immediately prior to addressing the assemblage of neophyte doctors, but even before she opened her mouth for her first words, she emitted absolute and total authority. They all knew she was "God" ... and they'd all be at her mercy for the next 60 days.

Ms. Costellanos rapidly explained to the group that the GAC was not intended to be an emergency room, but was similar in function to a general practitioner's office. Many of the patients had been coming to the GAC for more years than their GAC doctors' averaged ages. Most patients would not be seriously ill. Many would have only minor chronic medical problems. Some patients would have minor acute illnesses, and only a few would be sick enough to be hospitalized, and admitted to the hospital to be cared for by the "experienced doctors," she'd said.

After completing her brief general introductory remarks, the group learned the honeymoon was over. Ms. Costellanos ushered the new doctors individually to one of the dozen exam rooms sequentially located down the long central GAC hallway. At each door she instructed them to remain standing in the doorway, facing her in the hallway. There she issued to each man well-memorized *identical* instructions:

"Doctor, you will always address me as Ms. Costellanos. This room will be your room. Use the same room each day, so remember the number on your door. No smoking, eating, or beverages are permitted in the exam rooms. Keep your door open at all times unless doing an exam of a personal nature. Notify me if you need a chaperone for a personal exam. Do not leave the GAC unless you tell me you are leaving. I will tell you when it's time to go to lunch. The restroom you will use is the one at the end of the hall marked STAFF. Be advised that I also use that same restroom, so put the seat up when using, down when done, and aim well. I will personally escort patients and charts to your room. When you complete the exam, patient instruction, and charting, return the chart to the patient. Instruct him or her to return his or her chart to the table at the end of the hall. My private office is behind the unmarked door next to the staff bathroom. Always knock before entering either the restroom or my office. Do you have any questions Doctor?"

As each young doctor was instructed, Mark couldn't help but wonder why she'd been so inefficient. Why didn't she just assemble the whole group, and issue her rules (*commandments,* they'd soon call them) as a single statement for all to hear at once?

The answer soon became self-evident. After being instructed, each young doctor had somehow frozen in disbelief, and remained standing in the open doorway of his assigned GAC exam room. In so doing, each couldn't help but overhear her repeat the *same* rules verbatim some 12 times as she moved on down the line. As they all heard the commandment repetitions, they all knew she meant exactly what she'd said, and they'd better not dare claim they'd somehow not heard or forgotten a single rule.

After the last doctor was instructed, Ms. Costellanos announced to the group that they'd be seeing their first patients in five minutes. She then vanished from sight. Feeling they had a small break, and still in shock, they began to whisper to their nearest neighbors. Everyone remained frozen in their respective exam room doorways, poking their heads out just far enough to look up and down the hall.

"God, whatta bitch. Gotta be PMS," the neighbor to Mark's right whispered, with a slow Southern accent.

Mark heard a Northern twang to his left. "I musta taken a wrong freakin' turn gettin' here. This place must be freakin' Fort Benning! And she's the drill instructor!"

Though her looks were a little too good to accurately fit Mark's stereotype for a gay female, he heard himself whisper, "I think she's gotta be a bull dyke, and maybe she just isn't getting enough."

From several doors down, and way too loud for Mark's comfort, he heard another unfamiliar sharp Northern accent. "She wants our nuts, fellas. That bitch really wants our freakin' nuts! I don't know 'bout you guys, but I'm wearing a steel jock strap tomorrow."

Their conversations apparently went undetected, and their

whispering abruptly terminated when the first patient was delivered to exam room number one. Mark was located about halfway down the GAC hall. He had finally extricated himself from the door frame and sat quietly at the desk in his small exam room—just waiting for the delivery of his first-ever real patient. Mark discovered his palms were moist when Ms. Costellanos ushered the patient to the chair beside his desk. He had extended his own to shake the patient's hand, but Ms. Costellanos quickly interceded, and blocked the move by thrusting the patient's thick chart into Mark's sweaty hand.

She then introduced them. "Minnie Lee Bloodworth, this is your doctor—Dr. Telfair. He's new here, so please be patient with him."

Turning more toward Mark, Ms. Costellanos spoke without emotion. "Doctor, Minnie Lee's got a pretty bad UTI. Her UA's on the chart. Any questions?"

Before Mark could muster a reply, Ms. Costellanos left the room. He was now alone with his very first real patient as a real doctor. Minnie Lee was jet-black, and according to her chart, in her late 70s. She had been coming to the GAC some 30 years, several years longer than he'd been alive. She was dressed in what he assumed to be her Sunday best, but he noted her clothes were much too heavy for the season, and they embodied the strong fragrance of mothballs. Her head was crowned with a close-fitting narrow-brimmed black hat, one studded with tiny bright yellow plastic flowers. Except at her forehead, circumferential miniature snow-white hair plaits poked their way from beneath the hat's brim, and contrasted sharply with the color of her hat and skin. She kept a well-worn brown paper sack clutched in her lap with her left hand. Mark assumed the sack was her make-do purse. But despite her appearance, illness, and age, she was bright-eyed, and wore a very kind, warm, and knowing smile.

Without hesitation, Minnie Lee first broke the conversational ice. "Welcome to the Gradies Mr. New Doctor. I's so glad to knows ya, and don't worry yo'self none a'tall 'bout Ms. C ... 'cause she bark a heap worse than she bite!"

A feeling of relief crept over him. He felt lucky his very first patient had prior experience with Ms. Costellanos and with the GAC, and probably had experienced many other first-time real doctors to boot.

With the ice thus broken, Mark knew he needed to get down to business. Though he'd just had the patient handed to him prediagnosed by Ms. C as "UTI" (urinary tract infection), with supporting "UA" (urine analysis), he felt obligated to go through the motions of eliciting the proper patient history to record in the GAC record. To this end he began to question Minnie Lee.

"Minnie Lee, do you have any urinary discomfort when you void?" he asked with budding professionalism, Ray-Bans perched atop his head. He intently stared into the depths of her dark brown eyes.

After a long pause, and with a very puzzled expression, Minnie Lee replied with faltering words. "Uh ... say what ... now again ... uh, Mr. New Doctor?"

Sensing his question had missed the mark, he reformulated his query. "Minnie Lee, do you have any pain when you urinate?"

Another pregnant pause ensued, only to be followed by another "Say what now again, Mr. New Doctor?"

Frustrated, he again reformulated his question. "Minnie Lee ... does your water ever burn?"

He sensed his question may have finally hit the mark. She tightly closed her eyes, and seemed to be in the absolute greatest depth of thought. Eyes still closed, her head began to move slightly to and fro, almost as if she were in a hypnotic state. After a full 30 seconds of complete silence, her eyes still shut and head bobbing, Mark spoke to her again. "Minnie Lee? Minnie Lee, did you hear my question? Does your water ever burn?"

With her hypnotic thinking spell abruptly broken, her eyes popped open, and she blinked a few times before answering. "Doctor I hears yo' question all right ... but I don't rightly know now ya see, Mr. New Doctor ... 'cause *I ain't never really tried to set fire to it!*"

Literally choking on the impulse to burst into totally uncontrolled laughter, he rapidly excused himself, left the room, *closed* the door, walked several doors down the hall and allowed the laughter to come. It was either that or pee in his pants in front of his very first real patient. Unfortunately, his uncontrolled hysterics were heard by Ms. C. She instantly appeared out of nowhere to remind Mark that he'd just violated the "Keep your door open at all times" rule she'd personally issued to him only ten minutes ago. He knew he was really in trouble when Ms. C immediately invited him to explain himself in her private office.

Once in the confines of her office, all traces of his laughter were ancient history, his face now solemn. He related the questioning process he'd used with Minnie Lee as well as the responses he'd gotten from her. Poker-faced, Ms. C just sat there patiently listening to his rather lengthy explanation. She kept her hands in prayer position, her paired index fingers lightly touching her closed lips, her elbows resting on her desktop. Ms. C's unblinking dark eyes stared directly into his own as he anxiously explained himself. Initially no emotion on her part was apparent, then ever so slowly her eyes closed, and the corners of her mouth crept upward in a slowly evolving smile. Her smile quickly faded. She abruptly opened her eyes and spoke. "It just better not happen again, Doctor ... but I must admit, that's the funniest goddamn UTI history I've ever heard! Oh, and by the way, your name patch is on the *wrong* side of your jacket. Get your girlfriend or wife to fix it. Do not try to do it yourself. You surgeon wannabes can't sew worth a shit—at least not when it comes to clothes. And for God's sake get those silly looking sunglasses off the top of your head!" He quickly placed his sunglasses in his jacket pocket while being curtly dismissed. As instructed, he closed her door upon leaving.

As he stepped away, a little shocked at her language, he couldn't help but hear— and even feel—her hearty laughter. It literally reverberated off her thick closed office door. As he walked back down the long GAC hallway toward his abandoned first patient, he heard Ms. C's door abruptly open behind him. He turned to see her filling the doorway; she was no longer laughing, but motioning with her index finger for him to return to her office.

He again entered her office, closing the door behind himself. "Don't sit down," she quickly said. "This won't take long. If you don't have a wife or girlfriend to fix your jacket's name tag, give it to me when we close the clinic today. I'll fix it for you at home tonight, and I'll bring it back in the morning. And by the way, Dr. Telfair, most of these GAC patients are actually good Rooters, but you really need to learn to communicate with them on their own level. You'll never be effective if you speak above the patient's level of comprehension." Mark was sure Ms. Costellanos was now finally through, but he was mistaken. "And one more thing, Doctor, nothing that's done or said in my office ever leaves. Understood?"

Following a "Yes, Ms. Costellanos," and military-style about face, he started back to his abandoned first patient for the second time. As he again walked down the long hall he couldn't help but think about Ms. C: *Bull dyke? ... maybe. PMS? ... maybe. Bitch? ... definitely! Bark worse than the bite? ... Minnie Lee's right! But exactly what in the heck is a Rooter?* As a medical student visiting Grady, he'd heard the house staff occasionally use the word "Rooter" in reference to a Grady patient, but he'd noticed Rooter was never spoken in front of a patient, and he'd never seen it written down anywhere in the hospital record.

When Mark opened the door and entered his room, Minnie Lee was just as he'd left her—just patiently sitting there with the same Cheshire cat grin. "Sorry to leave you in such a hurry Minnie Lee, but I had to use the restroom," he lied.

"That be all right, Mr. New Doctor, but if you needs to leave again in such a hurry, jus' be sho you leaves dat do' open. You know Ms. C! She got dem rules. Jus' be glad she ain't caught you shettn' de do'. She got rules fo' ever'thing. She ev'n got rules for us'uns too, you know."

Due to delays of his own making, Mark had already spent 45 minutes trying to see his first patient. He rapidly completed Minnie Lee's history, then wrote appropriate notes in her chart. Next, he gave her prescriptions for her UTI, a lab request for a urine culture, and an appointment to return to the GAC in three days. He handed her the chart, and told her where to take it.

"I knows e'zakly where to take it, so don't you fret none. I get it there. But ain't you done fo'got sump'thin Mr. New Doctor?" she asked, no obvious criticism intended.

"Not that I know of Minnie Lee," he boldly replied, though secretly uncertain.

"De *sack* Doctor! You done fo'got to check my sack! That be one of Ms. C's rules fo' us de patient, you know. We always s'pose to show de doctor de sack, so dey kin check hit, you know." Minnie Lee dutifully handed the worn brown paper "pocketbook" sack to Mr. New Doctor.

As Mark accepted it, he was surprised that it was much heavier than he'd anticipated. He unrolled its frazzled top, and carefully emptied the contents onto the top of his desk. It contained all her medications. There were three prescription medications: digitalis, potassium, and a mild diuretic. All had been issued by the Grady in-house pharmacy, and all three drugs he'd earlier noted when reviewing her chart. The drugs had been prescribed for mild hypertension and congestive heart failure diagnosed at the GAC several years ago. The sack's remaining contents revealed an assortment of at least ten over-the-counter laxatives—plus a half-empty jar of Vick's Salve.

"Minnie Lee, please let me have your chart back just a minute," he said as he placed the medicines back in her sack. He opened her chart, and made a quick addition to the notes he'd just written regarding her UTI: "Check laxative use next visit." He returned the chart to her and smiled. "See you in three days ... OK?"

Minnie Lee started to leave. She turned in the doorway, still clutching both chart and sack, and presented a large warm smile. "If it be the Lawd's will, I sho be back Mr. New Doctor ... and I think we goin' to be gettin' along jus' fine!"

Minnie Lee had been gone mere nanoseconds when Ms. C appeared in the doorway with a second patient and their chart. Just as she'd done with Minnie Lee, Ms. C went through the same brief introduction and description of the patient's problem. Ms. C then paused, and turned to

Dr. Telfair. She looked at her large man's-style wristwatch, then spoke. "Doctor you'd better pick it up, or you'll never see the 20 patients I've got scheduled for you today—and you probably want to eat lunch before midnight tonight!"

CLINITEST TABLETS

Two weeks later Mark was adjusting to the GAC routine, as were his 11 peers. Regarding Minnie Lee Bloodworth's UTI, he'd seen her in follow-up on two subsequent occasions. All was going well with Minnie Lee. Her UTI had completely cleared. He'd simplified her laxative regimen, and had ruled out any serious underlying cause for her constipation.

The 12 GAC interns had elected to call themselves The Dirty Dozen (or Double Ds), thus distinguishing their group from the many other intern groups simultaneously doing their first rotations in other hospital areas. Each of the Double Ds had seen about 300 GAC patients apiece since their first day. All were now on a first name basis, even branding one another with nicknames. During lunchtime bull sessions in the cafeteria, most of the group had decided Ms. C really wasn't such a bad person after all. Knowing his girlfriend, Carla, couldn't sew clothing any better than he, Mark gladly accepted Ms. C's generous offer to fix his name-on-the-wrong-side jacket. She'd even washed, starched, and ironed it before returning it to him on the morning of his second day in the GAC. He had to admit Ms. C's stitching on the correctly placed name tag was *impeccable*.

About a week earlier, Mr. Eduardo Costellanos, Ms. C's well-dressed and extremely masculine husband, had come to the clinic. He had their two pretty early-teen daughters in tow. No one knew exactly why he'd briefly dropped by the GAC with their kids, but Eduardo's brief visit put the bull dyke issue to rest, or at least it did for Mark.

A few in the group now admitted Ms. C was a "damn good nurse," as if their neophyte experience qualified them to make such a professional judgment. Mark already realized she knew a heck of a lot more clinical medicine than he. If he'd just let it happen, she'd teach him something. He also knew she was what made the GAC work. She was the one who maintained the level of discipline and order—for both doctors and patients—essential to effective clinic function. He wished Ms. C was the supervisor of Grady's Surgical Outpatient Clinic, where he'd hopefully spend some time later in his internship.

Mark was sitting at his desk reflecting upon what his 14th day in the GAC might bring. *It certainly won't be anything I can cut on ... or sew up,* he thought.

His daydreams were abruptly erased by Ms. C. "Doctor, this is Alberta Brown. No middle name. We've got a bunch of Alberta Browns at Grady, so be sure the chart is for the correct one. Just be sure the address, age, hospital number, et cetera, are for the correct Alberta Brown. Alberta was in the Medical ER last night with dizziness, and was discovered to be diabetic. Her ER sheet and this morning's FBS (fasting blood sugar) are on the chart. Here is a sample of her urine that's about five minutes old. Any questions Doctor?"

Dr. Telfair had no questions, and promptly introduced himself to Alberta Brown. In terms of general demeanor, Alberta Brown seemed to be almost a carbon copy of his very first GAC patient with the UTI. Alberta was a little heavier, and not quite as old as Minnie Lee. Also, she wasn't carrying a sack. He'd already learned to check the sack—first thing—with each new patient.

Mark studied the fasting blood sugar lab report a moment, then spoke. "Alberta, I'm sorry, but it looks like you've got diabetes."

"You be a talkin' about sugar, ain't you Doctor?"

"Yes Alberta, I'm afraid so."

"Ain't got to take no sugar shots is I?" Her question told Mark she was obviously concerned about the possible need for insulin injections.

"Don't know just yet, Alberta. We'll first try to use some sugar pills. May come to sugar shots though."

With a sigh and resigned look, Alberta stared at Mark before speaking. "Doctor, I jus' knowed I'd catch it one day! I jus' knowed hit fo' sho. Ya see now, Mr. Doctor, on account a whole heap of my peoples, they got sugar too. And I sho is been bein' 'round 'em a heap here lately."

Mark elected not to even attempt to explain to Alberta that diabetes was not at all contagious. He found her analysis of the cause of her illness more sad than amusing, and began explaining—on her level—about diabetes in general, and about the additional and ongoing testing that would have to be done. He told her they'd start with some changes in her diet, and a low dose of oral medicine—a "sugar pill"—to lower her blood sugar. He next carefully explained how to "check her water" for sugar at home three times daily. Using a Clinitest Test Kit he kept in his desk drawer, he demonstrated the test for her in detail. Using the urine sample delivered by Ms. C, he placed the measured drops of her urine into the clear glass test tube, then dropped the aspirin-sized test tablet into the tube. The tube's contents vigorously boiled as the chemical reaction took place; like magic the tube's content turned a different color. He showed her how to compare the resultant color with a printed color scale card supplied with the kit. By comparing tube and card colors, she'd be able to read the urine sugar level over a range from negative to four-plus. She seemed to follow his instructions. To be sure she understood, he emptied and cleaned the tube, then had her repeat the test process, doing each step totally by herself. *She did it perfectly.*

"Any questions?" he asked Alberta.

"Jus' one, Doctor. Why do dat tube get so hot? I don't see no fire, but hit get so hot you can't ev'n hol' it at de bottom where it's a bubblin'."

Mark tried to be completely honest. "Alberta, I'm not really sure. I guess it's just a chemical reaction that gives off a lot of heat. After you get your own test tablets, just be sure you don't let any children get hold of them. Could be dangerous if they did."

Satisfied she'd be able to do testing on her own, he gave her a prescription for an oral medicine (Orinase) to lower her blood sugar. He also gave her a prescription for a Clinitest Test Kit identical to the one she'd satisfactorily used in his presence. A dietary instruction sheet and a sheet where she'd record her daily urine sugar readings were given as well. He also gave her a lab slip to have another FBS done about an hour before she'd be seeing him again in ten days.

Feeling confident he'd done a satisfactory job of explaining so much to her in just 20 minutes, Mark dismissed Alberta from his mind, and busied himself with the many other patients Ms. C would deliver on that and subsequent days. But instead of the ten days scheduled, Alberta Brown returned to the GAC in the early morning only five days later. When she was brought to his room by Ms. C, Alberta looked terrible. As she sat down beside him at his desk, she obviously didn't feel well either. Ms. C handed him a fresh urine specimen and Alberta's chart, both of which Mark placed on his desk.

With the specimen, chart, and patient thus delivered, Ms. C looked at Mark with a grave expression. "Doctor, I need to talk to you in my office NOW!" She immediately started walking to her office. Mark instantly became anxious as he followed her.

Once inside her office, Mark became defensive. "Just exactly what have I done now! I haven't broken any more of your precious rules!"

She placed a finger to her lips, indicating he should shut up. "Doctor, don't be so sensitive and defensive. Just calm down—don't get your Jockeys in a wad. Did I *say* you'd broken any of my 'commandments,' as I know you guys call them? Did I?"

"No. No, you didn't say that," Mark admitted calming down.

"Doctor, you're in my office so I can tell you Alberta Brown is one sick chick. This Rooter is *really* sick, and I didn't want to talk in front of her. It just might scare the crap out of her! So, Doctor, quickly go back to your room and find out what's wrong with her. Then come back to my office. OK?"

Mark nodded he understood, and left her office returning immediately to his sick patient.

"Good morning Alberta," Mark said, now deeply concerned. "You sure don't look like you feel too good today."

"Lawd, Doctor, I sho feels po' ... ev'n feels lower than a snake's belly in a wagon track. My thoat's a closin' up too, and I jus' feels bad all over."

Mark checked her vital signs. She had no fever, but her blood pressure was a little low, her heart rate and breathing far too fast. He looked inside her mouth. Her throat was definitely red, and he thought her tongue might be slightly swollen. He checked the FBS she'd had done in the lab about an hour ago. The report indicated her blood glucose level was substantially elevated. Even though she had no fever, Mark first thought she perhaps had some type of viral upper respiratory infection that was causing her diabetes to go wild.

Not really happy with the viral infection idea, Mark directed his mind down a different path. "Alberta, where is that paper I gave you to write down the sugar tests you did on your water?"

She handed him the brown paper sack she'd acquired since her first visit. Mark withdrew its contents: Orinase tablets, Clinitest tablets, color scale card, test tube, eyedropper, and her neatly folded urine sugar record sheet. He unfolded the paper. All dutifully recorded, but not a single test recording indicated *any* sugar in her urine at *any* time over the last five days. All negatives. Mark found himself puzzling in thought: *Could the FBS done in the Grady lab be in error? Unlikely. Could the Clinitest Tablets be bad? Also unlikely,* his mind finally concluded.

"Alberta, I know you feel terrible, but could you show me how you check your water for sugar? You know, just the way I showed you before?"

"Glad to, Doctor," she croaked with obvious painful hoarseness.

As she was doing the test steps, Mark was looking down while writing in her record; he was interrupted when she quickly completed the test. "Here it tis Doctor!"

Mark looked at the test tube she held in her hand. It held the correct volume of light amber liquid that covered the tablet submerged on the tube's bottom. No color change. No bubbling. No chemical reaction. *Ah ha! Bad Clinitest,* he thought—but then he looked a little closer. The undissolved tablet in the tube was a little too small to be a Clinitest Tablet, and its color not quite right. Almost in panic he rapidly repeated the test himself. He used a Clinitest Tablet from Alberta's bottle. A hot brisk chemical reaction ensued as the tube contents turned the four-plus sugar color! He felt his heart rate accelerate as his mind processed his observation: *My God! She's been taking her Clinitest tabs by mouth ... and checking her urine with her Orinase!*

"Excuse me," Mark uttered as he rapidly headed for Ms. C's office. He burst in without knocking and blurted out his findings. "Ms. C! Ms. C! She's been checking her urine with her Orinase, and taking Clinitest Tablets orally—three times a day!"

"Oh my God!" Ms. C exclaimed. "Know what's in that stuff?"

"I'm not sure, but I know the bottle label indicates the stuff is poisonous," Mark shakily replied as he looked over her shoulder. Ms. C was already rapidly thumbing through a thick drug manual that listed the chemical contents of many pharmaceuticals, including Clinitest Tablets.

"Bad news," she frowned. "The stuff's got a lot of sodium hydroxide in it. *Lye!* She'd have been better off taking a real healthy sip of Drain-O three times a day!"

"God, I really feel bad about this Ms. C, I really do. I thought I'd satisfactorily explained to her about how to use the stuff! On her first visit I even had her do the test in my presence, and she did it OK then."

"Doctor, quit giving yourself such a monumental kick in the ass. I'll do the kickin' when you need it! So take it easy on yourself. I reviewed your notes in her chart after her first visit with you, and I think you did an admirable job of explaining testing and treatment to her. If this is the worst mistake that ever occurs on your watch, consider yourself truly blessed by the Grady Intern God."

"I still can't believe it happened, Ms. Costellanos," Mark said staring at the floor, shaking his head in disbelief.

"Well it *did!* Even good Rooters like Alberta get their instructions screwed up. We can't change what happened, Doctor. You can't ever un-ring a gong, but we can take steps to try to get it fixed. We need to get Alberta admitted to thoracic surgery stat. T-surg will scope her, and I'll bet her esophagus looks worse than raw hamburger on the inside. I'll call the T-surg admitting resident, and he can get the other medical and surgical consults she'll need ... and *you*, Doctor, can get back to work! And just this *one* time, I'll overlook the fact that you initially addressed me as Ms. C when you burst in here without knocking. You've got to learn to remember rules—even my little simple ones. Even when you're excited. And stressed. And frightened. Understand, Doctor?"

3

THE SUPPOSITORY

Mark was now over six weeks into the first rotation of his straight surgical internship, and that meant less than two weeks left in the GAC. He was looking forward to the next two-month rotation of his internship: Grady's Surgical Emergency Room, now dubbed the Big SER by the Double Ds. *I'll be cutting and sewing soon,* he thought, as he pondered his SER rotation. Despite his ER-euphoria, he had some gnawing apprehension regarding going there. At times he felt he might wish to continue in the secure environment of the GAC; there, he'd managed to piss off Ms. C only a few times, and had only one tragedy he felt personally responsible for: *Alberta Brown.*

Some four weeks after she'd almost died from ingesting the Clinitest Tablets he'd prescribed, Alberta Brown was still in the hospital recovering. On lunch breaks he'd visited her almost every day. She was still in the thoracic surgery ward. Alberta held no malice toward him whatever, and only praised the "Gradies" and its doctors for saving her life. She profusely apologized for getting her medications "messed up in my head," she'd put it. In her hospital bed, Alberta had also made a very sad admission: "Can't read nary a lick!" While Mark accepted this as a root cause of the problem, he still felt he should have been more perceptive. Her diabetes remained under control with the regimen he'd outlined in the GAC, but she'd be left with an esophageal stricture caused by lye burns from the Clinitest Tablets. The stricture would probably require a surgical dilation of her esophagus at four- to six-week intervals the rest of her life, or so her T- Surg hospital chart indicated.

Worrying about Alberta got put on hold when Ms. C delivered Mark's fourth patient of the day. "Doctor, this is Mr. Rufus Johnson. He has problems with his rectum. He's OK, so you won't need a chaperone," she added, then winked her unspoken message: *This guy is straight.*

Rufus' whole demeanor said *I'm not a rocket scientist—maybe dumber than a sack of hammers—but I'm definitely not queer!* Mark thought. Rufus was pale, and dressed in less-than-clean dark blue work pants. His lighter blue work shirt had a logo name patch: Rufus Johnson - Johnson Electric. A good bath would not have hurt Mr. Johnson at all.

"Mr. Johnson, do you own an electric company?" Mark inquired.

"Yeah, Doc. Electrical contractor. But I ain't here to talk about my business—I'm here to talk about my ass."

Ms. C's words entered Mark's mind: *Talk to them on their own level.* So he formulated his question accordingly. "Rufus, tell me about your ass. What's wrong with it?"

"Well Doc, it's a bleedin' at times, and it hurts like hell when I take a shit. Know what I mean?"

Mark went through the textbook history, which narrowed the problem to lower GI bleeding, probably from the rectum or anal canal itself. "Mr. Johnson, we need to take a look up there with a proctoscope. That's a little lighted tube. It's smaller than that three-quarter-inch metal electrical conduit you guys use, and it's only about five inches long."

Rufus reluctantly agreed to the proctoscopic exam. "Damn, Doc! This is the only time in my life I wished I was a fudge-packer. Just go on and do it ... if that's the only way to tell what's wrong. Let's get it over."

Mark escorted Mr. Johnson to a more elaborate GAC exam room where he did the proctoscopic exam. After finishing, Mark spoke to the relieved patient. "Nothing too serious Mr. Johnson. Get dressed and come back to my room, number seven. We'll talk about what's wrong then."

When Rufus returned to room seven, Mark was still recording his proctoscopic findings in the chart.

"So," Rufus asked, "exactly what's wrong with my ass, Doc?"

Ms. C's *Talk to them on their own level* again entered Mark's mind. "Well Rufus, looks like you've got a crack in your ass, but it's not a very big one."

Rufus' face turned beet-red, his neck veins bulged with anger. "Shit Doc! I don't need some friggin' kid half my age to tell me I've got a fuckin' crack in my ass. I've had a crack in my ass all my life ... ever since I was born, matter of fact!"

Mark sensed he was having his first-ever encounter with a hostile patient. "Rufus, take it easy. Calm down before you have a stroke! I know your ass ... my ass ... well everybody's ass, has a crack. The crack in your ass is *inside*. It's in the lining of your ass, inside the hole. Understand? So you've got what we call an anal fissure, and that's an inside-the-asshole-crack. Know what I mean?"

Rufus immediately cooled off. "Think I understand now, but you shudda said that right up front. Sorry I blew up, Little Doc, but my ass has really been bugging me, and I took it out on you. Got some damn building inspectors on my case, even got problems with subcontractors and the union."

Mark acknowledged the apology, then explained the treatment process: There would be some changes in diet, daily stool softeners, and rectal suppositories to be used three times a day. He explained that his body heat would melt or "dissolve" the suppositories, and release their medication. They'd be wrapped in foil and should be kept cool until used. He even suggested that if they didn't have a refrigerator at a particular job site, the suppositories could be kept in a small ice chest carried to work. Mark gave Rufus prescriptions, and a return appointment that would fall a few days before his own last day in the GAC.

Mark had put Rufus Johnson—and his hostile explosion—totally out of mind. Routine GAC patients filled his days and thoughts ... until Rufus returned. The stocky redneck owner of Johnson Electric returned at his appointed time ten days later. He had a warm smile on his face, and said he was a lot better. He stated he was not having much pain, and hadn't noticed any rectal bleeding for about a week now.

"Rufus, it's really good to know you're coming along. I hope the progress continues, and you won't need any surgery," Mark stated.

"*Surgery?* Like an operation?" Rufus replied, wearing a concerned look. "Man I hope I don't need no operation. Hell Doc, just th' lookin' ... just pokin' that conduit up my butt was bad enough!"

"We won't rush into anything. Just continue the suppositories for another two weeks, and then we'll have another look up there just to be sure it's healed." As Mark spoke, he knew full well the follow-up proctoscopic would be done by one of the unfortunate new GAC interns who would be following his own time there.

"Doc, I'll need another prescription for them 'depositories,' but I really ain't sure that first batch was worth a shit. They all come back out whole, didn't dissolve like you said they would."

"Oh?" Mark questioned. "Didn't dissolve at all? Where'd you get 'em Rufus?" Mark asked, feeling the suppositories may have been old pharmacy stock, possibly dried out, and therefore defective.

"Got 'em right here at the Gradies Pharmacy ... right after I first seen you ten days ago."

Knowing the Grady Pharmacy would carry only current stock, Mark figured maybe the patient was expelling the suppositories immediately after insertion, and thus not retaining them in his rectum long enough for body heat to melt them.

"Rufus, how long does it take one to come back out?"

"Didn't time it Doc, but I'd say about a day, sometimes day and a half."

Mark was now more puzzled than ever. "Rufus ... what do they look like when they do finally manage to come out?"

"Well Doc, at least the ones I was able to see in the toilet, they was sorta shiny, but they was a lot more wrinkled-up than when I *swallowed* 'em."

For the second time in his GAC career, Mark Telfair had to rapidly excuse himself in order to keep his Jockey shorts dry. This time he remembered. He left his door open. He even remembered to knock on the STAFF bathroom door before he burst into its delightful seclusion. He first rolled off about ten feet of toilet paper, which he rapidly wadded into his mouth as a gag. Only then did he let the muted laughter come. It took a full five minutes for him to recover. After urinating, putting the seat back down, flushing, hand washing, and picking numerous residual bits of toilet paper from his mouth, a loud knock on the bathroom door startled him. "Occupied ... out in a sec!" he responded in a bold voice. With a totally straight face, he opened the door—and found himself face to face with Ms. C!

"Now *that's* more like it Doctor!" she said with a knowing smile. "Just share it with me in my office after we finish today ... OK?"

TROUBLE MAKING HIS WATER

Coming down the home stretch! I've only two more days in the GAC ... then on to the Big SER at last, Dr. Mark Telfair thought while patiently waiting for Ms. C to deliver his first patient of the day.

Still waiting, he lapsed into deeper thought: *The GAC is not as bad as I'd originally thought. I've seen some interesting problems here. But have I really learned anything from Ms. C? Yeah, I have. Obey rules, even little ones. Ms. C has taught me how to talk to folks who aren't well educated ... and I've learned how you can screw up by not being sure the patient understands instructions. I think I now better understand Grady, and its role in serving the inner city ... and just how much the Grady environment differs from Buckhead and the Emory campus. Have I changed as a person? Am I a Grady insider yet? When am I ever going to learn something about surgery? Will my GAC experience make me a better surgeon?*

His thoughts, mostly questions, abruptly vanished as Ms. C delivered the day's first *patients* ... plural, because *two* were delivered at the same time. This was a first in his GAC experience, but the situation was quickly explained by Ms. C.

"Little Antonio Stinchcomb here is the actual patient," Ms. C said as she pointed at the black male child, a two-year-old. "The woman here with Antonio is his aunt ... I think, but it really doesn't matter. Antonio was seen in the Medical ER last night, and *he* is the patient. Antonio probably should have been referred directly to pediatrics, but the intern who saw Antonio in the ER last night told the aunt to bring him to the GAC this morning ... so I'm counting on you, Doctor, to find out what's really going on. Let me know when you get a handle on it," she said. For some reason, Ms. C was wearing a subtle worrisome smile as she left Mark's side. Mark just smiled back at her as she left the room, then shrugged, feeling he'd never completely figure out Ms. C.

He turned his attention to the mid-40s woman holding chubby little Antonio in her lap. Mark began his attempt at getting the handle on the problem that Ms. C had requested.

"Ma'am what's your name?"

"Shirley ... and this here sittin' in my lap is Antonio. He cute, ain't he? Ain't quite sure how we related, but my sister up in Dee-troit, she send Antonio back down here to At-lanta for me to look after when one of her last husbands run off with another women, and—"

"Shirley," Mark abruptly cut off her further explanation of the family tree, "were you the one who took Antonio to the emergency room last night?"

"Sure was."

"What kind of problem was Antonio having when you took him to the emergency room?"

"Well Doctor, I ain't really sure, but I think Antonio is having trouble making his water," Shirley replied, as she stuck a pacifier in Antonio's mouth.

Wanting to expedite matters, Mark quickly spoke. "Ma'am you say you *think* he is having trouble making his water ... what makes you say that?"

After a long silence, Shirley finally replied. "Well Doctor, let me say this: It don't happen ever' time Antonio make his water, but two, maybe three time a week, his eyes they jus' roll back in his head, and his body go to shakin', jerkin', and strainin' all over ... both arms and legs too, you know. Then finally he make his water! Sometimes it take him 15 or 20 minute of shakin' and strainin', and then he'll finally pee. But then Antonio he be so bad wore out from makin' his water, he jus' go dead asleep for 'bout a hour or two."

The young Dr. Telfair was now stumped. Other than the ER sheet from last night, he had no prior Grady records regarding little Antonio. Last night's ER record indicated normal vital signs, a chief complaint of trouble making water, and the ER intern's brief summary note, which stated: "No acute distress. UA negative. To GAC in a.m."

Mark thought a few moments, then continued. "Shirley, did Antonio have any other medical history—any other problems you know of, while he was up there in Detroit?"

"No," Shirley responded, then paused. "Well now, only 'cept maybe 'bout one ... now that I think some on it. My sister did say Antonio had the smiley mighty Jesus when he were jus' 'bout a one-year-old up there. She say he almost died from it, but then he finally got well over it, she say."

"*Smiley mighty Jesus!* ... as in smiley mighty Jesus Christ?" Mark asked, seeking confirmation.

"Don't know fo' sure, but that be what my sister say they call it up there in Dee-troit."

Smiley mighty Jesus Mark thought, as he did a brief exam on Antonio to rule out meatal stenosis, a condition where the urinary opening is abnormally small, sometimes no larger than a pinhole. Antonio's opening was normal, even larger than normal. In fact, Mark Telfair was fully impressed by the size of the two-year-old's prepubertal phallus. *God what's that thing going to look like when he grows up!* he thought.

Willing his mind back to the matters at hand, and still having no useful thoughts, Mark knew he was going to need some help figuring out the problem. One option would be to call a pediatric resident and openly admit he didn't have the foggiest idea about what was wrong with Antonio. The other option would be to talk to Ms. C. In his mind, he felt Ms. C would be less condescending than the pediatric resident, who'd surely make him feel stupid regarding his inability to diagnose the problem.

Mark excused himself from Antonio and Antonio's aunt. He slowly walked down the GAC hall. With lingering reservation, he softly knocked on Ms. C's office door.

"Come," was the single bold reply on the other side.

"Ms. Costellanos," Mark said as he entered, "I need some help with Antonio. I've tried to figure it out by myself, but I can't."

Ms. C smiled at him the same weird way she'd smiled at him earlier. "I figured it'd be a challenge for you, as it was for me ... initially. But then again, I've got 20 years of experience in the GAC on my side."

"I'm not asking you to make the diagnosis for me. I just need some help figuring out what the heck the smiley mighty Jesus is ... if you don't mind telling me."

"Don't mind telling you at all, Doctor. The smiley mighty Jesus is a Rooter term for *spinal meningitis,* commonly caused by the *Neisseria meningitidis* bacterium, and a number of other bacteria too. Frequently viral also, as I recall from nursing school."

"But what's the trouble making his water all about," Mark humbly asked.

"I'm the nurse, you're the physician. I suggest you think *neurological illness,* Doctor," she said, still smiling at him in the same odd way.

"Thanks, I'll just do that!" Mark said as he left in an internal huff. *Yeah, thanks a lot for nothing you smiling bitch! You're just playing some kind of mind game with me!* he thought as he quickly stepped away. He knew he'd just gotten all the help he'd get short of begging, and that was totally out of the question, at least it was in his present state of mind. He'd now prefer to kiss the pediatric resident's butt rather than Ms. C's.

Walking to his exam room, Mark kept thinking *neurological illness ...*

neurological illness ...what kind of neurological illness would cause that poor child to have trouble urinating? Maybe Ms. C really meant to say urological illness? Wouldn't that make more sense?

As he entered his room, he was more determined than ever to figure it out on his own. *Neurological illness ... neurological illness,* kept rolling is his mind. Then without warning the answer exploded in his brain. *Seizure!* Generalized seizure! Poor little Antonio was having epileptic seizures, and urinary incontinence was frequently associated with such seizures. And the so-called postictal state—an unresponsive post-seizure interval that sometimes follows a generalized seizure—could explain Antonio's going "dead asleep," as Shirley had put it. And prior brain damage from spinal meningitis—a.k.a. the smiley mighty Jesus—could have left residual brain changes that were responsible for causing Antonio's epilepsy! All the pieces of the puzzle seem to fit perfectly now.

He immediately called the pediatric resident to relay his brilliant diagnosis. The experienced third-year pediatric resident fully concurred with Antonio's tentative diagnosis. "Telfair, that was a pretty sharp call ... for an intern! All the kid probably needs is some medication for his seizures, but we'll do a full neurological evaluation anyway. Thanks for the referral. I'll keep you posted if we find anything unexpected," the ped's resident had added at the end of the call. Hanging up the phone, Mark had a broad smile on his face. *Thank you Ms. C,* a small voice kept saying inside his head as his pride swelled to dangerous dimensions. But Mark Telfair wasn't overly concerned ... he knew he'd probably be humbled again, his pride reduced to normal. It would happen during his next intern rotation—the Grady Surgical Emergency Room.

5

ONE FOOT IN THE TOILET

Goodbye *GAC!* Mark arrived an hour early at the surgical ER—the Big SER, as all the Double-Ds now called it. He'd eagerly looked forward to this day, but at six in the morning only two patients were there. Each appeared to be sleeping face down on wheeled stretchers called gurneys; both were handcuffed to a side rail of their respective gurneys. Dr. Mark Telfair felt a little disappointed by not seeing anything that needed prompt surgical attention.

He'd never met Dr. Jerry Bacon, the Senior Assistant Resident (SAR) in charge of the ER. Presently, the SAR was calmly sitting at a long desk just chatting—mostly flirting—with the extremely good-looking student nurse seated at his side. As Mark approached the desk, Dr. Bacon terminated his flirting, and the student nurse promptly left.

"So you must be one of my new 'terns, aren't you ... Telfair?" Bacon asked as he read Mark's name tag.

"Yep, I'm Mark Telfair. Straight surgical. Did my first two months in the GAC."

Dr. Bacon stood. At five foot six he was about Mark's height, but must have weighed about 40 pounds more. "Well I'm Jerry Bacon, SAR in charge here," Jerry said, warmly extending a hand to Mark. "Welcome to the Pit. Just call me Jer. And don't mind those fellas over there on the gurneys. They've already had some minor stitching, and they'll both become guests at the APD Hilton as soon as they sober up a little more. And by the way, how did you and Ms. C get along in the GAC?" Jer asked, broadly smiling.

"Jer, I didn't screw up but a couple of times," Mark admitted with a sheepish grin.

Bacon smiled back. "Yeah, I heard about a couple of them. Really funny stuff ... especially that ain't-tried-to-set-fire-to-it story!"

Mark was a little incensed that knowledge of his blunders in the GAC, even if somewhat humorous, were already on the hospital gossip net. *Has Ms. C violated her own rules about things never leaving her office?* his mind questioned.

"Uh, Jer ... just how did you learn about anything that might have happened to me in the GAC?"

"I did a straight surgical internship, same as you Telfair. My first rotation was also in the GAC. So let's just say me and Ms. C are real close. We're 'real tight,' as the Rooters say. She's an authentic mother hen, and she tells me about each new 'tern I'll be gettin' ... at least the ones coming from *her* GAC to *my* Pit. She's really one great gal, and you'll find yourself appreciating her more and more each year you've been around this place. I know a lot of Grady docs, even senior residents, find themselves goin' back to talk to her in her famous private office from time to time—just looking for advice about stuff that's bugging 'em. I got invited into her office a few times myself, when I was a 'tern in the GAC, but I've been back on my own a time or two since. Just be assured very little ever leaves her office, and anything she may have told me about you will go no further. Period."

Jer Bacon seemed to sense that Mark was somewhat concerned about Ms. C's breach of confidentiality. "Now don't let this go to your head Telfair, but Ms. C told me she thought you'd someday make a darn good surgeon. 'He should definitely make a good cutter, but he's just not cut out to be a pill-pusher,' she told me."

Mark modestly ignored what he considered a compliment from Ms. C, and quickly asked Jer a question. "Uh, Jer ... a minute ago you called this place—the SER—the 'Pit.' Did I hear you right?"

"Right-O,"Jer replied. "I don't know where you got that SER crap from, but nobody who's anybody ever calls it that! Now there was a time during segregation—way before my time here—when Grady's two ERs were called either the White ER or the Colored ER. But that's all history, man. After integration, I think it was the White ER that became the Medical Emergency Room. And the one used by the blacks became the Surgical Emergency Room, I think, but I could have that reversed. But anyway, most of the staff don't call 'em ERs."

"Jer, you just told me you don't call it the SER ... so what's correct?"

"We usually call 'em the Medical Pit, and the Surgical Pit. And the Grady Pits are where the rubber meets the road of life. Down here, you'll learn that man is really only another animal ... he's just wrapped in a thin veneer of so-called civilization. And that stuff just falls off all the time, especially on Saturday nights. But Pit is an in-house term, sorta like Rooter. So never use Pit or Rooter in front of a patient, or write stuff like that in the hospital record ... OK?"

"No problem-O," Mark replied, already liking the more laid-back attitude he'd seen thus far in the Surgical Pit. *But I still don't know exactly what a Rooter is,* he thought, feeling too embarrassed to ask.

Mark looked around at his impressive surroundings. "Jer, you got anything you want me to do right now?"

"Not a thing," Bacon replied, then explained to Mark that his Junior Assistant Resident (JAR) and three other interns should be showing up at seven. Then they'd all have a conference in the office, before the day "really got rockin'," Jer had said, and then told Mark to feel free to look around the Pit.

Following Jer and Mark's exchange, the big-breasted blond student nurse promptly returned to the desk. Dr. Jerry Bacon immediately returned his full attention to her amorous blue eyes that followed his every move.

Checking his watch, Mark knew he had about 45 minutes to kill before the rest of the crew got there. He decided to check out the boundaries of his new environment. The Surgical Pit was indeed a large ground-level Grady Hospital area. Its overall dimensions must have been about 150 feet long, and perhaps 60 feet wide. He noted light-colored terrazzo floors throughout. Beige ceramic tile went up the walls to a height of six feet or so. More or less in the center of a large central common area, three huge tile-encapsulated support columns stood like frozen giants, only to disappear through the suspended acoustical tile ceiling. The ceiling held dozens of recessed brightly lit fluorescent lighting fixtures.

Down one side of the common area were eight large treatment rooms. Each room had its own wide door connecting it to the central common area. In addition, each treatment room had smaller lateral doors that permitted access to the neighboring rooms on either side. Each room had its own cabinet-mounted wash-up basins and storage cabinets. Piped-in wall oxygen and vacuum ports; overhead operating lights; operating room style tables; wheeled IV stands, and various electrical and communication gadgets were identical in each treatment room. As he explored the environment that would be his new home for the next two months, the facilities truly impressed Dr. Mark Telfair.

On the side opposite the series of treatment rooms, a long free-standing desk and counter served as a community staff workstation; Jer and his student nurse had resumed their side by side sitting positions there. He quietly walked just a few feet behind the sitting couple, hoping not to be a distraction to their flirting conversation. Mark silently opened a relatively narrow unmarked wooden door. It was a very small four-foot-square bathroom, containing only a wall-mounted lavatory and institutional toilet bowl without a water tank. *Cramped essentials only here,* Mark thought, as he quietly closed the door, then continued his exploration.

On the same side as the workstation and bathroom, but about 20 feet to one side of the station, Mark discovered another unmarked door; it was flanked by a pair of 20-foot-long wooden benches with their backs pushed tightly against the beige tile-covered wall. They looked exactly like church pews. *Those benches must be seating for ambulatory patients ... and that door between the benches must go into Dr. Bacon's office,* Mark's mind concluded, though he refrained from opening that particular door.

Except for several other areas he assumed to be for storage, Mark felt he'd fully explored his new home. Still having some time before Jer's meeting at seven, he decided to walk over to the Medical Emergency Room—the Medical Pit. It was separated from the Surgical Pit only by the 20-foot-square foyer between the two ERs. Mark soon learned both ERs had the same basic equipment; the Medical Pit was simply a mirror image of the Surgical Pit. The foyer—in addition to the opposing swinging doors that went into the respective ERs—had its own large glass doors that opened directly outside to a large covered ambulance bay. The foyer, on its remaining wall, had an empty elevator, its door standing fully open. *Maybe that elevator is broken,* Mark thought as he checked his watch. *Shit, I'm late!* his mind panicked.

"Yo 'Tern—get your butt in here. It's time to boogie! Conference in my office starting *now!*" Jer Bacon yelled, poking his head through the Surgical Pit's swinging doors and spying his missing intern ... who was blankly staring into the foyer's open empty elevator.

Silently, Jer led Mark to the mystery door in the Surgical Pit, the one between the church-like benches Mark had earlier suspected might go into Jer's office. When Jer opened the door to the sizable room, a fairly large assemblage of staff was already present. Counting himself and Jer, there were some 13 ER staff members assembled. Most were already seated in folding chairs loosely arranged in front of Jer's large desk. Dr. Bacon quickly sat down behind his desk, which was totally covered by a hopeless mess of paperwork. Undisturbed by the clutter before him, Jer spoke: "OK, folks ... looks like we've *now* got all present and accounted for. Looks like we've always got at least one person who's always a tad late," Jer said as he smiled at Mark Telfair, who was desperately trying to open a folding chair that was obviously stuck shut!

"I get that for you Doctor," whispered a huge black man dressed in whites that did little to hide his muscularity. Without any apparent effort, the giant man pried the reluctant chair open. He then placed it, and motioned for Mark to sit down. Just as Mark sat, wearing his sheepish grin, a little nervous titter rippled through the group. Extending his huge hand to Mark, the hulk spoke: "Doctor, I'm Mose. Mose Mallone. I been an orderly at the Gradies for over 30 years ... and best I remember that same old sticking-chair was over at the old Gradies, way back when I first started out!" The whole group burst into hearty laughter. Mark felt his face turning red, but his own laughter was the loudest in the group.

Jer's two-fingers-in-the-mouth whistle brought the entire group to instant silence. "Introductions first," Jer said. "I see Dr. Mark Telfair here, one of our new interns, has just met Mr. Mose Mallone, who's our 7:00 a.m. to 7:00 p.m. orderly. I think the rest of the group has also met them both in the process. I might add that in private we call Mose Mr. Clean. Folks, just look at his bald shining head. Just check out those massive biceps! Can you believe this guy is 62? But, Mose here ... well he's got a little more 'tan' than that guy pictured on the bottle of that commercial cleaning stuff. Tell 'em what you do when you're not working here, Mose."

Mose promptly stood to speak, obviously taking no offense at Jer's reference to his skin color. "Well I teach wrestling, boxing, and bodybuilding to a bunch of teenage ghetto kids three night a week. Ten year ago, the city give me an old rundown warehouse, to use as my gym. At my gym I try to get the kids to respect they body ... try to get 'em to where they don't feel they need drinkin', drugs, knives and guns jus' to be somebody—or to protect theyselves. I jus' hope that maybe someday we'll have less shootin' and stabbin', and a lot less heartache for the families, and maybe less hard work for the Gradies," Mose summarized.

After the spontaneous heartfelt applause from the group died out, Jer resumed. "Thanks Mose. Oh, and folks ... if you get a problem patient—especially if it's a black patient creatin' the problem—don't take matters into your own hands. Fortunately this integration thing is going down pretty smooth here in Atlanta, and the powers that be—I'm talking about hospital administration here—have told me in no uncertain terms, that we'd better not do a single thing down here in the ER that disturbs that process. Mose here is a true master at dealing with disgruntled patients, especially blacks. So please call him when you even *think* you may have a problem. Mose can defuse a potential racial incident in a heartbeat, and hopefully keep the Grady ER off the front page of the *Atlanta Journal*.

"And when you need the law, you call Shorty," Jer continued. "Shorty Smith is with the City of Atlanta Police Department. He's the one over there with the gun, cop's uniform, handcuffs, radio, nightstick and stuff." Shorty stood up, smiled and nodded, but didn't speak. Shorty was indeed short. About five foot two, he was a light-skinned freckled black, thin as a rail. "And folks, Shorty here ... well he stutters pretty bad, so be patient when you're trying to talk to him," Jer explained. Shorty sat back down smiling, obviously relieved he didn't have to try to speak. Reading between the lines, it was obvious to Mark that Jer Bacon was somewhat unimpressed with Shorty being the APD representative in the Surgical Pit.

"Next we have our ER clerk, Betty Bullock," Jer informed. Betty remained seated, but timidly smiled, revealing buckteeth that would have given most orthodontists a heart attack. "She's our Paper Queen. She's the one who fills out all that biographical stuff on the ER sheets, and she'll deal with any other paper problems you might have." Though in her mid-30s, her ring finger was bare. *Old Maid ... maybe? No, definitely!* Mark's mind quickly concluded.

"Let's see—" Jer stopped, as he looked at one of the several hundred pieces of paper on his desk. "Well that covers Mose, Shorty, and Betty," he mumbled. "I guess I can dismiss you three to run the boat till the rest of us can get out there and help." As if on cue, Mose the orderly, Shorty the cop, and Betty the clerk simultaneously stood, then left Dr. Bacon's office in single file.

"OK, let's see now," Jer said as he consulted his notes. "Oh ... and I'm Jerry Bacon, the Senior Assistant Surgical Resident in charge of this ship. And that fellow over there with the pubic metastasis on his upper lip, a.k.a. moustache, is Dr. Terry Brinson. He's our Junior Assistant Surgical Resident, and he's second in command of our boat." Those that remained smiled, but did not laugh at Jer's attempt at moustache-humor. "So either myself or Terry will be here at all times during our shift. Terry and me are where the local buck stops, and if we can't deal with a problem we'll kick it up to one of the specialty chief residents that are always in-house, or even on up to the attending Emory doctor who's on call for the ER, if necessary."

Mark yawned and was getting a little bored while Jer finished the introductions. There were two seasoned RNs assigned to their 12-hour ER shift, plus two second-year student nurses (SNs). One of the SNs was the attractive girl Mark had seen with Jer earlier. Of the new interns introduced by Jer, only Zack Paslaski was familiar to him. Zack had served with Mark in the GAC. On their first GAC day, Zack had been the one who'd indicated he was afraid Ms. C "wanted our nuts," or something like that, Mark recalled.

Mark was sure Jer's meeting was finally over, but it had one final gasp. "Since it's a Monday, it'll usually be pretty quiet, but you never really know. We're all here to teach one another. You RNs can orient the SNs, and me and Terry will get the interns off on the right foot. Now let's all go out there and boogie—see what the day brings!" Jer said, then stood, indicating the meeting was over. *At last!* Mark thought.

In addition to the two drunks handcuffed to the gurneys, some ten new patients had accumulated during Jer's long-winded meeting. Betty the bucktoothed Paper Queen had their Grady ER patient forms filled out with pertinent biographical data; the RNs and SNs had recorded the patient's vital signs, along with the patient's chief complaint, or CC as it was called. Resident Doctors Jerry Bacon and Terry Brinson quickly evaluated each new patient, then assigned several patients to each of their new interns. Mark was elated when Jer assigned him two laceration patients, plus a teen with a possible broken arm. After the interns had been assigned their patients, Mose approached Mark. "Doctor Telfair, your cut patients are in the last two rooms, but you needs to start with number eight ... he's still bleedin' pretty bad."

As Mark Telfair, Zack Paslaski, and the other interns went to work on their assigned patients, they each had almost constant supervision from either Mose, the RNs, or the two residents in charge. Mark was amazed at how well the process worked, and even a little amazed at his own ability to sew up real people ... especially considering almost all his prior experience at suturing had been in the medical school physiology lab, and largely limited to a few anesthetized experimental animals that would be euthanized upon experiment's end. He'd done a little people-suturing as a med student, but that was limited to sewing up episiotomies during his student OB experience. As a medical student he'd also been in operating rooms both at Emory and Grady, but had always been there simply as an observer, or a lowly redundant retractor holder, thus never really an essential element in the surgical procedure.

As the day progressed the patient load got heavier and heavier. Four gunshot wounds (GSWs) had come in over the course of the day; those were cared for by the experienced residents. Strictly as directed, Mark simply assisted either Jer Bacon or Terry Brinson with the GSW patients' emergency care. All were first stabilized, then admitted to the hospital for other experienced doctors to manage. Mark wondered when he'd be among the experienced. He already longed to be there, but knew he'd just have to wait his turn. *Earn my turn,* he thought.

Mark was just finishing his 15th minor suture job of the day in room four. He heard a loud *POP! ... POP! ... POP!* followed by yelling and screaming. Out of curiosity he poked his head out the treatment room door to investigate the strange sounds. What he saw rapidly accelerated his heart rate in response to instant and total fear. *Staggering around in the center of the common area, a young glassy-eyed shabby white male was firing a large silver handgun!* At first he appeared to be firing at random. *POP! ... POP!* He fired into the ceiling. Electrical sparks flew. Exploding fluorescent bulbs rained glass shards to the terrazzo floor. The crazed youngster then unsteadily aimed at various staff and patients, wobbling as he shot. Yelling and screaming, everyone seemed to be running in random directions, but the general flow, at least for the staff, seemed to be toward the staff bathroom located directly behind the workstation. Jer was barking orders and directing traffic: patients to the exit doors, staff to the tiny bathroom. Mark rapidly followed the flow, praying he didn't get hit by a bullet in the process. As Mark ran toward the bathroom, he saw Jer in a low crouch behind the workstation. *POP! POP!* Instantly two quarter-sized divots appeared in the ceramic wall tile— barely a foot over Jer's head! Jer pointed to the bathroom when he saw Mark. "In!" he commanded.

Mark didn't question the order as he rapidly forced his way into the tiny space he'd investigated earlier in the day. Jer was last to squeeze in just as a single bullet struck the thick wooden door. Jer had barely managed to close it in time. Except for everyone's rapid breathing Mark heard nothing. Then a loud sentinel metallic click let Mark know someone had managed to lock the bathroom door. A frantic jiggling of the door knob was followed by loud bangs on the lower part of the door, presumably frustrated kicks by the shooter. *POP! POP! POP!* Bullets again slammed into the thick door, but did not penetrate it fully. *Mark silently thanked God for thick doors ... especially ones with locks. Other than the bathroom shelter chosen by Jer, Mark hadn't seen a single lock on any other door in the ER!*

Now only rapid breathing could be heard in the dark relatively minuscule space. Mark's college days popped into his head. He recalled his Emory SAE fraternity brothers seeing just how many pledges could fit into a single telephone booth, or a VW Beetle. The gunfire had been a far more efficient incentive than the fraternity brothers' hazing paddles. They were so tightly packed, movement was virtually impossible. Jer's shaky but reassuring voice broke the silence.

"Roll call everybody!" Jer did indeed recall every staff member's name. All were present and accounted for—except Shorty the cop. At least 12 of the ER crew were now safely crammed in. *Shorty is dead,* Mark thought.

A frightened young female voice said, "Uh, can anyone turn on the light?"

"Sure can't, Sugar ... some dumb electrician put the switch on the *outside!*" Jer responded. Mark was almost sure the voice belonged to Jer's pretty girlfriend. He couldn't help but wonder if Rufus Johnson—his GAC patient—might have been the electrical contractor who wired the ER.

"Hey! Watch where you've got those hands buster!" said an older female voice. *One of the RNs,* Mark thought.

"I know exactly where I've got my hands," a male voice responded, "but I can't move nothin' I own ... and I'm doin' damn good just to breathe in here." The male voice was one definitely recognized by Mark as belonging to Dr. Zack Paslaski, his fellow intern from the GAC.

The temperature in the totally dark confined space was rapidly rising. Mark was sweating, and even worried about there being enough oxygen if they all stayed in there very long. *Will I live to see Carla again?* Mark's mind asked, his fears soon sidetracked by another female voice.

"I don't know just exactly who you are, but keep your hands exactly where they are ... uh, just as long as necessary of course." Mark was almost certain the voice belonged to the ER clerk, Miss Betty Bullock, the Paper Queen.

"Hey ever'body, I got my hands in my pockets," came the unmistakable resonant bass response from Mose the orderly.

A very loud voice outside the door startled the bathroom's captives. They immediately fell silent as the loud voice repeated the message: "Police! OK to come out now. I've got him cuffed."

Jer verified the authenticity of the voice; it belonged to Fuzzy McInnis, the APD cop from the Medical ER. McInnis had apparently heard the commotion, then responded. Satisfied, Jer issued an order to his captive audience: "Whoever can find the lock, open the door."

As the door finally opened, the unpacking of the tiny room was indeed a slow process of disentanglement—similar to a major pileup on a football field. The bright light and freedom was savored by each occupant as they finally disengaged themselves. Each was greeted by air that seemed like a Canadian cold front, one laced with the pungent odor of cordite produced by the multiple gunshots. Mark was last to exit. Only then did he realize his soaking-wet left foot had been firmly wedged in the toilet bowl! He was thankful no one had caused a flood by activating the flush valve ... but not nearly as thankful as the young SN who had a neat bullet hole punched in the peak of her starched nurse's cap. "It's OK Sugar," Jer said, consoling and embracing her while her tears flooded, causing her mascara to run on Jer's white coat.

Still stunned, Mark quickly surveyed the ER. He fully expected to see pools of blood, dead patients, and a dead ER cop. Except for the dazed ER staff, Fuzzy McInnis, and the shooter, the ER was now completely empty. *Where did all the patients go?* Mark's mind wondered.

In the middle of the common area, Fuzzy had the cuffed shooter pinned face down on the glass-littered terrazzo floor. With his 250 pounds sitting on top of the squirming shooter, Fuzzy desperately summoned Shorty by handheld radio. "Shorty, Shorty. McInnis to Shorty. Perp subdued in Surgical ER. Shots fired. Nobody down or injured. Assistance needed. Over." Mark heard McInnis repeat an identical radio call several times.

Shorty casually ambled through the Surgical Pit's doors. He became wide-eyed, freezing stone still, his brain processing the scene.

Spotting Shorty, McInnis yelled, "Where the fuck were you, man? I've been trying to raise your ass on the handheld!"

Shorty checked his radio. "Uh, I g-g-got it turned off. Went out s-s-side. Smoke break."

"Damn it, Shorty! Turn that son of a bitch back on! And call an APD unit to take this perp in. And for God's sake don't you mess with this evidence ... like that .357 on the floor over there, or any of these scattered shell casings," McInnis angrily demanded, still sitting on the cuffed face-down perp, and using his handheld radio's antenna to point out scattered scene evidence to Shorty.

And this is just my first day in the Surgical Pit, Mark thought, still very unsettled ... still very frightened ... now oblivious to his wet left foot.

MISTER CLEAN

At 7:00 a.m., two weeks following the shooting incident, the Surgical Pit was empty. Mark remained disturbed as he entered to begin his ER shift. Though Dr. Telfair had signed up for military service with the U.S. Air Force, his active duty had been deferred until he completed his surgical training. Now, days after the shooting incident, Mark continued quietly to wonder if he'd not be better off to forfeit his active-duty deferment, and go directly to Vietnam. A strange thought occurred to him: *I should have gone to Georgia Tech—mechanical engineers don't get shot at in Atlanta!*

In an apparent attempt to keep the incident quiet, it was rumored a private investigation firm had been hired by the hospital. ER personnel had been instructed by administration not to discuss the incident with anyone other than the private investigator they'd hired. But Mark Telfair had not honored those instructions. He'd secretly spoken with APD Officer Fuzzy McInnis, who in turn probably violated APD rules by giving Mark some information: "Off the record, Doc, the perp is a known heroin addict. He's in his late teens—a son of one of the hospital's board members. He violated parole, left his rehab facility, and apparently came to the ER looking for drugs. And you never heard any of this from me!" Fuzzy had whispered. Mark was dying to tell Jer and the others, but didn't. Couldn't. Wouldn't. He'd given Fuzzy his word. Local papers never published anything about the incident. Even the physical damage done by some 12 bullets had been repaired.

As Mark had surmised while a bathroom prisoner, Rufus Johnson had had a role in the original wiring of the hospital. Rufus had come to the ER a week earlier and repaired the damaged lighting in the ceiling. Spotting Rufus, Mark had asked him if he could relocate the bathroom light switch— so it'd be located on the *inside.* Rufus had immediately recognized Mark.

"Oh, hey there Little Doc ... good to see ya. My ass is great now, thanks to you. But I really didn't appreciate that other doc that came after you in the clinic. You know, looking up my butt to be sure it was healed? I think he musta used four-inch conduit, not that little three-quarter-inch job like you used. But I'm really sorry I can't relocate that light switch for ya without a work order. I knew we shudda put that switch on the inside back in '58 when we first wired this place—but you can't argue with them damn building inspectors. They think they know *everything!* Gotta get back to these shot-up lights. See ya."

Mark continued his reflections about his first two ER weeks. He'd certainly come to appreciate Dr. Jerry Bacon's ability to think and act quickly in emergencies, surgical and otherwise. Jer's outward appearance certainly didn't allow him to come off as a polished genius with upper triple-digit IQ. He reminded Mark of Colombo, the TV detective. *Stupid like a fox,* Mark thought. He even tried to hang the Colombo nickname on Jer, but it just wouldn't stick.

No matter what you called Jer, Mark knew Jer's cool head, and getting everyone in the tiny bathroom—and patients out the door—probably saved some lives. But hospital administration didn't see it that way; the results of the hush-hush private investigation apparently never openly revealed how any gun—other than Shorty's—got into the ER in the first place. As Senior Assistant Resident in charge of the ER, and therefore captain of the ship, Dr. Bacon received most of the blame for the incident. For reasons unknown, Shorty escaped any criticism and all blame. The shooting did result in slightly better screening for weapons, but few effective changes were made that Mark could tell. Mose, the orderly, had privately summed it up: "Ain't never gonna stop all the dope, guns, and knives ... no matter what you do. But that sorry Shorty could do a heap better if he jus' would. So we jus' gotta do the best we can, and pray to the Lord it ain't your time for one of them crazy folks to get you." Mark was continuing to reflect upon Mose's wisdom, and coming to a tentative conclusion: Some risk is always present, no matter where you are, no matter who you are, no matter what you're doing. *Might the ER be a little safer than 'Nam?* his worried mind asked.

Now it was 6:30 p.m. and Dr. Telfair was bushed. His day had been filled with stab wounds, gunshot wounds, car wrecks, fractures, concussions, contusions, abrasions, and burns. It all left him ready to see his shift end. Sitting at the workstation, writing up what he hoped would be his last patient, Mark was startled by the very loud familiar Yankee voice of Dr. Zack Paslaski.

"I ain't puttin' up with this shit! I just ain't puttin' up with this shit no more!" Paslaski had just stormed out of treatment room number four.

Jer, who was sitting at the workstation alongside Mark, also heard Zack's excited voice and foul language. Jer instantly focused on Zack's vulgarity. "Paslaski! To my office *now!*" Jer commanded.

Mark turned just in time to see Jer and Zack disappear through the office door—a second before it loudly slammed shut. Mark wished he could be a fly on the wall in Jer's office, but resigned himself to shelving his curiosity, and resumed the paperwork at hand. Mark was about to finish his write-up when Jer poked his head out the office door and yelled. "Hey Telfair! Find Mose and get him into my office. You come in here too when you find Mose. OK?"

Mark made no reply, but quickly located Mose, then went to Jer's office with Mose trailing close upon his heels.

Jer began by explaining his actions. "Telfair, I've got you here as a *witness*. Mose you're here for your *wisdom*. And Paslaski you are here to go over what happened out there again, even though I didn't give you time to finish explaining it the first time. So let's have it from the top. Again. OK?" Jer said, staring at Zack with obvious displeasure.

"Well Jer, like I said before, that drunk piece of shit in room four first spit in my face. He did it just as I was startin' to suture a small laceration on his forehead ... a laceration inflicted by a cop's club when they had to subdue the dude at some juke-joint brawl. I was just goin' to bandage it up, but the cop who brought him in insisted we sew it up before they took him to jail. 'No open wounds allowed in jail,' he said. Seems they've had too much trouble with them startin' to bleed again once they get 'em in the clink."

"That still don't justify the language you used in front of the patients when you came stomping outta that treatment room Dr. Paslaski! You don't simply say 'I ain't puttin' up with this *shit*' in front of a bunch of fuckin' patients—no matter how pissed you are! I don't care what you say in private, but you don't *ever* do that in front of patients. You might get by with that crap up in New York where you went to med school, but you can't get by with that shit in Georgia. OK? Sorry I interrupted, Zack. So go ahead," Jer finished.

"Well the SN set up another sterile surgical tray, because his spit contaminated the first one. Then the jerk sat up on the table and dumped the second tray on the floor!" Zack explained.

"And?" Jer prompted.

"The prick then grabbed the SN's blouse, right between her big tits you know, and ripped that sucker right off. Just like that!" Zack demonstrated, rapidly jerking his arm to one side.

The mention of the SN definitely caught Jer's attention, and it was obvious to Mark the story had just progressed beyond the endpoint of Zack's private first-telling ... just beyond the point where he and Mose had been invited in for their *witness* and *wisdom*.

"Which SN was it?" Jer asked, with visible anxiety.

"Sylvia ... er ... Banks, I think her name is, Jer. You know that cute little blond with the really big knockers?"

Mark thought Jer might explode. His eyes bulged, his neck veins distended, his face reddened—even his bald spot turned scarlet with anger. Mark didn't know if Jer's anger was fueled by Zack's crude reference to his girlfriend's chest, the ripping-off of her blouse, the patient's spitting, Zack's cussing in front of patients, or all factors in combination. In a rage Jer instantly started for the door, but Mose's massive black hand shot out like the head of a striking snake to grab Jer's arm, then jerked him back.

After glaring at one another for a full ten seconds, Mose finally delivered some of the wisdom Jer had earlier solicited. "Doctor, let *me* get in the middle of this mess. Please sir ... please! You already in enough trouble 'bout that gun gettin' in here, and you don't need no new troubles. We sometime don't think clear when someone's a messin' with our woman, you know."

While Jer's brain was processing the wise words from Mose, the orderly's iron grip on his arm remained steadfast. Jer finally took a deep breath, then slowly exhaled through tight lips. Jer knew Mose was right. Completely right. And possibly saving his future at Grady ... if the gun incident hadn't ruined it already. Mose cautiously released his grip on Jer's arm.

Now outwardly calm, Jer spoke. "Zack, is the guy who spit on you black or white?"

"Black. But what difference does *that* make?"

"Perfect," Jer said, leaving Zack puzzled, and the question unanswered.

"Mose, I want you to go straighten that son of a bitch out!" Jer ordered.

"My pleasure, Dr. Jerry," Mose said as he removed his starched white jacket and hung it on a hook located on the back of Jer's office door.

For the first time Mark fully appreciated Mose's massive chest muscles; they were clearly outlined beneath a spotless tight-fitting white T-shirt. *Mr. Clean indeed,* Mark thought. In a slow deliberate manner, Mr. Clean left Jer's office to accomplish his mission.

As Mose closed the door, Mark quickly fired a question. "Jer, is there any way me and Zack can watch what Mose does?"

"Nope!" Jer instantly responded. "At least not officially. I know I ain't about to watch what happens. That way I can honestly say I haven't seen a thing. But off the record, if you two guys go into room three next door, you two just might *hear* a little something. Get my drift?"

Mark and Zack bolted from the office like white-clad rabbits. Fortunately, room three was still vacant and its lights off. They entered, closed the main door, and silently moved to the small closed lateral door that connected rooms three and four. With ears pressed to the closed door, they heard the drunk loudly speak with slurred words: *"Hic* ... well if it ain't ... *hic* ... Mr. Fuckin' Clean!"*

"God, I wish I could see something," Zack whispered as he looked at the door's small painted-over eye-level window which transmitted some light into room three. Zack soon discovered a small scratch in the semiopaque white privacy-paint on the window. The small area of missing paint allowed him a peephole view into room four. "Holy shit!" Zack exclaimed in a whisper.

"Let me have a look," Mark whispered back.

"Not a big enough area for us both to look. You just keep listening, and I'll do the looking. We can compare notes later," Zack whispered.

Mark was dying to look, but decided since Zack was the one who got spat upon, he definitely was entitled to the looking-rights. He'd be content with listening, and if they both didn't quit whispering so loudly, they'd be discovered and miss everything. Mark pressed his ear to the door. All he could hear was Mose clearing his throat, a series of *bump-bump-bumps* repeated several times, plus a few more "holy shits" softly spoken by Zack as he peered through the scratched window. Mose was speaking so softly, Mark caught very few of his words through the thick door. He did finally hear the drunk loudly say "Yes sir" several times, and finally Mose's full bass voice boomed: "Now that's a lot more like it son! See you at my gym this coming Friday night!"

"Let's split! I think Mose is through," Zack urgently whispered to Mark in the darkness of treatment room three.

The two interns rapidly left their spying place, arriving in Jer's office a moment before Mose left treatment room four. When they entered the office, Jer just smiled at the pair, staring in anticipation. "Well?" Jer said. But they had no time to answer Jer's query. They had just barely seated themselves, when Mose returned to Jer's office to retrieve his white coat still hanging on Jer's door. Mose did not look the least bit out of sorts, his demeanor unchanged, clothes pristine as always.

"Everything's OK now, Dr. Zack. You can go on back in there and finish your work." Mose remained totally calm as he put his jacket on, then held the door open for Dr. Zack Paslaski, who confidently returned to room four.

When Zack entered the treatment room, he saw a great transformation. He first spied Sylvia Banks, the SN. She was now dressed in a green surgical scrub suit top that replaced her ripped-off uniform blouse. A third sterile surgical suture tray was now in place and the patient quietly lay on the table without visible evidence of trauma inflicted by Mose. Zack did note the neckband of the drunk's T-shirt had been stretched to a point that the thin shirt now barely covered his shoulders. The neck hole in the T-shirt now resembled some type of feminine off-the-shoulder attire. Also, the patient now appeared three shades less drunk, and his remodeled attitude impressed Zack.

"Well now ... let's start all over again, shall we?" Zack said with mock pleasantry.

"Yes sir, *Doctor,*" was the patient's now-humble reply.

With Sylvia Banks' assistance, Zack quickly sutured the drunk's laceration and applied a sterile dressing.

"You'll need to come back to the Surgical Outpatient Clinic in seven days to get those stitches out," Zack said, and handed an appointment slip to the transformed patient. "And I'll have the nurse here give you a tetanus shot ... then you can go to jail," Zack added.

As Sylvia Banks cleaned the tetanus toxoid injection site with an alcohol swab, she had only to slide the T-shirt's neckband a little farther down the patient's right shoulder. Watching the injection the patient said, "Ma'am, I'm really sorry about your dress, and I'll buy you a new one soon as I get some money." Sylvia ignored the comment, and busied herself with the room's cleanup.

The drunk then turned to Zack. "Doctor, sir, if it'll make you feel any better, you can spit in my face before they take me to jail."

"That won't be necessary," Zack responded, but secretly he'd been dangerously close to accepting the patient's invitation.

While Shorty escorted the patient out of the ER to a waiting APD car, Zack immediately headed to Jer's office to compare his looking-notes with Mark's listening-notes. Jer had waited there as long as he could, but had left at eight o'clock to attend a residents' meeting.

Zack was obviously excited as he entered the office. "Man, you just ain't gonna believe this shit! That Mose is something else! He just caught that guy by his T-shirt's neckband ... right up front under his chin, ya know. Then he just started winding it up—just twisting it up with his hand—just like he was goin' to choke the dude to death with his own freakin' shirt! I swear, man. When Mose got it really tight, that guy's jugular veins popped out as big as my thumbs. His eyes was red as a fire truck! And with just the chokehold-hand, old Mr. Clean just started shakin' the fella's head, and bangin' it on the table pad. And all the while Mose had his head real close, just whispering something in the dude's ear. Man, I thought I was about to witness a murder! I thought Mose was going to kill him, but I finally realized Mose knew exactly how far to push it. Then the drunk said something I couldn't hear. Mose unwound his chokehold, got the dude a cup of water to drink, and smiled. Then Mose just casually washed and dried his hands.

Now what did you *hear!"*

"God, after that I'm afraid I don't have much to contribute," Mark said. "All I could actually hear was the bumping of the guy's head on the table, a couple of 'yes sirs' from the patient, and Mose saying at the end 'That's more like it son. See you at the gym Friday night,' or something close to that," Mark replied.

Dr. Zack Paslaski and Dr. Mark Telfair then enjoyed a good long laugh together in the privacy of Jer's office. Mutually deciding it was time to leave, Mark spoke. "Come on you trash-mouthed Polack, I'll buy you a beer!" Still smiling, and walking silently together toward Mark's car in the Grady parking lot, Mark Telfair had but one dominant thought: *If that fellow is out of jail by Friday night, he'd damn well better show up at Mose's gym!*

I EATS BROOMS

D r. Mark Telfair was still trying to adjust his life to the Surgical Pit's routine: twelve hours duty, then twelve hours off, seven days a week. The two hours he wasted in Atlanta's commuter traffic each day became frustrating. If he got in any reasonable amount of sleep during his off hours, that left only three or four hours to eat, bathe, shop, study, and socialize what trivial amount he could. Both mentally and physically, he always felt totally exhausted when arriving at the apartment he shared with Carla Lay, his girlfriend.

In contrast, Carla worked nine to five weekdays as an office manager at Frito-Lay. She was well paid for her skills. Carla definitely was the significant breadwinner in their relationship. When she got off work, or on weekends, she always felt rested and ready for social outings, or physical attention from Mark. With increasing frequency, Mark found himself neglecting Carla's needs. Following his first day of ER rotation, their love life had completely fizzled.

A week earlier Carla had abruptly announced she was moving out of the apartment they shared. In a few words she'd politely told Mark she had given up on him and his impossible work schedule: "Mark, I'll always care about you and remember the good times we've had together. I'm really sorry, but my mind is made up. I'm leaving because I can't live in a social and sexual vacuum for the next five years," she'd said before departing. *Well, she's left me,* Mark had thought. His mind quickly did a one-eighty: *No, I'm the one who left ... just abandoned her.*

Mark knew he could no longer afford the apartment they had shared in Northeast Atlanta's Brookhaven, a pleasant area just a few miles north of his old familiar Buckhead stomping grounds. Over four years earlier he'd acquired the Brookhaven apartment when he first started med school. Recently, the landlord had notified all tenants their rent would be increasing by 25 dollars a month, beginning next month. Though he'd never considered his old 1956 PV 444K Volvo a gas hog, the daily 32-mile commute between Brookhaven and Grady Hospital generated expenses far larger than he'd anticipated; he simply could no longer afford to stay where he was, at least not on his intern's salary alone.

Considering possibilities, Mark knew one option would be to move back home to the Buckhead area. He knew he could live there in the family home with his widowed mom. She lived alone. Mark's father, a workaholic CPA, had been the senior partner in a large Atlanta accounting firm, when he suddenly died of a coronary. Mark was a junior in medical school when it happened. While growing up, and even through college and early med school, his dad's work schedule had not allowed them much time to interact as father and son. But when they did have their infrequent lengthy father-son talks, Mark shamelessly shared all his secrets with his dad. Whatever he told his dad remained there: their man-to-man secret. It had always been his understanding father who accepted Mark the way he was. It had always been his father who tried to impart some practical bits of worldly wisdom, striving to keep him on a path that would prepare him for life in the real world. Mark treasured the meager bits of fatherly advice he'd received prior to his dad's untimely death. These bits of wisdom had been invaluable to him. He'd forever regret there hadn't been more time to receive a lot more of it.

On the other hand, Mark's mom presented an entirely different picture. During his upbringing as an only child, and well before his father's death, his mom had certainly been the dominant parent. She had dutifully tried to make up for Mark's frequently absent hard-working father. At 62, his mom remained in good health, and continued to live in the family home unassisted. The family home was located in the Garden Hills section of Buckhead, and several miles closer to Grady. Despite their recent and past differences, Mark knew he'd always be welcome there. *Perhaps a little too welcome,* he thought. Even as a teen he'd resigned himself to the fact that his mom would always consider him her "little boy." Perhaps she actually did want the best in life for him ... or was it the precious family name she wanted to keep untarnished? At times she could be too domineering, too controlling. Mark had always found her obsessed with outdated social appearances and social properness, much more so than his very practical dad who'd accepted the '60s well.

Mark had often wondered why his mother was so socially obsessed. Perhaps it was because life in Atlanta contrasted so sharply with her own rural roots, of which she was not particularly proud. As one of five daughters in a poor South Georgia logger's family, Mark's mother, Anne, was the only one with a college education. She was the only one to ultimately break rural bonds and move away to live in a large "cosmopolitan city," as she so delighted in calling Atlanta. Apparently ashamed of her background, she had conveniently minimized all knowledge of her rural South Georgia upbringing. In Atlanta she'd quickly become Queen Anne, completely enthralled with its social life. She reveled in the achievements of her CPA husband and her pride-and-joy son, now a *doctor.*

While considering a move back to Buckhead to live with Mom, Mark recalled a situation that suggested that choice was a definite "no." Two years earlier, Mom had paid a surprise visit to his Brookhaven apartment. Despite the fact that her little boy was then in his second year of med school, and in his mid-20s, she had become thoroughly distraught when she discovered her son was shacking up in his Brookhaven apartment with a girlfriend. Just *seeing* Mark's girlfriend had caused Mom to leave the apartment in a total huff.

The next day he'd phoned Mom to see if she'd settled down. She hadn't. "Son, I've suffered through—even facilitated, at times—your fascinations for hot rods, rockets, snakes, insect collecting, and bombs. Those things were trying enough, but when knowledge of your attraction for that redneck trailer-park trash you're living with gets out—and it *will*—it'll be a blight on the Telfair name. *Your name,* son. You'll find that hussy, her miniskirts, and those low-cut dresses have just ruined any chances you ever had of becoming a prominent surgeon ... at least here in Atlanta! I'd even been told they were keeping an eye on you for an Associate Professorship at Emory's Winship Clinic. But be assured, that'll never happen now ... and you'll never be invited to join the Piedmont Driving Club, Atlanta Athletic Club, Capital City Club, or East Lake Country Club!" Mom had slammed the phone down in disgust.

Mark knew his mom's opinion of the hussy would change, if only she'd bothered to ask the girl's name before storming out of his apartment that day; Hussy's daddy *owned* Frito-Lay. As the daughter of the potato chip and corn chip genius, she was well respected, but not solely because her dad was a multimillionaire snack-food giant. In Mark's eyes, Carla Lay was respected on her own. She had an MBA degree from Agnes Scott College with honors. She was rapidly becoming an outstanding business team member of the multimillion-dollar Lay dynasty. *But who gives a flying fuck about the Queen's opinion!* he clearly recalled thinking after his mom had stormed out. Mark knew the Queen would never change with the times, but he was determined not to let that destroy his own ability to change with them, nor diminish the basic love he'd always feel for his socially infatuated mother.

His present thinking about his ex-girlfriend and Mom was not solving his most pressing present problem: *finding a place to live.* The 14th floor of Grady offered free quarters for interns and residents, but they were in very short supply. The rooms were nothing fancy, yet were comfortable. They had the accommodations you'd expect to find in a nice semiprivate college dormitory room. The Grady rooms were very similar to ones he'd experienced in his dorm at Emory as an undergraduate. Grady's staff rooms each had two single beds, two desks, private bath, phone, and a place to keep clothes, books, and limited possessions.

Mark's cohort, Dr. Zack Paslaski, had lived in Grady's dorm since the day he and Mark had started out together in the GAC. Zack had no roommate. Daily, Mark and Zack continued to work together in the Surgical Emergency Room. Aware of Mark's situation with his girlfriend and apartment, Zack kept pestering Mark to move in with him at the hospital. The unused bed in Zack's room was the *only* one left.

"Look at it this way," Zack had finally said. "Where else can you live on the lousy 79 bucks a month they pay us interns to work here? Granted, we get free meal tickets, free maid service, free laundry service, and health care at no cost. And a *free room!* Just where else can you get all that shit free, and still get paid 79 bucks a month? Where? Just tell me ... huh?"

Mark knew Zack was completely right, but wasn't sure he could live with Zack. Their pre-Grady worlds had just been too different. Mark had grown up in one of Northeast Atlanta's more desirable neighborhoods. He had attended Emory University and Emory University School of Medicine—the so-called "Harvards of the South," according to some in the academic world, as well as his mom, Queen Anne. In college and med school he'd been at least an average student, and had socialized with peers having similar backgrounds. Though certainly not sexually innocent, nor entirely naive otherwise, Mark realized he had led a somewhat sheltered life. He had been born into Southern ways that made him gentle in manner and soft in speech. Though he did frequently "cuss in his mind," he rarely used profanity openly.

In sharp contrast, Zack Paslaski was of Polish background, growing up in a poor neighborhood in Harlem, New York. Zack almost never spoke softly. He cursed like a sailor. Zack's father had been an automotive mechanic. By the time Zack was ten he could hot-wire any car made, and fix almost anything mechanical that had broken down. Strangely, Zack had first attended college at Albert Einstein, then Albany Medical College—both on full scholastic scholarships. Although Mark hated to admit it to himself, Zack was definitely smart. Brilliant, actually. He was both academically smart and streetwise, a chimera, an unusual combination of traits that did not fit Zack's skinny six-foot frame and reddish-blond hair. Mark knew he could live with Zack's freckles and beanpole appearance. But Zack's mouth was another story.

"OK, OK, OK!" Mark heard himself finally say to Zack. "But you gotta help me move. My apartment lease runs out in three days. I'll get 125 bucks back from the security deposit. That'll be enough to make about three payments on that old Volvo I've got. But after that money runs out, you gotta help me with the payments if you want to use the car. OK?"

"Hey Man, no problem," Zack allowed. "I ain't spent but 15 bucks since I've been here, saved the rest. And you bought me the last beer I had. Was on that day after Mr. Clean straightened out that spittin' piece of shit in the Pit! I mean old Mr. Clean really cleaned that guy's fuckin' clock!"

Mark ignored Zack's reference to Mr. Clean but not the language. "And one more thing Zack—do you *always* have to cuss so frequently?" Mark added, feeling that if he moved in with trash-mouthed Zack, the arrangement would—by association—negatively reflect upon his own character.

"Well no ... I don't guess so," Zack responded. "But ya see Mark, I grew up talking just like I talk. Whole family and all my friends did too. What you Southern folks call cussin' we'd just call plain talkin' up in New York. Hell, up until I was six years old, I thought my name was Asshole, 'cause that's what Pops always called me. I didn't even realize my name was Zack until I got to the first grade. First grade teacher said my name was Zachary and that Zach was OK, if it had an *h* at the end. So when I told Pops my name was Zach, I remember he said 'That fuckin' teacher-bitch can't even spell worth a shit!' And I'm sure I pissed off Jer that day he heard me say shit in front of those patients in the ER, and to this day I ain't said another fuckin' cuss word in front of a patient!"

Though he still had serious reservations about his decision, Mark's move from Brookhaven to Grady went off without a major hitch. Zack had helped Mark cram his limited worldly possessions into the ancient Volvo which Zack promptly labeled: *The Bomb*. At 3:15 a.m. they finally put the car in the Grady parking lot after the final trip of Mark's move. Zack slowly walked around Mark's parked Volvo, apparently doing a final inspection. "I ain't seen an old '56 PV 444K in years, but ya know Mark, I'm surprised this piece of shit is still street legal. Wouldn't be up in New York, you know."

"Well this piece of sh ... uh, car, is now in *Georgia*, Zack. And it beats the heck out of what you're driving!" Mark shot back, finding pleasure in knowing Zack didn't even own a car. Mark was even more pleased he had denied Zack the pleasure of hearing him say "shit."

"Here's a car key," Mark said as he handed Zack an extra Volvo key he kept in his wallet. "Just remember you promised to help with the payments."

"Well since we're now attending the Exchanging of the Keys Club, here's a duplicate key to our room," Zack remarked, as he also removed a spare key from his own wallet. "All you gotta do is pay your half of the rent!"

With arms full, the pair entered the building. They caught the elevator to the 14th floor and stacked the last load of Mark's limited possessions in semi-neat piles. They arranged them so they'd at least be partially out of their way. By the time they'd finished arranging the piles of Mark's things, it was close to 4:00 a.m., and both were totally exhausted. As they crashed into their beds they both knew they'd better grab what sleep they could, while they could. The 7:00 a.m. starting time for their ER tour was rapidly closing upon them. *God, what have I done?* Mark thought, as he fell into the deepest sleep he'd had in quite some time.

A little over two hours later, Mark jangled awake as their room's phone loudly rang. Being disoriented in his dark new environment, Mark knocked over a couple of piles of his books and other belongings; they made substantial crashing noises as they hit the hard vinyl tile floor. He finally located the light switch and answered the phone on its fifth or sixth ring.

"Good morning! It's six a.m. Dr. Paslaski. My goodness! We sure are quick to answer today aren't we?" the pleasant singsong operator's voice said. Mark couldn't respond because she'd instantly disconnected, and was now in the process of waking up perhaps 50 or so other doctors with similar standing wake-up requests.

Mark first heard Zack groan, then heard a yawn as his roommate stretched. Zack sprang out of bed and yelled at the top of his lungs: "GOOD MORNING VIETNAM!" Mark jumped at the unanticipated loud pronouncement. Mark soon learned Zack could go from the sleep of the dead to a state of being hyperawake in a mere five seconds. The real problem in waking Zack was simply breaking through the barrier of his sleep. Mark would quickly discover the reason for the operator's "My we sure are quick to answer..." comment: It was because it usually took 10 or 15 rings to shake Zack loose from sleep's grip, but once accomplished, Zack was instantly awake and ready for the day.

Despite a small traffic jam during their morning shave-and-shower routine, Mark found that living-in was really going to be a timesaver. It actually added some two hours to his free time each day, the time he'd formerly spent commuting in Atlanta's traffic.

Mark and Zack boarded the elevator together at 6:30 a.m. They were headed for Ptomaine Plaza, as some unjustly called Grady's third-floor cafeteria. The pair ate a tasty breakfast, and by 7:00 a.m. had gone down to start their day shift in Jer's Pit.

The workday that followed in Dr. Jerry Bacon's ER had all been routine—except for the very last patient of Mark's shift. Tired from last night's move to Grady, and having only a couple hours' sleep, Mark was feeling totally exhausted as he neared completion of his shift. But in terms of Mark's learning something new, his last patient had been his best one of the day.

Close to the end of the shift, a black male in his late 50s had come in with a small wound to his right lateral chest. The patient was having extreme difficulty breathing. The wound to the chest looked like a small puncture wound of some sort, but since the patient claimed he'd been asleep and in the dark when it happened, he stated he had no knowledge regarding the kind of object that may have caused the puncture wound. In addition the patient denied having any information regarding the circumstances of his wounding. "Jus' woke up ... this away," the patient repeatedly explained between rapid breaths. Though Mark listened carefully with his stethoscope, he could hear no breath sounds on the right side of the patient's chest. A portable chest X-ray rapidly confirmed Mark's clinical diagnosis: total pneumothorax, or a fully collapsed right lung.

Dr. Jerry Bacon had shown Mark how to make a small incision and place a thoracotomy tube through the patient's chest wall into the space between the collapsed lung and the inner chest wall. Jer had then shown him how to secure the tube to the patient's chest with heavy sutures and wide adhesive tape, thus making an accidental dislodgement of the tube virtually impossible. He had patiently shown Mark how to connect the tube to a regulated vacuum system that would re-expand the collapsed lung. Mark had been surprised how easy it had been to do, and how quickly the patient's labored breathing returned to normal. Upon completing the tube's placement, he even allowed feelings of pride and self-confidence to creep into his thoughts.

With the patient fully stabilized, Jer had left the treatment room. The patient rested comfortably while waiting in the ER's treatment room until an orderly could come down from the Thoracic Surgery Department, and transport him upstairs to spend a few days on the T-surg ward. Still glowing in his achievements, Mark sat on a stool at the patient's side. He was completing lengthy notes attached to a clipboard when he heard a loud knock on the closed treatment room door. Expecting a transport orderly from thoracic, Mark loudly and proudly said, "Come on in!"

46

Instead of the expected T-surg orderly, a five-foot-tall elderly woman—the ugliest Mark Telfair had ever seen anywhere—popped through the treatment room door! She had stringy yellow-white disheveled hair that almost reached her waist. She nervously clutched a filthy brown paper sack in her hands, and kept it drawn to her chest. Her dark black face was covered with warts the size and texture of unshelled black walnuts. Her rumpled long-sleeved dress was entirely black except for a small filthy white collar that surrounded her skinny wart-covered neck. Her crooked smile had only two visible teeth, one upper and one lower. Her left eye was non-seeing and a uniform gray color; the other eye was jet-black, piercing, and rapidly surveying everything in the treatment room. Mark first detected an offensive smell, not unlike that of a dead rat, then felt a definite *chill* crawl over his entire body.

"Is he still a livin', Doctor?" the witch-like creature asked as she abruptly fixed her one good eye on the patient. Upon hearing her high-pitched voice, the patient suddenly closed his eyes tightly. In a way Mark couldn't blame the patient. Something about this lady horrified Mark too. He wished he could join the patient, close his own eyes, and make the whole chilling scene go away.

Stunned by her grotesque appearance and shrieking voice, it took Mark several moments to muster a reply. "Uh, yes ma'am, he's definitely alive ... be good as new in just a few days."

Though still unsettled by her appearance, he continued to feel traces of a rapidly fleeting warmth; for the very first time in his life as a doctor, Mark felt his *own* actions, his own hands, even if directed by Jer, had actually saved a person's life.

Mark finally recovered his composure. He cautiously spoke to the woman. "Do you know the patient?"

She turned and stared at him with her good eye as though it were an evil laser capable of looking directly into the depths of his soul. With apparent reluctance she finally answered. "Well Doctor, I's the woman what he stays with. He done stole some of my mojo ... and throwed hit away! And you don't *never, never, never* do that to somebody what's got the *power!* So I try my best to kill him graveyard dead while he was a sleepin'. Did hit early this mornin'."

During Mark's initial dialog with the witch, the male patient appeared to be quietly sleeping on the treatment table. Upon hearing the woman's voice again, the patient became agitated, started squirming, but then rapidly froze in apparent mortal fear. He was totally unable to speak or move, refusing to open his eyes. Mark felt his own pulse quicken. His mind sensed he was about to experience another chilling introduction to life's perils. *God, I hope she doesn't have a gun in that sack!*

The witch—or whatever she was—reached into the paper sack she was carrying. From it, she withdrew a red-handled ice pick. She lunged toward the patient. Mark tried to restrain her. He found she was a lot stronger than he'd anticipated. She grabbed the patient's chest tube with her free hand, frantically trying to pull it out. With the edge of his clipboard, Mark whacked her on the back of her bony hand that gripped the tube. She glared at Mark, but at least she'd released the lifesaving chest tube she seemed so determined to dislodge. Laughing, she next tried to bite Mark on his restraining hands and arms. Having only two teeth she did little harm, but she did succeed in causing Mark to drop his clipboard—*his only weapon!*

With an unexplained burst of energy, she broke Mark's restraining hold. *She promptly stabbed him in his right shoulder with her ice pick!* In disbelief, Mark looked at the small expanding red spot on the shoulder of his white coat, but he felt no pain. Desperately searching for another weapon—*a weapon of any kind*—Mark grabbed a straw broom which leaned against the wall in a corner of the treatment room. He swung it at her head as hard as he could. The broom's straw smacked into the side of her head with a solid thud. She dropped the ice pick to the floor, but not the sack. The witch quickly retreated into a corner, yet remained totally intent on her mission. Squatting on the floor in the corner, she incessantly cackled with a piercing high-pitched laugh. Mark kept her in the corner by repetitively jabbing the broom in her face, hoping to disable her one good eye. Between Mark's broom-jabs the witch managed to retrieve a *second* ice pick from her sack. She stood and hurled it at him with lightning speed. The thrown ice pick whizzed past his right ear with such speed he actually heard a swishing sound and felt the disturbance in the air as it flew past. The pick harmlessly buried its point into a wooden cabinet door directly behind him. For a few seconds, the pick made a resonant vibrating sound similar to a fading bass note on a guitar string.

Not deterred by her missed target, she extracted from her sack what appeared to be a large bird's foot. The foot, a pale yellow one with black claws, had a fuzzy yarn-like red string about three feet long tied to it. She held the free end of the red string between the same fingers of her hand that clutched the sack, then extended the bird's foot toward him at arm's length with her other hand. She shook the bird's foot at Mark's face. While jiggling the foot, she uttered totally unintelligible words, all spoken between periods of hoarse cackling laughter. Still clutching her sack, but apparently having no more weapons, she suddenly bolted out the treatment room door.

"Shorty! Shorty! Help!" Mark yelled for the ER's cop, as he chased the witch through the length of the ER common area. Using his broom as a weapon, he continually swatted as he chased after her. She ran through the ER's swinging doors into the foyer, and quickly stepped into the open elevator that always waited there on the ready. Since his first day in the ER, Mark had learned that this elevator went only to the second-floor X-ray department, or up one additional floor to the third-floor operating rooms. Either the "two" or "three" button had to be pushed before the elevator doors would close and permit the elevator to leave the ER's ground-level foyer. *Got you trapped in there now bitch!* Mark thought. But the witch quickly pushed one of the buttons. The doors started to close. Mark panicked. *Oh God! What if she gets loose in X-ray, or worse—the OR!* Instantly he started moving his broom side to side, alternately striking the elevator's black rubber door edges, trying to defeat the multiple jerky attempts the elevator doors were making at closure. "Shorty! Shorty!" Mark yelled again ... and again ... and again. All to no avail.

The witch was now hunkered down in a back corner of the foyer's elevator, laughing, cackling, mumbling, and consulting the remaining contents of her sack. Mark kept batting the elevator doors with his broom and yelling for help. The witch finally stood up with something balled up in her right fist. She stared at Mark with her one good eye, and screeched loudly. *"I eats brooms, White Boy! You hear me! I eats brooms and I shits broom straw!"*

As his adrenalin surged, renewed fear struck Mark. He heard his own pulse rapidly pounding in his ears. His right shoulder now began to throb severely. The red spot on his white coat had expanded to the size of a dinner plate. He found himself sweating profusely, mostly from fright. The exertion of the constant broom motion needed to keep the elevator door open—and keep the witch at bay in the back of the elevator—was alone enough to lead to rapid exhaustion. At the moment Mark felt he could no longer keep it up, help finally arrived. Mark saw two familiar huge black hands reach from behind him. They grabbed the elevator's door edges and kept them apart.

"Miss Lucifer, put that mojo down—NOW! You know I got the *power* too!" Mose spoke with unquestioned authority. The witch promptly dropped the sack held in her left hand, then slowly opened her clenched right fist. With a soft thud, a dead blood-encrusted toad dropped to the spotless elevator floor.

Mose then entered the elevator and pressed a button that canceled the elevator's repeated attempts to leave the ground floor. In a nonthreatening and tender way, Mose extended his giant hand to the witch-woman. She quietly accepted it. Mose gently led her away and said, "Missy, it's time to go home now."

THE CUE BALL

Mark had two weeks remaining on his ER rotation. His encounter with the witch had left him a little paranoid, especially regarding patients who carried a sack of any kind. His mind kept bringing up the bad things: *I've been shot at. I've been stabbed with an ice pick. My roommate has been spat upon. A student nurse had her blouse ripped off. Stuff like this never happened in Buckhead!*

After 27 years of sheltered life, the troubled young doctor was beginning to personally experience a side of life he'd only heard rumors about. *A side of life that doesn't actually exist in Atlanta,* he recalled thinking prior to his extended stay at Grady. The environment of his upbringing and education had left him essentially unexposed and ill-prepared. Daily he vacillated between canceling and continuing his military active-duty deferment ... between leaving Grady to assume active duty with the Air Force ... or remaining at Grady to tough it out.

Zack, Jer, and Mose had all recognized Mark's despondent state. Each tried to help him in their own way. Initially, Zack had patiently explained he'd seen much worse things happen on the streets of Harlem. When Zack felt Mark had almost made up his mind to leave Grady, he finally spoke to Mark quite bluntly: "You can't live like a chickenshit Buckhead pussy forever. Just tough it out, and quit bein' such a candyass!"

Jer had insisted he care personally for Mark's shoulder wound. He gave Mark a tetanus shot, X-rayed his shoulder, put a small surgical drain in the ice pick wound, and placed him on antibiotics. Jer even did bacterial cultures from the ice pick that had stabbed Mark—the pick that had shared the sack with a stinking dead toad, a chicken's foot, and only God knows what else. Jer's final advice to Mark was also fairly concise and blunt: "Shit happens. Get over it!"

But more so than anyone else, it would be Mose that came to Mark's rescue and helped him out of his doldrums. Mose had started taking his lunch breaks at the same time Mark did. Over lunch together, Mose would answer some of the questions that disturbed Mark Telfair. A few days after the ice pick incident, Mose and Mark were sitting alone in the cafeteria eating lunch.

"How's that shoulder feelin' today, Doctor?" Mose inquired between bites of cornbread.

"Still painful, but less so today than yesterday. It's only been four days you know.   X-rays didn't show any chipped bone, and Dr. Jerry doesn't think the pick actually went into the joint space. So I'm hoping it won't amount to much ... especially if the cultures from the ice pick don't reveal any antibiotic-resistant bacteria," Mark summarized, trying to sound upbeat enough to hide his depression from Mose.

"Guess you wondering about that old gal, Miss Lucifer, ain't you?" Mose said as he easily read Mark's troubled mind.

"Well yes Mose, matter of fact. But I'm also wondering why you just simply led her away that night, just told her to go on back home. Why'd you do that, Mose? Why didn't you give her to the police? What if I'd wanted to file assault charges? What if she tries to stab her husband again?"

"Well let me tell you a little about her before I answer your questions. You see, Doctor, we don't really know who she actually is, not ev'n how old she is. And if you look real close at her hands, you can see she ain't ev'n got no fingerprints! But she been 'round since I was just a little boy over in the housing projects. Rumor is, she come up to Atlanta from down in New Orleans. Come up here when she was just a little tiny baby—had all them warts and one dead eye, e'vn way back then. And she s'pose to be a *juju*, an evil spirit of some kind, and a conjurer too. She don't ev'n have no birth certificate that we knows of, and she don't have no real name—no legal name—that we knows of. So I jus' calls her Miss Lucifer, or Missy, only 'cause that's what the folks over in the housin' project decided to call her."

"Well Mose, you still haven't answered all my questions," Mark responded, as he absorbed Mose's comments on Miss Lucifer's background. *Is Mose avoiding my question ... the one that concerns me the most?* Mark's mind asked.

Politely, but defensively, Mose spoke. "Doctor, I know you upset at me 'cause I jus' let her go that night. But jus' let me say this: You think you could file charges against a no-name old lady for stabbin' you, and ain't no witness 'cept you? Or the *possible* stabbin' of her husband with no witness? And ain't ev'n got no fingerprints? Then you think you goin' to take them charges to a mostly black jury, with half of 'em still believing in that voodoo and mojo root-stuff? Think serious Doctor. Think on that just a minute."

Mark knew he had just been politely injected with a healthy dose of real-world ... a vaccine containing some of Mose's mojo-wisdom. But he still harbored concerns about the old lady harming someone else. "Mose what if she stabs someone again?" Mark countered.

"Ain't goin' to happen, Doctor. Unless she stab an inmate down at the Central State Hospital in Milledgeville. She'd been in there before, and after she stab you and that fella what she stays with, I called some special folks I know. And when she got home that night I walked her outside, they was already there ... jus' a waitin' for her at her house. They took her straight back on down to Milledgeville that very night!"

Mark's mouth popped open like a toad expecting to catch a June bug. A meager "Thanks Mose" was all Mark managed to get out, before an additional less-troubling thought entered his mind: *Rooters ... exactly what are they?*

"Mose, think I can ask you just one more question, before we go back down to the ER?"

"Let me hear it quick, Doctor," Mose said, as he checked his watch.

"I'll be quick, Mose. Could you tell me exactly what a Rooter is? I've heard the term Rooter since I was a medical student here ... and I'm really embarrassed to say, I still don't know exactly what one is."

"Oh Lawdy, Dr. Mark!" Mose exclaimed, but then chuckled softly wearing an amused grin. He'd obviously been expecting a serious question. Mose dropped his voice to a whisper. "Doctor, years back, we'd called 'em *Grady* Rooters. But these last few years, folks is jus' callin' 'em *plain* Rooters. It all got started way back, 'cause a heap of the folks what come to the Gradies believe in voodoo, mojo, and root ... jus' like that witch what stab you with the ice pick. But Rooter today don't mean e'zactly same it did way back then. Today, Doctor, Rooter mostly mean any folk what's completely trustin' of the Gradies, and wouldn't never consider goin' to no other hospital 'cept the Gradies—*not for no reason!* Now I know some folks'll say you got to be a nigger to be a Rooter, but that jus' ain't so. We got a heap of white Rooters runnin' 'round here too. But you ain't never s'pose to say Rooter to they face, or write it down nowhere. Understand?"

"Sure, Mose. I'd never do that anyway. But if we've got time, could you tell me just one more thing? Exactly how did Grady become the *Gradies?* Like plural, you know?"

Mose again looked at his watch. "We ain't got but about five minute left, but I try to be short, Doctor. The very first Grady Hospital, she were built over 60 year ago. Gotta be so, 'cause that's where I was born at ... the first Grady, just down the street on the corner of Coca-Cola and Butler.

But this new hospital, where we at now, it replace the old one. New one, she were finish-up about 1959, best I remember. So, ya see, they was a short time, 'round 1958, when Atlanta had *two* Grady hospitals, and the Rooters wasn't sure if it should be the old Grady or the new Grady, where the ambulance should be a takin' 'em, you know. So they simply say: 'Take me to the Gradies,' 'cause they knowed the ambulance would know which one to take 'em to."

"Thanks, Mose." *And I've still got an awful lot to learn about the Gradies, and the real world,* Mark's mind told his embarrassed brain.

"Well you most welcome, sir," Mose said with a warm smile. "But Dr. Mark, this lunch time she is gettin' mighty short now, and there's jus' one more thing I'd like to say before we go back down to the Emergency Room."

"Shoot," Mark said as he stuck a spoon in his bowl of egg custard dessert.

"I know a lot of bad stuff been happenin' lately in Emergency Room. Come in spells, you know. It's been four or five year since we've had so much bad stuff happen so close together. Might not happen again for a very long time. But what worries me, Doctor, is I see you gettin' all discouraged. I see you gettin' down in your mind. I hear you talkin' 'bout leavin' the Gradies and goin' on in that U.S. Air Force. So let me ask you this: Just what you think you'll be doin' when you gets in that Air Force? You got that M.D. degree, and less than four month of the internship—and that's *all you got!* They'll put yo little inexperienced nonspecialized white butt in one of them Vietnam helicopters, just like what you see on the TV. You ain't gonna be in some big fancy hospital far away from the fightin' over there. You goin' to find them peoples over there is ev'n more crazy than some of the peoples what comes to the Gradies ER. Some of the older boys at my gym—least the one or two what did make it back from over there—say them folks is so crazy they eats dogs and cats. So if you decide to go over there, I think you goin' to find you jus' jumped straight from the frying pan into the fire—that's what!"

Mark wasn't sure Mose was totally correct about the Asian diet, or the Air Force assignment he'd get ... but it sure gave him a lot to think about while he and Mose quickly headed back to the ER in silence. For some strange reason—he felt it totally silly—his mind couldn't help but wonder: *Does Mose have the mojo power ... or some other strange power that allows him to read my mind?*

Upon entering the ER, Mark started reflecting about the time of day the bad stuff happened. He had already learned to respect the final hours of his 7:00 a.m. to 7:00 p.m. shift; that was when most of the quirky or unusual things happened, usually between 5:00 p.m. and 7:00 p.m. He'd often talked with the interns that pulled the ER night shift. Frequently, they'd still be wrapping up the night's loose ends when he came on duty at seven in the mornings. Mark had learned the night shift was usually much worse than what he'd seen during the days. Finally, feeling somewhat fortunate, his troubled mind accepted Mose's lunchroom-wisdom. Zack and Jer's advice quickly blended with Mose's wisdom. His mind decided: *By God, I'm going to tough it out at Grady!*

Just when Mark felt he'd decided on his future, and figured out the most likely hours for dangerous or unusual things to happen, he heard Dr. Jerry Bacon's voice call him. It was only 12:30 p.m., and Mark put his figuring-out on hold.

"Yo! Dr. Telfair ... we got a really unusual problem in room three. Come take a look! I ain't never seen anything like it before," Jer smiled.

Jer and Mark quickly entered room three. Having previously surveyed the situation, Jer didn't say a word. He wanted to give Mark an opportunity to evaluate the patient's dilemma on his own.

Initially, Mark was at a complete loss. There before him, sitting on the treatment room table, was an obese white male in his 20s. He reeked of alcohol and swayed a little while sitting. His head was constantly cocked to one side. In his right hand, he held a kidney-shaped stainless-steel basin to one corner of his mouth. A steady stream of saliva dribbled from the corner of his mouth into the waiting metal pan. His mouth appeared to be forced wide open by a smooth white object that totally filled all visible space behind his upper and lower teeth. Small nonbleeding skin tears were present in both corners of his mouth. The patient was unable to speak, but he could make a humming noise through his nose: He used either a *umm* for a yes, or an *umm-umm* for a no. His nose-breathing appeared to be adequate, unhindered. Mark put on a rubber glove and touched the object in the patient's mouth. It felt hard as a rock, locked in solid, and totally immobile to firm pressure. A switch clicked in Mark's brain: *It's a damn cue ball ... a regulation-sized cue ball!*

"Jer! That's a cue ball stuck in there! How'd it get in there?" Mark immediately asked.

"Not our problem, Doctor. The real problem is how do we get it *out!* We need some real ingenuity here. We can't put him to sleep. He's got a belly full of beer, pickled eggs, and pretzels. That's the only useful information we were able to get from the guy that brought him in from Cooter's Cue Room ... you know that little joint about five or six blocks from here. I've already talked with the Chief Anesthesia Resident, and he says it's too risky to put him to sleep with a full belly—just too risky he'll vomit and suck all that stuff back into his lungs. Nasal intubation probably won't work because the thing is jammed too close to the back of his throat. We could even cause him to vomit by stimulating the back of his throat with the nasal tube."

"Jer, what about pulling a few of his teeth?" Mark asked.

"Been there, done that," Jer shot back. "I already talked with the Chief Oral Surgery Resident, and he had no useful suggestions except pulling about half his teeth, provided he could even get his extraction forceps on the teeth. Then he said maybe—just *maybe*—there'd be enough room to get it out, if we could figure some way to grab hold of the sucker!"

"Well, what about first doing a trach?" Mark asked. (Secretly, Mark was anxious to have Jer show him how to do a tracheotomy—a surgical opening made in the front of the neck that goes directly into the windpipe). "Jer, a trach would insure we had a good airway for him. And they wouldn't have to worry about all that stuff getting into his lungs during a general anesthetic in the OR. Under general, and using muscle relaxants, that ball should come out. They might have to make some small incisions at the corners of his mouth, just so they could get their fingers around it though."

"'Tern, I've already considered all that," Jer said. "Don't you think doin' a trach is sorta drastic? I mean like for a conscious patient who's breathing OK at the moment? Besides, even if we started doing a trach, and even if we had already made the incision into his trachea, he could still vomit and suck all that stuff into his lungs *before* we could even get his trach tube inserted and sealed off with its inflatable cuff. Pretty big risk for a simple procedure. But we can't wait several hours for him to naturally empty his stomach either. By then, he'll probably have enough swelling in the back of his throat he won't even be able to breathe through his nose."

Mark thought a moment. "I don't have any other ideas, except to try to get something behind that cue ball. Maybe something thin, like a sling. Something that would not even touch the back of his throat, and cause him to vomit by reflex. We could then pull like heck, accepting the fact we might break a few teeth."

"Be my guest, 'Tern—give it a try!" Jer exclaimed, eyebrows arched, hands thrown in the air, indicating he obviously had little confidence in Mark's idea.

Mark got a surgical tray out of the cabinet. From the tray, he selected a pair of Kelly clamps, similar to large curved hemostats. He next unfolded a square multi-ply gauze sponge, then refolded it to make a multilayered foot-long gauze ribbon about two inches wide, but less than one-eighth inch in thickness. With the aid of the two instruments Mark was finally able to gently "fish" the thin gauze ribbon behind the cue ball, and out the other side—all without touching the back of the patient's throat. They now had "handles." Jer restrained the patient's head, while Mark simultaneously pulled on the two free ends of the gauze sling. Mark pulled as hard as he could, creating a tug of war between himself and Jer, with the patient's head caught in the middle. Finally there was a sudden give. Mark flew back against the wall, then fell to the floor, unhurt. His hopes crushed, Mark studied the frazzled gauze that had abruptly given away. *Well shit! Triple shit!* he thought, now really concerned their patient would suffocate if they couldn't come up with something quickly.

"Nice try, 'Tern," Jer said in desperation, again dramatically throwing his hands in the air.

"Where's Zack?" Mark asked, still sitting on the floor and studying the frayed gauze ends like someone had just popped his toy balloon.

"He was sitting at the desk last I saw," Jer informed.

"Jer, mind if I ask Zack to come in here?"

"And what makes you think Mr. Trashmouth could solve the problem?" Jer asked.

"Well, Jer, Zack's got a brilliant mind, especially when it comes to mechanical things. I think it's worth a try."

"Go get him," Jer ordered, unconvinced, concern edging into his voice.

It didn't take Mark but a few seconds to find Zack, and get him into the middle of the dilemma. Mark and Jer both quickly briefed Zack on the problem—and their own failed attempt at extracting the ball using a gauze sling.

After being filled in on the situation, Zack remained silent for a full ten seconds while thinking. Even when Zack's brain was in low gear, it was faster than most folks' high gear. Zack cleared his throat, indicating he was through thinking. "This ain't Mission Impossible, ya know. If all you guys need is a firm handle on that cue ball, you really ain't got no problem."

"Whatdaya mean, *no problem?*" Jer shot back with a skeptical look.

Zack ignored Jer's question and replaced it with one of his own. "This place got a shop ... you know, a maintenance head-shed, or something like that?"

"Yeah I'm sure it does, but I don't know exactly how to contact them," Jer lamely replied.

Saying nothing, Zack picked up the wall-mounted in-house phone in the treatment room. He dialed a single number. Zack kept the phone glued to his ear while Jer and Mark silently wondered what Zack was up to. "Hey, Baby Doll! It's Zack Paslaski here. You know, your 15-ring 6:00 a.m. wake-up call?... Same to you Baby Doll, but I need a real special favor. Can you somehow connect me to the shop or maintenance HQ for this place?" Mark and Jer stood by silently while the operator transferred the call. A few seconds later, Zack spoke: "Uh, hello ... you the shop guy?" A brief pause ensued before Zack spoke again. "Yeah, you sure can man. I need a quarter-twenty tap, a good quarter-twenty hex-head bolt about three inches long, an electric drill, and drill bits up to one-quarter. You got that? Oh, and a pair of large Vise-Grip pliers too," Zack added, but then paused while listening before speaking again. "No I ain't exactly *new on the job here!* I'm Dr. Zack Paslaski, and we need that stuff in room number three in the Surgical Emergency Room. *Stat!* OK?"

Zack quickly hung up with such a cool confidence that it had Dr. Jerry Bacon—and now Dr. Mark Telfair—extremely anxious about the decision to call Zack in on their predicament. But if Zack had been any calmer, he would have been in a coma. Except for small talk unrelated to the problem, a full five minutes passed in relative silence.

A somewhat mystified silver-haired fellow in a gray uniform next appeared in the treatment room. He had a tool box in tow. "Uh ... Dr. Paslaski?" the fellow said, uncertainly looking around at everyone present.

"Right here," Zack said. He reached for the bright red tool box, then opened it. Zack was quite pleased to find all the items he had requested.

"Plug this in," Zack abruptly said to Mark, and handed him the end of the electric drill's power cord. "Let's see," Zack mumbled as he selected a drill bit and chucked it into the electric drill. "I need you guys to hold the patient's head *real steady* while I drill a hole in that cue ball. OK?"

Neither Jer nor Zack said a word, just did as they were told. Jer was concerned about the future of his residency as Zack skillfully drilled a hole in the center of the exposed part of the cue ball. As the drilling continued, and the drill's depth increased, Jer and Mark became absolutely petrified with a thought: *Zack might accidentally drill all the way through the ball—and into the back of the patient's throat—and cause the patient to suffocate on his own blood!* Jer was reaching to snatch the drill from Dr. Paslaski's hand, when Zack yelled out, "OK! That's deep enough! Now let me tap that sucker." Zack quickly used the tap and expertly cut clean threads into the sides of the deep hole he'd just drilled into the stuck ball. He next rummaged around in the tool box, found the requested quarter-twenty hex bolt, and promptly screwed it into the now-threaded hole. Zack then applied the self-locking Vise-Grip pliers to the exposed hex bolt's head. With a smile, he turned to both Jer and Mark. "OK doctors, here's your handle!"

Jer was first to try the new handle. It was indeed secure. Jer gave it an estimated 50- or 60-pound pull, but slacked off because the patient was rapidly humming *umm-umm* through his nose, attempting to tell Jer to stop pulling.

"Zack," Jer said, "I really appreciate your brilliant help. It's a great handle ... really is. Only problem is, we're going to tear all his teeth out. Or break his jaw. Or both!"

"Uh Jer," Zack piped up. "Sorta like Newton said ... 'what goes *up*, must come *down*,' and sort of like common sense, what goes *in* must come *out* ... or else none of us in this room would still have a dick! Know what I mean?"

Jer flushed with anger. "Doctor, you're out of line. We've been over this before. You know—the language-in-front-of-the-patient thing. Remember?"

"Yeah, sorry Jer. And I ain't tryin' to change the subject on ya, but have you ever read Dr. Bronson's book, the one called *Human Myophysiology*?"

"Can't say I have," Jer tersely replied, his exasperation mounting regarding Zack's mouth.

Zack ignored Jer's annoyance, and replied with absolute confidence. "Well unless Bronson's book is wrong—and it ain't—if we pull on that handle about 15 minutes with steady force, the jaw muscles will fatigue, give up their spasm, and that cue ball *will* come out, same way it went in!"

"OK," Jer smugly replied. "Just what do you suggest now, Mr. Myophysiologist?"

"A steady 15-pound pull using orthopedic traction weights," Zack immediately shot back.

"OK, Zack, you go ahead and rig the traction stuff up. Just do your thing! But if that cue ball ain't outta there in 15 minutes flat, I'm going to call the Emory attending who's on call for the ER. Understood?" Jer said.

"Well at least start the clock *after* I've got the traction hooked up," Zack begged.

Jer said nothing. Mark just stood there, silently wondering if his roommate was just as crazy as Miss Lucifer.

Using an IV stand, orthopedic traction rope, pulley, and weights, it took Zack about five minutes to rig the device. One end of the traction rope was securely tied to the handles of the Vise-Grip pliers that were locked onto the bolt screwed into the cue ball; the other end of the traction rope had been passed through a pulley, suspended overhead by an IV stand. Finally, the rope attached to a standard platform designed to hold various numbers of orthopedic traction weights.

"OK, Jer! You can start your clock right ... NOW!" Zack said, at the instant he loaded the last of three five-pound saucer-shaped cast-iron traction weights.

The room was quiet except for the patient's nasal breathing, the occasional slurping of a suction catheter, and the shuffling sounds of three anxious doctors' feet pacing around the treatment table on the hard terrazzo floor. Zack now had the patient flat on his back, his head strongly secured to the table with several wraps of wide adhesive tape. Zack had inserted a small suction catheter to one side of the ball, and it was continually "slurping" as it removed the patient's excess saliva. *Sorta sounds like that thing they use in the dentist's office,* Mark thought.

Jer kept consulting his watch. Finally he spoke. "OK Zack! That's it. Exactly one minute to go, and I'm calling the Emory attending."

Still studying his watch, Jer reached for the treatment room's wall phone. He instructed the hospital operator to get the Emory attending on the line: "Line's busy. Want me to try again, Dr. Bacon?" the operator said into Jer's ear a moment later.

Jer's reply to the operator was interrupted by a loud metallic clang. *Fifteen pounds* of cast-iron orthopedic traction weights hit the terrazzo floor with an earsplitting crash! The noise was so deafening it completely shocked Jer, who'd been looking down at his watch when the weights actually hit the floor. Jer had instantly dropped the phone when startled by the noise.

"HOT SHIT!" Zack immediately exclaimed after the cue ball popped out. It continued swinging on the rope's end like a clock's pendulum, still firmly attached to the bolt held by the Vise-Grips. "And he's still got all his teeth!" Zack blurted.

"Hello ... Hello ... H-e-l-l-o!" were the audible words coming from the dangling wall phone's receiver. Flushed, Jer quickly retrieved the phone's receiver, and said, "Uh ... no operator, don't try again. Thanks anyway, it won't be necessary now."

After Jer hung up, the room remained silent. Zack was frozen with his eyes tightly closed, and his hands tightly pressed over his own mouth. Zack just realized he'd said "hot shit" in front of the patient ... and even worse, in front of Dr. Jerry Bacon. Keeping his hands firmly over his mouth, he opened his cat-like green eyes one at a time. Zack's eyes met

Jer's dark eyes focused upon his own with a stare that would bore through steel. Eyes locked, they froze for a full 30 seconds. Mark was unable to read the thoughts of either. The fellow from the maintenance department silently stood by with his hands in the pockets of his gray uniform, just waiting to get his tools back. Finally it was the patient who broke the uncomfortable silence and ongoing stare down between Zack and Jer.

"Hot shit, holy shit, God Almighty I'm glad that motherfucker's out!" the obese patient finally sputtered with slurred words of relief as he wiped the cue ball drill-dust from his chin. Wearing an expression of gratitude that defied description, the patient worked his fingers around the restraining adhesive tapes to massage his sore jaw muscles.

The patient's own "*S* words", and worse, must have been Jer's subconscious cue. "That really was some HOT SHIT!" Jer found himself loudly saying, his own face immediately becoming crimson, as he realized what *he* had just said ... *in front of a patient*. Jer burst into laughter. He quickly embraced Zack, next held him at arms length. Shaking his head, Jer said, "You're something else, you ... you ... Dr. Polack!"

All five of them—Zack, Mark, Jer, the patient, and maintenance man—soon became totally engulfed in laughter that lasted several minutes.

It was subsequently learned that the cue ball had gotten in the patient's mouth as the result of a 50-dollar wager made at Cooter's Cue Room. The patient had bet another of the poolroom's patrons that he could put a cue ball in his mouth. Though the patient did have a large mouth, despite his best efforts he had still been a few millimeters shy of success. A third patron—one who'd been pulling for the patient to win—had "assisted" the patient by forcefully pushing the almost-in cue ball with his palm. Though the ball went in, the patient lost the bet ... because the assistance rendered was considered cheating!

ICE WATER, PUS, AND GOLDFISH

Atlanta was getting cooler, the November daylight much shorter than the hot July day when he'd started at Grady. Dr. Mark Telfair was beginning the fifth month of his year-long straight surgical internship. The first two months in the General Admissions Clinic, followed by two additional months in the surgical ER, were behind him. He'd gotten over his paranoid concerns about getting shot at and being stabbed with an ice pick. He'd finally come to realize just how invaluable his Grady ER learning experiences would be. *Assuming I survive them all,* he thought.

The Grady straight surgical internship program permitted each intern to take a two-month elective rotation during the intern year. Such electives could be taken on any hospital service—surgical or nonsurgical—provided that the service was accredited for teaching purposes. Taking the advice of some of his senior peers and favorite professors, Mark had decided to spend his elective time on the Internal Medical Service. He knew all surgeons need to know a little bit about the whole patient; they needed to be able to at least evaluate minor medical problems that would arise in surgical patients from time to time. He didn't want to become merely a technician—*a body mechanic*—as some of the non-surgeon doctors demeaningly called their surgical colleagues.

Mark had even overheard one internist speaking to another: "Give the surgeons prediagnosed patients with dotted lines painted on their bodies. That's the only way they'll know exactly where to cut!"

Despite the insults he'd heard about his chosen field, he decided to take his internal medicine elective with an open mind, and a thick skin. As was his habit, he arrived a little early on 5-C, the internal medical ward that would become his new home for the next two months. He found the Chief Medical Resident's office without difficulty. The door was open. He entered to find the Chief Resident studying EKG strips and intently making notes. Mark knew the man had to be only 29 or 30 years old, but his salt-and-pepper hair made him appear much older. His neatly trimmed moustache and beard seemed somewhat out of place, especially when contrasted with the outdated flattop cut perched upon his large egg-shaped head. Extremely thick glasses with black rims made it impossible to evaluate his dark eyes. Mark studied the resident's white shirt with button-down collar, conservative tie, brown slacks, and well-shined dark wingtip shoes. At least a dozen pens and pencils bristled from his crisp white jacket's breast pocket, protected by a clear plastic pocket-liner device. A huge stethoscope was casually draped around his neck. *This guy is the picture-perfect nerd if ever I saw one!* Mark thought, struggling to keep an open mind about his nonsurgical colleagues.

Upon entering the Chief Medical Resident's office Mark had loudly cleared his throat several times. The resident didn't even look up from the EKG strips he was reading. *Fine reception ... sure different than Jer's greeting in the Surgical Pit,* Mark thought.

Determined to communicate, Mark finally spoke. "Hello there ... I'm Dr. Mark Telfair."

"Well I'm Dr. Thomas E. Wellington III, Chief Medical Resident," the nerd finally replied without emotion or even looking up. "Who did you say you were again?"

"Dr. Mark Telfair. Straight surgical intern. I'm here to do my elective on internal medicine. I just finished two months in the Surgical ER with Dr. Jerry Bacon."

Obviously resenting Mark's intrusion, the Chief Resident finally glanced up. "Can't you see I'm very busy right now? Come back around nine, and I'll try to get you off on the right foot—if that's ever possible with surgeons!" Dr. Wellington promptly resumed his EKG reading as though Mark Telfair didn't even exist.

Mark needed no further prompting to leave the "hospitality" of Dr. Wellington's office. He decided to have a look around the medical area. Ward 5-C was one of four similar medical wards located on Grady's fifth floor. Mark noted that most of the semiprivate room doors were open, and almost all beds were filled. Many patients appeared to be elderly and unresponsive. A number had nasal oxygen catheters connected to their noses. Some had feeding tubes and IVs. *Really got some sick folks in here,* Mark thought, continuing his exploration, punctuating it by periodic checks of his wristwatch and passing time until nine. Hopefully, Dr. Wellington would then find time to get him oriented on his new job.

Mark returned to Dr. Wellington's office precisely at nine. By then several medical interns and medical assistant residents had shown up. Dr. Wellington introduced Mark to the assembled staff and immediately informed *his interns*—the straight medical interns—that Mark would be available to them to do any scut work they might wish him to do.

Mark became incensed. For reasons unknown, a bit of his deceased father's advice suddenly bolted into his mind: *Son, folks will use you for a doormat—but only if you allow it.* Mark lowered his head. Totally out of character now, Mark Telfair felt like a bull ready to charge. Till the very last moment he held his tongue. Finally, he glared upward at Wellington and the little bull hidden within him charged out. "Look, Dr. Wellington! I didn't come here as an intern on elective to do the scut work your own interns may not want to do for their own patients! I came here to—"

"To do what *I* say you do!" Wellington interrupted, glaring.

"Not on your life sir!" Mark shot back. "*I* came here to learn some clinical medicine, not to be a slave to your medical interns. Don't you worry sir, I'm not here to steal your most intellectually stimulating cases—the patients with weird and exotic diseases. I came here to learn about simple common medical illnesses. Just assign me my own patients that have the boring stuff ... like simple cases of pneumonia, hypertension, diabetes, and stroke. I'll gladly do what scut work my *own* uninteresting patients may need done."

"Well—" Wellington started.

"Well you had better believe I'm not about to become a mere goddamn lackey to your precious medical interns!" Mark interrupted, trembling, astounded at his own lengthy outburst, and uncharacteristic open profanity.

The room fell silent. Apparently no one had ever really told off Dr. Thomas E. Wellington III, and he was obviously both shocked and pissed. Wellington cleared his throat, and swallowed before speaking. "Very well, Dr. Telfair. I think you've made your point ... or at least a lot of rude noise. You may soon regret your words, so don't come whining to me in a few weeks when you get bored with the mundane patients you'll be getting. On this service you have to *earn* the interesting patients ... and I'd say you're off to an extremely bad start!"

While Wellington angrily pointed at Mark, he turned and addressed the medical interns to reveal his sinister plan: "I want each of you medical interns to select one of your own patients, and transfer that patient's care to Dr. Telfair here, our outspoken on-loan intern from the Department of Surgery." Wellington ceased pointing at Mark, placed his hands on his hips, and turned glaring at Mark as he continued. "And furthermore, Dr. Telfair, today we'll be having Grand Rounds at two o'clock with the noted visiting British Professor of Internal Medicine, Dr. Charles Cromwell. He's from London, England. Cromwell's rounds on 5-C will be the very first Grand Rounds he's ever conducted at Grady.

You'll be expected to concisely recite your patient's entire medical history, physical examination, laboratory data, and X-ray findings during Grand Rounds ... all without the aid of bedside notes, I might add. Understood?"

Still angry, Mark simply nodded affirmatively, afraid he'd have another outburst if he actually spoke to Wellington. *What a complete and total asshole!* Mark thought while trying to keep a lid on himself.

Dr. Wellington and the assistant residents left the room, leaving Mark alone with the three medical interns. He'd met none of them before. All three were smiling, and Mark wasn't quite sure why. *Maybe they've already decided which one of their own undesirable patients they'll soon dump on me,* he thought.

In reference to now-absent Dr. Wellington, one of the medical interns spoke: "Well it's about time someone put that pompous self-proclaimed genius prick in his place. Man, that bastard's ego is second only to God's!" A second then commented: "Hey man, we'll even give you some easy patients. Won't we fellas?" Another intern chimed in: "You'll only have three patients. We'll help you learn the history and that other stuff cold, and do it well before Grand Rounds start this afternoon. That should blow old Wellington's socks off! And that British prof, that Dr. Cromwell, don't sweat him. I've talked to some of the guys in the Emory program. Cromwell started making Grand Rounds at Emory three months ago, and they say he's cool, that he's a real hoot! Got that dry British sense of humor, and he makes Grand Rounds a lot of fun while you're learning."

Mark smiled, then cautiously thanked them for their support. He knew he was the new kid on the block—the new rooster in a strange henhouse, so to speak. He just hoped the medical interns were indeed sincere. A bit of paranoia seeped into his thoughts: *I hope these guys are not just setting me up to make a total ass of myself during Grand Rounds in front of their Chief Resident Wellington, to whom I've just shown my newly found rebellious side ... or perhaps worse, to make a total ass of myself in front of that Professor Cromwell, who's gotta be the International God of Internal Medicine!*

For three hours Mark visited the patients the medical interns had elected to give him. He personally met and examined each one of his three hand-me-down patients. Indeed they were all nice routine medical patients with nonexotic problems, but their charts had grown quite thick during the several weeks each had already been hospitalized at Grady. One, a diabetic, was almost ready for discharge, probably the next day. Another was recovering from pneumonia, and the third was a minor stroke patient who would probably have little residual functional damage.

Spending several hours cramming for Grand Rounds, Mark had abstracted the three charts, putting the essentials on separate handwritten notes regarding each patient. Working from his abstractions, he then memorized the details of each. Over lunch with the three medical interns, he did some practice runs on the presentations he'd soon be making before Chief Resident Wellington and Professor Charles Cromwell. The various medical interns helped him refine his presentation. It soon became apparent to Mark that Wellington was their common enemy, and the interns were indeed fast friends and allies ... allies that wouldn't simply cave in to his Lordship Nerd Wellington. Mark's mind soon came to a further realization: *His Lordship, Captain Thomas E. Wellington III, MD, is very close to experiencing a mutiny aboard his 5-C Grady Hospital frigate!*

As the 2:00 p.m. hour for Grand Rounds approached, Mark witnessed a flurry of strange activity. Dr. Wellington shined his shoes with a paper towel, then checked the trim of his moustache and beard. He even clipped a few of his nasal hairs. He used a tiny pair of surgical scissors and a mirror kept hidden among the many pens and pencils in his plastic-shielded breast pocket. The assistant residents and interns also checked their uniforms and appearance, but with much less obsession than Chief Resident Wellington. Nurses tidied up their coiffures and their nurses' station, and checked their assigned patient rooms for properness. *Jesus, it's as if they're expecting a visit from God Almighty Himself!* Mark thought.

Precisely at 2:00 p.m., Professor Cromwell's rotund body entered Dr. Wellington's office. He wore a long rumpled white lab coat bearing recent food stains, among other unidentified soils. The unbuttoned lab coat revealed a large round belly covered by the vest of his three-piece tweed suit, complete with classic gold watch fob. Looking at his fat flushed jowls, perhaps enhanced by evening brandies, Mark could not resist a thought: *This guy looks exactly like a combination of Winston Churchill and Alfred Hitchcock.*

While rising from behind his desk, Dr. Wellington almost tripped over his own feet as Professor Cromwell entered the room. Wellington, with a grin and bowing gesture, extended his anxiety-dampened hand to Dr. Cromwell. "It's my deepest pleasure, sir, to meet you sir, Dr. Cromwell, and I must tell you I've really enjoyed your latest book, *The Basic Principles of Internal Medical Care.* To call it a masterpiece is indeed an understatement," Wellington added with ass-kissing awe. "And please know, sir, we here on 5-C are honored by your presence today, and we're quite ready to start Grand Rounds when you're ready, sir."

Professor Cromwell finally extracted his hand from Wellington's. "Dr. Wellington, exactly what edition of my book do you have?" Cromwell asked, in proper BBC English, while wiping his Wellington handshake hand on his already-soiled lab coat.

"Oh the latest one I'm sure sir," Wellington smiled.

"Then you must have the *third* edition. The edition we *export* from the UK. I must confess, I was rather unimpressed by my own work in edition three, but then you're entitled to your own opinion I suppose ... especially if you haven't availed yourself regarding editions one and two."

Not knowing how to respond to Cromwell's self-criticism, and his own lack of knowledge regarding the earlier volumes, Wellington simply said, "Shall we start rounds now, sir?"

"In just a moment, Dr. Wellington. First, I'd very much appreciate a large glass of iced water ... before we begin rounds, if that's possible. Doctor, how might I acquire that? I'm sorry to be such a bother, but that bloody awful American ale I had at lunch has left such a foul taste!" Cromwell explained.

Dr. Thomas Wellington quickly stepped to his open office door, extended his arm into the hallway, and loudly snapped his fingers. An attractive young nurse immediately appeared. "What do you need Dr. Wellington?"

"A large glass of iced water, for Dr. Cromwell here ... *stat!*" Wellington commanded.

The nurse returned a few seconds later carrying a large glass filled with water and ice cubes. She approached Dr. Cromwell and apologetically explained as she extended the glass toward him: "Dr. Cromwell, we just got a new ice machine here on 5-C, and I hope you don't mind the type of ice cubes it makes ... you know the kind that have a hole in the middle?"

"Oh that's quite all right, miss. You see I'm quite familiar with ice cubes that have a hole in the middle. I've been married to one of *those* for 25 years!"

The nurse turned crimson in embarrassment. Snickering among the medical interns rapidly spread to Mark, then on to the assistant residents. Finally the whole group burst into laughter—except Dr. Wellington, who'd totally missed the humor of Dr. Cromwell's response to the nurse.

"Did I miss something here?" Dr. Wellington innocently asked, looking around in total confusion.

Professor Cromwell himself responded to Dr. Wellington's question. "I'm afraid so, lad. Missed it completely, I'd say. I think you were a bit involved in adjusting all those pens and pencils in your breast pocket.

Let's start Grand Rounds, shall we, Doctor?"

The entourage quickly left Dr. Wellington's office to proceed with Grand Rounds on Grady's 5-C. A slightly less pompous Wellington now led the brigade. The rounds progressed uneventfully through the first several rooms. Details of each patient were first spouted by the medical intern, then elaborated upon by the assistant residents and Chief Resident Wellington. The esteemed Dr. Cromwell made pertinent observations regarding each patient presented. As rounds approached the next room, Mark realized it was now his time to show medical people what "inept" surgeons could do.

From memory, Mark precisely presented the status of his inherited female diabetic patient. She had been admitted in a coma due to acute diabetic ketoacidosis (ADKA) but was now well stabilized on a regimen of diet and insulin, and ready for discharge the next day or so.

After Mark's presentation to visiting Professor Cromwell, the respected British doctor warmly smiled at Mark, then excitedly spoke. "Jolly good, lad! Very precise! You seem to know how to summarize well—get to the heart of the matter quickly. I wish I could say that about all the previous presentations. But since you've been so quick and precise in your presentation, that leaves time to ask a theoretical thought-provoking question for anyone here to answer. Suppose ... just suppose now, if you would ... that you had *no laboratory* available to you, and also suppose you had a patient you suspect might be in ADKA. Assume that they are in full diabetic coma, so you cannot communicate with them a'tall ... can't even ask them if they're diabetic. As a physician, how would you diagnose ADKA and diabetic coma using *only* your own human senses?"

When it looked like no one was going to take the bait of Dr. Cromwell's question, Mark felt obligated to at least respond to the cheerful professor who'd just praised his presentation.

"Dr. Cromwell, sir," Mark said, "I'd try to smell their breath. If it smelled like fruit ... you know, like bananas or a cheap fruit-based wine, I'd certainly consider diabetic acidosis, especially if the patient was breathing rapidly."

"Excellent, laddie!" Cromwell commented. Mark could now see Chief Resident Wellington rubbing his temples.

"And how would you evaluate the possibility of the patient's urine having glucose in it ... again with no help from the laboratory?" Cromwell asked, pronouncing it la-BOR-a-tory.

"I really don't know, sir, but historically glucose in the diabetic's urine was first discovered by ants. That's where the term 'piss-ants' originated ... but if you waited until piss-ants told you the patient had sugar in their urine, the patient would probably be dead, sir!"

Cromwell erupted with laughter, and as it subsided, he smiled at Mark. "Jolly good, Doctor! I see you've read either the first or second edition of my book, *The Basic Principles of Internal Medical Care*. That's where I posed this same question, and expounded upon the very existence of piss-ants!"

Mark couldn't recall exactly where he'd read about piss-ants, but he was sure it wasn't Cromwell's book. He could not bring himself to tell Dr. Cromwell he'd never heard of—much less read—his books. Not any edition of them.

Feeling he was on a roll, Mark decided to respond with a thought that had just popped into his head. "Dr. Cromwell, I know the thought is repulsive, but what if the physician could actually *taste* the patient's urine. You know, just to see if it tasted sweet. Do you think that would work?"

"Dr. Wellington, just where did you find this brilliant fellow?" Cromwell asked.

Wellington winced, then replied. "Well, sir, he's sort of ... uh ... on-loan. He's a surgical intern that's taking his elective on internal medicine. I'm very sorry to say we probably won't be able to keep him among our ranks. But let me say his comment about tasting urine for sugar content has merit. Do you think a tasting might be in order, sir?"

"Well I certainly have no objection," Cromwell replied, "but the diabetic patient just presented here by Dr. Telfair is now so well controlled, there's probably not enough sugar in her urine to be detected by any human's sense of taste."

Dr. Wellington desperately wanted to see his enigma, Dr. Mark Telfair, taste urine on Grand Rounds. "Dr. Cromwell, sir, we have another patient admitted earlier this morning in ADKA. That patient still has a urinary catheter in place, and she should still have extremely high levels of glucose in her urine. Would a sample of urine from that patient suffice for the taste test?"

"Surely it would, Doctor," Cromwell replied to Wellington. "Have someone go fetch a sample, and we'll conduct the taste test out here in the hallway." *Uh-oh,* thought Mark.

Less than a minute later a nurse from the Grand Rounds crew returned with several ounces of fresh urine from the new still-uncontrolled diabetic patient on 5-C. The nurse handed the clear glass urine sample container to Dr. Mark Telfair. He looked at the urine container he held in his hand. *It was still warm.* A tactic for delay quickly occurred to Mark, and he immediately spoke up.

"Uh, Dr. Cromwell, don't you think this experiment would have much more scientific validity if all present here tasted the urine? Individuals vary so greatly in their senses—their ability to see, hear, smell, taste, and feel. Statistically, wouldn't we have a more valid sampling if we *all* did the taste test, then averaged the results?"

"Couldn't agree more, laddie. I'll start the experiment," Cromwell stated as he stuck his own finger into the warm urine sample Mark was holding. Cromwell promptly inserted his finger into his mouth, making little sucking noises as he did the taste test. Cromwell then dried his sampling fingers on his white lab coat.

Mark held the urine sample container while some nine other individuals—including Wellington—repeated Dr. Cromwell's finger-dip urine-tasting technique. Mark was the very last to do the test.

"Well, now that we've all sampled, has anyone formulated an opinion yet?" Cromwell beamed as he asked the question.

"I have, sir," Mark immediately replied.

"Oh?" Cromwell responded. "What did you taste, Dr. Telfair?"

"Absolutely nothing, sir. And neither did you, sir. But I can't speak for the others."

"Well just how do you think you can speak for *me*—for what *I* alone tasted?"

 "Well, Dr. Cromwell, I simply followed your example. I put my *index* finger in the urine, then tasted my *middle* finger. The other seven tasted the *same* finger they put in the urine. So you'll have to ask them, sir!"

Cromwell burst into laughter, and patted Mark on the back. "Always good to have a keen observer on Grand Rounds! *Observation* is the key. Observation is the essential element in any physician's diagnostic ability. Lad, you have just restored my faith that perhaps a few young doctors still possess the ability to critically observe!"

Grand Rounds continued that day without additional hilarity, but Chief Resident Wellington appeared nauseated, looking as though he might lose his lunch at any moment.

Days passed. Temporary though it may be, Mark felt he was still on a roll. Putting down Dr. Wellington on Grand Rounds had made him realize that stupid cut-on-the-dotted-line surgeons could hold their own amid intellectuals, if forced to do so. He just hoped he had not offended the medical interns who indeed seemed genuine in their efforts to help him survive his 5-C internal medicine elective. Mark quickly learned the medical interns remained on his side. Medical intern James Foster, his favorite of the three, told him so while they were eating lunch alone. In confidence, Dr. Foster also had indicated he was planning some mischief for the next Grand Rounds with Cromwell.

Two weeks following the urine-tasting Grand Rounds, time for the next Grand Rounds with Dr. Cromwell was upon them. Mark's four patients for today's Grand Rounds would, he thought, all provide straightforward presentations to the visiting British professor. What made Mark anxious about today's Grand Rounds was a prank scheme Dr. Foster had first mentioned to him in the cafeteria several days ago. Foster had decided it would be a neat idea to put a goldfish in one of his patient's IV bottles ... and have it just swimming around inside the bottle during Grand Rounds. Mark admitted he thought Cromwell would have a lot of fun with the prank, but he also felt it could be *dangerous* to the patient.

To that end, Mark had immediately spoken up. "Foster, I agree that would really be a neat prank. But the bacteria in the fish poop might really give the patient some serious disease ... especially if they got it IV." Dr. Foster had promptly assured Mark—his sole confidant—that it would actually be a fake IV, one having no needle that actually entered the patient's vein. The closed-off IV tubing would simply "disappear" beneath a small bandage on the patient's arm, thus simulating a real intravenous infusion. Foster had further explained the type of glass IV bottles used at Grady were easy enough to uncap and recap; all one had to do was substitute ordinary tap water for the IV bottle's normal content, and then insert the fish.

As Grand Rounds started, little did Mark know that one of his own patient presentations to Dr. Cromwell would create hilarity equal to the goldfish prank Dr. Foster had planned. Mark's straightforward presentation was a stroke patient who'd been transferred to Grady from a nursing home. She had been transferred primarily because she'd had an extension, or worsening, of the original stroke that occurred several months ago. She also had acquired a bedsore over her tail bone area while in the nursing home.

As Mark was concluding his stroke patient's presentation to Dr. Cromwell, he added a final note: "She also has a shallow infected bedsore located in her presacral area. It's only a little over a centimeter in diameter, but has a pussy drainage, which I've already cultured. Bacteriology lab results are still pending, sir."

"Laddie," Cromwell said, "I remember you quite well from the urine tasting two weeks ago. I felt you were quite bright, but today you give me some cause for concern."

"What do you mean *cause for concern*, sir?" Mark responded, puzzled.

"Well, your descriptions of the stroke patient's neurological events

71

and findings were absolutely superb ... it's just your description of the bedsore that gives me concern. You described the infected bedsore as having a pussy drainage, did you not?"

"Sure, that's how I described it ... but what's your point sir?"

"Well just exactly how do you *spell* 'pussy,' Dr. Telfair?"

Mark mentally did the spelling and could feel his face becoming beet red. Then came an additional blow: Mark watched Dr. Wellington's evolving shit-eating grin—*a silent nerd's revenge!*

Cromwell placed a fatherly hand on Mark's shoulder. "Dr. Telfair, except for vulgar slang referencing the human female pudendum, or referencing domestic cats, or certain species of willow plants, proper terminology—medical or otherwise—does not recognize such a word. The proper medical term to describe a drainage of pus from a wound, or body orifice of any type, would be to reference such a discharge as being a *purulent* discharge. P-u-r-u-l-e-n-t! Well ... unless, of course, we were making Grand Rounds on the GYN ward!"

Cromwell's correction of Dr. Telfair's medical terminology brought the house down. In fact, the laughter had barely ceased when Grand Rounds reached the goldfish room. Mark knew the medical intern, Dr. Foster, had still been working on the details of the prank shortly before Grand Rounds began. He'd even talked the obese jovial female patient into going along with his Grand Rounds prank—fake IV, goldfish, and all. Though it had taken several attempts, Dr. Foster finally taught the patient how to pronounce the medical term *ichthyosis*, an easily diagnosed severe human dermatologic disease that causes the patient's skin to become covered with silvery scale-like flakes of dead skin. Foster was positive the patient did not have that disease. If a human patient develops *ichthyosis,* their skin closely resembles the scales of a fish, thus the medical designation derived from the Greek root word for fish: *ichthyo.*

When Grand Rounds entered the goldfish room, Mark refrained from looking directly at the IV bottle where the little fish was casually swimming around in lazy circles. He knew if he looked at the IV bottle he would certainly laugh, alerting Dr. Cromwell and others that something was amiss. The Grand Rounds group intently looked on. Dr. Foster presented the fat lady's history, physical, and laboratory findings. Fortunately, the patient was pain free at the moment, but some elusive autoimmune disease was causing this unfortunate woman to experience intermittent episodes of excruciating generalized joint pain. Dr. Foster, even with help from Chief Resident Wellington and the assistant residents, had been unable to establish any definite classification of the patient's obscure illness.

At length, Foster presented his problem patient. Dr. Cromwell intently listened and observed. Cromwell calmly removed his spectacles, cleaned them with a handkerchief, then replaced them upon his nose. He then moved a little closer to the IV bottle. Quite casually, he glanced at it from several angles, but said nothing. Mark was in a position to see Cromwell's eyes as they discreetly followed the IV tubing, which appeared to be properly connected to a vein in the patient's right forearm. With a stone face, Cromwell finally spoke. "Your presentation was excellent, Dr. Foster ... but I'm afraid I have some bad news. I, too, cannot establish a diagnosis ... at least not a diagnosis based upon my observations thus far. Does anyone in this gathering have any suggestions or ideas?"

A number of people in white clothing stood clustered around the patient's bed. Some rubbed their chins, others scratched heads in thought. As an absolute certainty, no one in the group—except Foster, Mark, and the patient—knew of the presence of the goldfish. But Mark Telfair was almost positive the sharp-eyed old British professor hadn't missed seeing the fish. In anticipation of what may come, Mark firmly held his hand over his mouth to keep from laughing. The painfully long silence was finally broken by the jovial patient's voice. Speaking to Dr. Cromwell she said, "Uh, Mr. Head Doctor ... is I in this gatherin'? And if I is in this gatherin', can I say what it is I think I's got?"

"Oh certainly Madam! You're the foremost reason for this gathering in the first place. With difficult cases such as yours, we don't turn down help from any source. So please ... please go ahead and say what you will. Tell us your thoughts regarding your illness."

"Well, Mr. Head Doctor, I think I's got the *ichthyosis!* Now what you think 'bout that Mr. Head Doctor?" The patient had indeed pronounced *ichthyosis* perfectly.

Dr. Cromwell said nothing, his face flushed slightly, his abundant belly began to jiggle as his laughter rose to his throat. "By Jove! *I think I've been had!*" That was all he managed to get out between his rolls of laughter ... a laughter that immediately engulfed the entire group, including the huge patient, whose laughter was so violent it was visibly rocking her bed.

As the hysteria resolved, Dr. Cromwell removed his glasses, and wiped his tears of laughter on the sleeves of his perpetually soiled white la-BOR-a-tory coat. "Jolly well, my lads. Can't wait to take this sham back to London! Think you can keep that bloody goldfish live long enough for me to take him back 'cross the Atlantic next month?"

10

FISH AND SPIDERS

Afew days after Christmas, Dr. Mark Telfair found himself nearing the end of his two-month internal medicine elective and eagerly anticipating his upcoming rotation to orthopedic surgery. He had adjusted to living in the hospital with his roommate, Zack, who was completing the last few days of his own orthopedic rotation.

Because he roomed with Zack, Mark had already learned the working hours on the orthopedic surgery and internal medicine services were drastically different. On orthopedics Zack worked 36 hours on duty, and 12 hours off ... keeping Zack's biological clock confused. Zack no longer really knew if it'd be daylight or dark when he awoke from his off-duty sleep. In contrast, Mark's internal medicine rotation allowed him to keep fairly regular hours, but he never felt completely sure when he'd find Zack in the room they shared. Whenever the two did find themselves in the room at the same time, they eagerly compared notes regarding their respective intern rotations.

At six in the morning it was still pitch-black outside. "Hey Markie Boy!" Zack remarked upon entering their room, and actually finding Mark there.

"Zack, you look totally beat, man. You feel OK?" Mark asked his haggard roommate, an edge of genuine concern in his voice.

"Yeah, I'll recover. Just feel like I've been run over by a train. You're going to absolutely love orthopedics when you get there next month, but let me tell you ahead of time—their schedule is a real killer-bitch! With 36 on, 12 off, your head gets so screwed up, you feel just like you're constantly jet-lagged or somethin'. But I've learned so freakin' much about orthopedic traction and stuff, I bet I could now get a stuck cue ball outta some redneck joker's mouth in five minutes flat!"

"Zack, what service are you going to take your elective on?" Mark asked, when Zack stopped for a breath.

"Haven't decided yet. If it wasn't for their crazy killer schedule, I think I'd definitely take another shot on orthopedics. May do it anyways. That would give me four months' orthopedic experience just for the intern year, you know. But I don't think my elective comes up till May and June. I'll decide by then. You still glad you did your elective on internal medicine?"

"Yeah," Mark replied. "Overall it's been a very good experience. That Dr. Cromwell—the visiting British professor I told you about—he's a smart cookie, and has really taught me a lot. But Dr. Wellington, the 5-C Chief Medical Resident, he's a nerd. A real prick! The medical interns are good guys, and all the assistant medical residents are OK too. Should you decide to choose internal medicine as your elective, I wouldn't go to 5-C if I were you. Just pick one of the other medical wards, so you can go where Dr. Wellington *isn't!*"

"I appreciate the advice, man. I'll think it over. But right now I've gotta catch some *Z*s." Zack immediately went to sleep still fully dressed ... just passed out as if he'd been given an IV injection of pentabarbital.

Though Mark wanted to talk with his roommate further, he didn't dare try to keep Zack from seeking his needed rest. He showered, shaved, and dressed as quietly as possible. He silently left their room at 6:30 a.m., heading for the cafeteria before going to 5-C to finish yet another day of his few remaining there.

Mark had gotten what he asked for when he came to 5-C. He'd requested patients with simple medical problems he'd likely encounter in his future surgical patients. But as his two-month medical elective was drawing to a close, one of his simple patients suddenly presented a puzzling problem.

The one with such puzzling hospital-acquired behavior was a white male in his early 30s. He was a professional house painter by trade. His admitting diagnosis was bacterial lobar pneumonia, and his history indicated he was a heavy smoker. Mark knew the patient also constantly breathed paint fumes during the course of his work. Certainly, neither helped his present pulmonary problem. The patient admitted having a couple of beers each day, but claimed he was not a heavy drinker, didn't do drugs, and generally enjoyed very good health. "Haven't been back inside a hospital since I was born," the patient had bragged upon admission.

The painter's lobar pneumonia was responding well to treatment, but as Mark made his rounds on the morning of the patient's fifth hospital day he found something had dramatically changed.

"Morning Little Doc," the patient whispered. "Close that door. Don't let nobody see where I'm catchin' these fish!"

"What *fish?*" Mark asked, totally confused.

"Th' ones right over there, Doc! All largemouth bass. Look at the size of them sum'bitches!" the patient exclaimed as he pointed to an empty corner of the room. "That's where they've been bitin' the best. I got a whole mess of 'em over there in the sink."

Mark stepped to the lavatory, and looked in the sink. It was half-filled. A dozen strips of brown paper towel floated on the water's surface. Mark quietly turned to observe the patient. The painter sat on the side of his bed. He held a black pocket-sized hair comb in his left hand. At intervals, his left thumb nail repetitively raked across the comb's teeth, resulting in a cyclic chirping sound. This chirping sound was synchronized with a circular winding motion the patient made using his right hand held close to the comb. *That's his fishing reel!* Mark decided.

Mark said nothing to the patient. He just continued to observe in silence. According to Professor Cromwell, *observation* was the key to diagnosis. It was really fascinating to watch the patient make a left-handed cast with his imaginary fishing rod, one that was obviously connected to the equally imaginary comb reel. The painter periodically gave a sharp jerk to set the hook, then started winding in, comb chirping away.

The painter patient had just made a loud grunting noise as he aggressively set the hook on yet another fish, then started madly thumbing his comb reel. "Good Godamighty! This one's a monster! God, please don't let him get off!" He anxiously continued to play his imaginary monster fish, started to perspire profusely, and was becoming extremely agitated. As much as Dr. Mark Telfair was enjoying the show, he knew it was time to bring it to an end.

"Here, fella," Mark volunteered, "let me give you a hand with this big one." As Mark approached the bedside to assist, the patient immediately snapped back, and fell flat in the bed. Mark thought he'd passed out, but the patient quickly sprang back up to his sitting position again. He was now trembling all over, drenched with perspiration, and shaking his head side to side.

"Too late Doc!" the patient exclaimed, both hands clutching his chest as though he might be in severe cardiac pain.

"What's the matter?" Mark instantly fired his question of genuine concern. "Are you having chest pain? Any pain in your arms, neck, or jaw?"

"Nah, Doc. I'm OK Doc ... it's just ... it's just that sorry fuckin' Kmart fishing line. It broke! *And right here at the goddamn boat!*" the patient lamented, patting his bed, and almost in tears. "And that was the biggest one I ever hooked! But Doc, thanks anyway for tryin' to help me get him in the boat here," he said, again patting his bed.

Like some epileptics who experience the warning given by a pre-seizure aura, Mark Telfair had learned to recognize the strange feeling he'd get when he was going to be struck down by one of his own convulsive fits of laughter. This was such a time. He was in the process of rapidly excusing himself from the patient's room, but just as Mark reached the door, the patient yelled to him. "Hey Doc, that's a good mess of fish in the sink ... take a couple home with you!" Mark quickly grabbed two strips of the paper towel floating in the sink, and exited the room still holding his breath.

It took Mark about five minutes to recover from his laughing fit, which he totally expended in the privacy of an empty patient room just across the hall. Now fully composed, he re-entered his patient's room, still holding the two strips of wet paper towel. He calmly told the painter he was going to put the two fish in a refrigerator, and he'd be back in a few minutes.

Mark quickly located one of the assistant medical residents and relayed his observations. Mark was told he'd probably just witnessed his first case of DTs, or *delirium tremens*, a condition precipitated by abrupt alcohol withdrawal. An additional diagnosis was added to the painter's chart, and appropriate treatment quickly instituted.

The episode had indeed sparked Mark's interest in the problem of DTs. Though he'd certainly heard of DTs before—and considered the problem trivial—his further reading on the subject indicated it could be quite serious, *even fatal* if left untreated for an extended period. He also realized it could be an unanticipated problem for recovering surgical patients, especially the ones who inaccurately claimed "only a couple of beers" regarding their alcohol intake history. In his mind, Mark defined the problem: *What is needed is a simple bedside test, one that would detect the possibly of impending DTs before the full-blown clinical picture evolved. Early detection would allow preventive treatment to be instituted well before the full-blown—possibly fatal—clinical picture developed.*

Mark also learned that patients in DTs are frequently highly suggestible to many sensory stimuli, especially visual stimuli viewed in dim light. He learned that a patient in incipient DTs could appear totally normal and mentally clear, yet still be suffering from severe hallucinations. Mark decided where he'd start with his attempt to develop an early detection test for DTs.

It took a trip to the Emory library to find a realistic photograph of a spider. Mark checked out a large book on arachnids, one that had excellent life-sized and larger spider photos. He made a quick trip to an office supply store in Buckhead, and purchased a few supplies. After returning to the privacy of the room he shared with Zack, Mark studied spiders at length. He selected one of the life-sized tarantula photos as being the most desirable for his purposes. With a supply of unlined white three-by-five-inch file cards, and using black drafting ink and very fine drafting pens, Mark drew a realistic picture of one of the large hairy tarantulas featured in the Emory library text. Mark, no artist, was proud of his life-like reproduction on the white card; all the fine body and leg hairs, and even the small facets in the spider's eyes, had not escaped his attention. He placed the finished product on his white bed sheet, and squinted his eyes to simulate dim light. Indeed, the white card seemed to disappear, leaving only the "spider." Mark stood back, still squinting and admiring his art work, when he heard Zack put his key in the room's door lock and burst into their room.

Zack immediately went into the bathroom without noticing Mark's spider-card. While Zack continued a lengthy urination, Mark transferred the card to Zack's white pillow.

"God what a day ... didn't even have time to take a decent leak," Zack said as he finally finished and moved toward his bed. "Holy shit!" Zack exclaimed, and sprang back, the instant he spied the spider. "Where the fuck's Orkin when you really need 'em!"

Zack removed a shoe to smash the spider—and poised, prepared to strike—when he suddenly realized it was fake. "You little ass wipe!" Zack said, in reference to *Mark*, not the spider. "Now is that any way to treat your old buddy here? The one who's been working 36 straight?" Zack then burst into laughter, and picked up the card to move it closer to the light.

"Hey Mark, that's pretty damn good. I think I should get you some green ink, and paper just the right size, and I think you can solve any money problem we may have. Know what I mean? And we're gonna need several hundred bucks real soon. Last time I used the Volvo, I noticed a whine in the transmission. Bad bearings."

Mark knew Zack was joking about getting into the counterfeit money business, but completely serious about the Volvo's need for a transmission overhaul. Mark also knew Zack was utterly exhausted, but he just couldn't refrain from telling Zack a condensed version of his DTs patient and the fishing episode. He also added a brief explanation of how he planned to use the card as a test for DTs.

When Zack's laughter subsided, he immediately went to bed, still smiling while falling asleep. Mark heard Zack's final faltering pre-sleep words: "I'm gonna be pissed at you, if I dream ... about that ... that son-of-a-bitchin' ... s-p-i-d-e-r..."

When he quietly left Zack sleeping in the room, Mark really didn't know if the spider would work or not. Nonetheless, he'd decided to give the "tarantula" a clinical trial that night. His own patient—the DTs fisherman—was now out of DTs, so he had to seek some assistance from the medical 5-C interns. They each had at least one patient in obvious DTs; more importantly, they also had a number of other patients—ones with no outward signs—who just *might* go into DTs. While the medical interns listened intently, Mark explained how he wanted to proceed with the experiment.

"Fellas," Mark began, "glad you all agreed to help me. This is what I've got in mind: We go into a possible DTs room, then just lay the card down on their bed in dim light. We then carefully observe the patient's reaction. If they ask us why we put a card on the bed with a *drawing* of a spider on it, then we assume they are *not* in DTs, and that would be a negative spider-test. But if we have a possible DTs patient who *backs away* from the card, OR *appears to totally ignore* it, then either of those responses would be considered a positive spider-test. Wanna give it a try?"

The three medical interns were all eager to assist, especially Dr. "Goldfish" Foster, as he'd been immediately nicknamed following the earlier prank on Grand Rounds. They gave all known and all possible DTs patients on 5-C the test. With the help of other medical interns, they expanded the test to the three other medical wards at Grady. By midnight, they had spider-tested some 27 patients.

It took several days to evaluate the results of Mark's spider-test. They had 11 patients who had tested positive, yet had no obvious clinical DTs at the time of testing. *All 11 developed full-blown clinical DTs within 72 hours! Those that tested negative didn't.*

Word rapidly traveled on the hospital gossip net. Mark couldn't draw spiders fast enough to satisfy demand. Finally, he'd sweet-talked a secretary in the business office into making 25 photocopies when her supervisor wasn't looking. Despite the exhaustion due to his orthopedic rotation, Zack insisted he help with sales: He sold the photocopies for a dollar a piece; hand-drawn originals went for five bucks; signed originals were ten dollars; signed originals with instructions on the back went for fifteen. The TDT test (Telfair Delirium Tremens test) was born!

11

HOT BODY, BONES, AND DNA

January in Atlanta can produce some bone-chilling weather ... the kind that scraped on Dr. Mark Telfair's Southern nerves. But he really didn't mind winter so much this January. He rarely had time to go outside the hospital anymore. After the first week of his orthopedic surgery rotation, Mark truly understood what his roommate, Zack, meant when he'd described the "killer-bitch" orthopedic work schedule. Mark had not been outside the hospital in over a week now and conceivably might not go outside again until his orthopedic rotation was over. He found that after working 36 hours straight he felt like doing only one thing during the 12 hours off: *sleep. Maybe it's a good thing my relationship with Carla ended when it did ... while I was still in the ER. My orthopedic schedule would have finished it off anyway,* he thought, knowing his ex-girlfriend had not been unreasonable, only human.

At 6:00 a.m. he'd just arrived on Grady's seventh floor, the orthopedic surgery floor, to begin his 36-hour shift. He could always be found on the seventh floor, or down on the third floor in surgery, or on the second floor in the Orthopedic Outpatient Clinic. The only sleep he might get in the next 36 hours would be an occasional catnap on a vacant gurney or an X-ray table ... chances of any real sleep were completely nonexistent.

Nonetheless, the work schedule—and lack of sleep that went with it— was the only negative thing Mark found about orthopedics thus far. His very first day on the service contrasted sharply with his first day on internal medicine elective. Unlike the nerd Internal Medicine Chief Resident, the Orthopedic Chief Resident had *seemed* to be a great down-to-earth fellow from day one. Only a week ago now, Dr. Dyson DeJarnett, the ortho Chief, had welcomed Mark to the service with open arms. Mark's mind flashed back to that first day:

"Welcome to orthopedics, Dr. Telfair," Dr. Dyson DeJarnett had said with a smile as he rose from his desk's chair, then warmly extended his hand to Mark. "We're always glad to get some good help around here. Just call me Dyson. I've seen you a time or two before, but we didn't actually meet. I think it was down in the Pit ... when I was down there jaw-jackin' with ole Jer Bacon about some of the broken bones."

"Well it's my pleasure to meet you, Dyson," Mark said. "My roommate, Dr. Zack Paslaski, said I'd better come prepared to work though!"

"So *you're* Paslaski's roommate?" Dyson asked with unreadable facial expression.

"Yep ... I'm afraid I am," Mark said, having no idea regarding DeJarnett's opinion of Zack.

Dr. DeJarnett gave a knowing smile before he replied. "That Zack Paslaski, he's a real boss-hoss. He even worked *my* butt off! He's a trip all right. No, I take that back. He's not exactly a trip ... he's a whole dang vacation! I know he talks a little rough now and then, but he's smart as a whip. I think I've even got him talked into specializing in orthopedic surgery, but he said he wanted to have a look at the other surgical services before he makes his mind up. Might get him back again this coming May and June, when his elective comes up."

"Yeah, Zack's a character all right," Mark admitted, relieved that Dr. DeJarnett had a positive impression of Zack.

"Telfair, you want to scrub on a hip-nailing this morning ... in just a few minutes?" Dyson asked.

"Sure!" Mark replied with a grin. "But you need to know I've never been in on one of those before."

Though obviously elated, Mark was a little nervous. This would be his first trip to the Grady OR since he'd become a real doctor. He was six months into his straight surgical internship and *finally* he was actually going to see the inside of an operating room.

As Dr. Dyson DeJarnett's Hollywood-handsome, yet very masculine, six-foot-two frame ambled toward the elevator, he whistled *Just a Closer Walk with Thee*. Mark silently followed. While waiting for the elevator to take them down to the third-floor operating suites, Dyson turned to Mark. "Telfair, you like to sing?"

"Sure," Mark replied. "But I really can't carry a tune ... not even in a five-gallon bucket."

"Shoot, don't worry about that! Lots of folks can't sing too well ... but singing in the OR is sort of an orthopedic tradition around Grady. Now we don't sing during every operation, just do it now and then. Do it especially when we're all tired. Sorta keeps our spirits up when we're beat, you know. Guess that's why the black folks used to sing when pickin' and choppin' in the fields back home in Hickory."

"Hickory? Like Hickory, North Carolina?" Mark asked.

"Yep, I'm from Hickory. My daddy is a GP there. Of course my daddy didn't have any slaves himself, but his daddy did in his early years. When I was just a little boy, Granddaddy use to tell me how much he missed sittin' on the porch and hearing the darkies singin' in the fields. My daddy sings at church in Hickory, even got me to singin' there too. That was back before I started my residency here at Grady, you know. I just love to sing."

When its bell announced the elevator's arrival on the seventh floor, Dyson seemed to sense Mark's apprehension about going down to the OR only minutes after he'd arrived on the service. Dyson didn't know Mark's foremost apprehension: He might be expected to *sing* while in the OR.

"Now don't you worry, Mark. I'll be the surgeon, and you'll only be second assistant on this one. Dr. Ed Faulkner, my SAR, will be the first assistant. Only reason I'm doin' this particular one is because it's a subcapital fracture—just below the femoral head, you know. And they can be real tricky to nail. But you'll soon be doing the simple ones as the primary surgeon. Here at Grady we got a rule: '*See One ... Do One ...Teach One.*' Your buddy Zack really got the hang of it. I bet he's the only surgical intern who's nailed six hips during a two-month orthopedic rotation."

Mark wasn't sure he'd be able to fill Zack's shoes, but decided he'd give it his best. Though Zack had never mentioned singing in the OR, Mark decided he'd learn to do it ... if that's what it took to keep the Chief happy.

When the elevator stopped and opened on the third floor, Mark followed Dr. DeJarnett into the doctors' dressing room and they immediately started getting into ancient sets of green surgical scrubs. While dressing, Dyson commented, "You might want to take those skivvies off, Telfair. Nailings get a little bloody sometimes. Goes right through your gown and scrubs, even onto your underwear sometimes." Mark followed Dr. DeJarnett's example and walked to the OR totally naked beneath his scrubs.

During the mandatory ten-minute scrub, Dr. DeJarnett was whistling *Onward Christian Soldiers* beneath his surgical mask. Dyson would pause now and then to exchange pleasantries with the parade of shapely nurses passing by. Nurses somehow seemed drawn to him. Not a single one passed without some flirting comment. *Must be because he's the Chief* Mark thought, then realized he was only kidding himself: *It was because Dr. DeJarnett was every woman's perfect black-haired blue-eyed hunk.*

At the end of scrub, Mark again followed Dyson's example. He turned off his scrub sink's water using just his elbows to close the special faucet levers. Keeping his forearms vertical, he followed Dr. DeJarnett into the adjoining OR. The patient was already asleep, and positioned on an operating table specially designed for hip-nailings. Dyson was handed a sterile towel by the scrub nurse; he dried his hands, then gowned and gloved in a series of rapid fluid movements.

Mark stepped forward to receive his own sterile towel from the attractive scrub nurse. Then disaster struck. A slight tickle from some lint on the inside of Mark's surgical mask suddenly caused him to violently sneeze. The waist drawstring on his well-worn scrub pants snapped, his loose-fitting pants promptly slid down his legs to greet his ankles. *His rapidly shrinking manhood was now hanging out in a cool brightly lit room full of women!*

Mark's face got so red it was beyond crimson, more like purple, and probably a dark shade of that color. He was so embarrassed he was speechless. But Dr. Dyson DeJarnett saved the day.

"Hey, Telfair ... when you're through showing your personal real estate to all these good-looking nurses, how about you giving me and Dr. Faulkner a hand with the prep and drapes."

Dyson's casual handling of the "disaster" gave Mark time to find the courage to speak. Not wanting to pull his own pants back up—and contaminate his sterile hands, and then go through *another* mandatory ten-minute scrub—Mark heard himself speak to the pleasingly buxom circulating nurse: "Hey you dumb broad, there's a draft in here! Pull 'em back up."

The circulating nurse didn't appear to take offense to Mark's coarse reference to her being a "dumb broad." She promptly knelt on the floor before him with a large safety pin clinched in her mouth through the gauze of her surgical mask. She was so close Mark could actually *feel* her warm breath ... on his *manhood!* Her absolutely beautiful hazel eyes were only a foot away from his *thing ... his most private thing!* But she dutifully raised his pants, then pinned the waist securely, all without a word spoken. She'd acted as though this might be a routine occurrence.

While gowning, a thought entered Mark's head: *She has absolutely beautiful intelligent hazel eyes. The most beautiful eyes I've ever seen. God, what made me say what I said?* He immediately wished he could retrieve the demeaning words he'd uttered in his embarrassing moment of masculine insecurity. He didn't dwell on his faux pas. Mark quickly directed his full attention to the surgical task at hand.

The hip-nailing went off without a hitch, no singing required. Dr. DeJarnett made the surgery look so simple. The technical aspects of the procedure fascinated Mark, and he tried to take in every detail. But other than hold a retractor, to keep the lateral hip incision widely open, and facilitate exposure for both surgeon and first assistant, Mark did little else until the metal femoral neck pin (the "nail") and its side plate had been installed. X-rays confirmed perfect position. As primary surgeon, Dyson

DeJarnett then dropped out of scrub and left the OR.

Dr. Ed Faulkner and Mark finished the procedure. While closing the incision, Dr. Faulkner spoke to Mark. "Just look at those X-rays—perfect position! That Hot Body is a slick operator isn't he?"

"Uh, *Hot Body?*" Mark asked, seeking clarification.

"Yeah ... you know... Dr. DeJarnett. That's what we all call him. Well some call him *Corpus Calor* ... just trying to be fancy with their Latin, you know."

Mark was pleased that Dr. Faulkner was letting him put in the skin stitches, but he couldn't resist asking the obvious question: "How in the heck did Dr. DeJarnett get the name Hot Body?"

Dr. Faulkner was clipping the skin suture's excess free ends as Mark placed and tied them. Leaning very close to Mark's ear, Dr. Faulkner whispered through his mask. "Just watch the *ladies,* man. Look at the way they *watch* him! If cherries were worth a dollar apiece, he'd already be a millionaire! I know an old guy in the Grady Pharmacy. Been there for years. He says Hot Body has written more birth control prescriptions for Grady nurses than any Grady doctor he's ever known. Including the GYN docs!"

Getting the message, Mark smiled in thought beneath his mask. *So Hot Body is a legendary ladies' man ... and probably has been legendary since his first day at Grady six years ago.*

After the patient's incision was fully closed, and sterile dressing applied, Dr. Ed Faulkner and Mark headed for the dressing room. To Mark's surprise a little of the patient's blood had soaked through to his skin in various places. The two showered and dressed, then headed straight to the cafeteria for a very early lunch at 10:45 a.m. Mark's mind immediately recalled some of Zack's recent sage advice: *Mark, when you get on orthopedics, you'd better eat when you can, hungry or not ... 'cause you never know when you'll get the next chance.*

While sliding his tray along the stainless-steel rails of the cafeteria line, Mark recognized a few of the personnel involved in the just-finished hip-nailing. They were also taking their lunch break. He hoped he wouldn't be recognized, now that he was back in his whites ... and minus the disguise afforded by his surgical attire. He kept looking for the attractive hazel eyes that had come so close to his "thing" after his scrub pants fell off. He didn't see her. He knew one day he'd find those eyes, but didn't know exactly how he'd handle the situation when he discovered who she was—or *she* discovered who he was.

A week had passed since Mark's participation in the embarrassing hip-nail procedure. Mark was preparing for the rounds Dr. DeJarnett would soon be making on the seventh floor. As low man on the totem pole, Mark was expected to carry all the ancillary stuff needed for on-the-spot repairs or modifications of various orthopedic appliances. Among other items, Dr. Telfair's baggage included: cast saw, cast spreader, several rolls of plaster, stockinette, sterile dressings, tape, traction rope, assorted traction weights, and several tools used to tighten or loosen various screws and bolts on orthopedic appliances. In the standard intern's uniform, there simply was not enough pocket space to carry all the supplies Dr. DeJarnett expected him to carry on rounds. To solve this problem, the day before, Mark had briefly left the hospital and braved the cold to walk to a little store on nearby Decatur Street; there, he'd purchased a pair of white bib overalls—the kind frequently used by house painters. On today's rounds, Mark Telfair would be fully prepared. He looked like somebody from maintenance at NASA. He had all the required paraphernalia conveniently stowed in the many pockets of his spotless white bibs. When Dr. DeJarnett noticed Mark's new attire, he could not help but comment.

"Now that's what I call *innovation*, Telfair!" DeJarnett said. "Your buddy Zack Paslaski solved the same problem by stealing a shopping cart from the Piggly Wiggly Grocery Store down the street. But I gotta tell you, Dr. Telfair, what you've gone and done ... well it just looks a heck of a lot more *professional!*"

Mark beamed at the compliment, but knew the room they'd next enter on rounds would be a sore spot for Dr. DeJarnett. It was the room of the 73-year-old female who'd had her hip nailed the very first day Mark had arrived on the service. Technically, she was doing fine. No wound infection. In-bed X-rays still showed perfect fracture alignment. But she had absolutely refused to eat a single mouthful since surgery. She would not ambulate with her walker when the physical therapist and the nurses tried to get her motivated to recover from her perfect hip-nailing.

Dr. Faulkner sadly summarized at the patient's bedside: "Chief, despite everything being so perfect, she just does not seem to be motivated to recover at all. What in the world can we do?"

Dr. DeJarnett thought for a moment, then spoke as he was removing his shoes. "All she needs is a little stimulation ... and a reason to live."

That said, Dr. DeJarnett promptly climbed onto her bed, and stood towering over her pale white body. He faced the head of her bed. Each of his sock-clad feet were firmly planted on each side of her pelvis. As the patient looked up at Dr. DeJarnett, her eyes were now widely open, and in total disbelief of what she was seeing.

"Ma'am this fellow here is Dr. Mark Telfair," Dr. DeJarnett politely said, as he looked down upon her, and pointed to Mark in his white bib overalls stuffed to the gills with orthopedic supplies. "Ya see ma'am, Dr. Telfair came to us here at Grady from a doctor-rehabilitation program. He was bad to drink, and even started taking dope ... but he's tryin' his best to go straight, and he participated in the surgery for your broken hip. He even put a lot of your stitches in. So please ma'am ... please don't disappoint him. He just might not be able to accept the failure if you don't get well. He'd probably just go on back to his old ways, you know."

Still standing over her on the bed, Dr. DeJarnett then began to slowly spring up and down. Her body was now gently bouncing up and down with Dyson's rhythmic motions. All the while Dr. DeJarnett was softly singing *"Jesus loves me, this I know ... For the Bible tells me so ..."*

Mark was petrified and in as much disbelief as the wide-eyed patient. Dr. Faulkner and the others on rounds did not seem the least bit disturbed. Some even joined Dyson in singing a few verses of *Jesus Loves Me* to the patient.

Mark's mind was in overdrive; he absolutely refused to believe what he was witnessing! He thought perhaps the long hours had tinkered with the very roots of his own sanity ... or possibly Dr. DeJarnett's. *Why hadn't Zack told me what really happens on orthopedics!* Mark thought, still doubting his own eyes and ears.

The very next day, Mark had occasion to return to the same patient's room. He was totally embarrassed as he entered, and tried to avoid direct eye contact with her. The patient was in a semi-sitting position in her hospital bed. The over-bed table held her breakfast tray. He couldn't help but note the open well-worn *Holy Bible* at one side of her food tray. She was apparently reading it ... as she devoured her breakfast! Bits of bacon were scattered on the open book's pages, making tiny grease spots where they rested. The patient finally looked up when she realized Mark was standing at her bedside.

"Well good morning, Dr. Telfair! Have you had any dope today?" she cheerfully asked.

"Uh ... no ma'am. No I sure haven't," Mark replied, still avoiding her eyes.

"Well, have you had anything to drink today?"

"No ma'am. Nothing except for coffee and orange juice at breakfast."

"Well, I've sure been praying for you. And it seems I'm a lot better too! I walked the entire length of the hall yesterday with my walker, and I plan to walk it three or four times today ... if the dad-burned nurse will *let* me!"

Mark removed her dressing while she was talking and gobbling the rest of her breakfast. The patient peeked at the wound and said, "Those are some pretty neat stitches in my skin there. They look OK to you?"

"Just fine ma'am, if I do say so myself," Mark commented, a little embarrassed at admiring his own work.

"That Dr. DeJarnett's something else, isn't he? Do you know if he's married?" the elderly patient asked.

"Yes ma'am, in more ways than one." *In more ways than you'll ever know, lady. Yes he is something else ... and yes he's married to orthopedics ... and yes he's married to every damn female nurse in this hospital building!* Mark thought, as he left the room to pursue his next task.

At 11:00 p.m. some 14 hours had elapsed since Mark had changed the dressing on the now-motivated hip-nail patient. Mark was sitting in the office with Dr. DeJarnett, who was reading the *American Journal of Bone and Joint Surgery.* Mark reflected upon the strange things that happened on orthopedics, but he had to agree with Zack; he'd never learned so much so quickly, nor worked so hard in all his life. As primary surgeon, he'd done his first hip-nail yesterday. Prior to that, he'd done a number of closed reductions of simple fractures. Basking in the glow of his recent accomplishments, Mark continued checking off items on his scut list and making notes in various patients' charts. The phone on Dyson's desk rang.

"DeJarnett speaking," Dyson quickly responded. After listening a moment, Dyson spoke to the caller. "Sure Jer, I'll be down there in just a few minutes." Dyson hung up, then turned to Mark who was still writing in a chart. "That was Jer Bacon down in the Pit. He's now working the night shift, and he's got a few bones he wants me to look at. Apparently they're really swamped with a lot of nonemergency stuff too. He wanted to know if we could help him out if we weren't too busy. I think he's also got a few folks from general surgery coming to help too."

"Can we do that?" Mark asked. "Just go to *another* service ... one we aren't even assigned to?"

"Sure can. We do it all the time on the surgical services. When one of us gets swamped, we *all* help out. Admin has never said a word about it that I know of, and I know for a fact they know it happens. So, do you want to go down there with me?"

"Yeah, sure!" Mark replied as he closed the chart where he was making notes.

When Dr. Dyson DeJarnett and Dr. Mark Telfair entered the Surgical Pit it was an absolute zoo. Granted, it was a Saturday night, but this was worse than the worst Mark had seen during his earlier two months there on day shift. All the church-like benches along the walls of the ER's common area were filled to capacity. A few patients had temporary bandages or ice packs applied to various areas of their bodies, but they seemed to be in no distress at all. All six of the ER's gurneys had patients on them, but they were obviously not really sick either; they would periodically sit up to talk and laugh with their neighbors, then lie back down again. In fact, Mark didn't see a single acutely ill patient in the lot. Most had no visible abnormality at all. The vast majority were smiling, chatting, and laughing like they were attending a Saturday night cocktail party. The alcohol fumes in the ER's air were enough to give the nondrinker a buzz. A thick stack of the triplicate-copy ER blue sheets sat in the to-be-seen wire basket on the workstation counter. From the thickness of the stack, Mark knew there were at least 50 patients in the ER.

"Thanks, fellas," a harried Jer Bacon said as he spied Dr. DeJarnett and Mark among the oppressive but festive crowd. "I think I've got two forearm fractures and a couple of broken ankles for you, somewhere in this mess, if we can just find them."

Dyson surveyed the scene for a full minute, then made his statement: "Jer, just give me that whole stack of blue sheets for a few minutes. We need to find out exactly who's really sick, and who's just down here for their Saturday night entertainment."

"I couldn't agree more, but just how do you plan to do that?" Jer smiled despite his fatigue.

"In my humble saw-bones opinion, allow me to show you what needs to be done." Dyson smiled back at Jer with a devilish grin.

Against his better judgment, Jerry Bacon handed the entire stack of blue sheets to Dyson. Dr. DeJarnett quickly went behind the workstation counter and got three old-style Coca-Cola crates, wooden yellow ones with red lettering. Those same old crates had been around Grady for years, and were usually used by various short folks as a foot rest when seated on the tall stools behind the counter. Carrying the crates and ER blue sheets, Dyson elbowed his way through the crowd. He proceeded to the very center of he common area. There he stacked the three crates to make himself a pedestal, then stood upon it. He was now about seven and a half feet tall. His shrill whistle brought all conversations and laughter to an immediate standstill. He loudly cleared his throat, then spoke.

"Ladies and gentlemen ... sisters and brothers ... please let me welcome you to the Grady Memorial Hospital Evening Healing Service. I'm Reverend Dr. Dyson DeJarnett, and just by the *laying-on of my hands*, I'll personally be healing each and every one of you this very evening. But before we begin the actual healing service, won't all of you please join me in singing *Amazing Grace, How Sweet the Sound?*"

As Dyson started singing, a few of the patients started joining in. By the time "Reverend" DeJarnett's splendid singing voice reached the third verse, participation from the flock was almost a perfect majority. The baritone voice of ER orderly Mose Mallone was truly fabulous; it resonated beautifully with the terrazzo-and-tile acoustics afforded by the ER. But Jer Bacon was not singing *at all!* He was just staring in astonishment, looking both exhausted and frightened at the same time. Mark hadn't seen Jer Bacon so scared since the day Zack Paslaski was drilling a hole in that cue ball jammed in a patient's mouth. The singing finally ended, but when the word got out, Jer Bacon was certain his residency at Grady would definitely be going up in smoke ... *holy smoke!*

Jer started to lunge at Dyson and snatch him off the Coca-Cola crate pedestal, but found a huge hand grasping him around his left arm's biceps. He turned to see Mose wearing a huge smile, fully determined to hold his arm securely.

Before Jer could talk Mose into letting him go, Dyson again started to speak, as final scattered "amens" flickered through the crowd.

"Oh, thank you! Thank you brothers and sisters! I'm sure that beautiful singing pleased the Lord, but it's getting late, so let's get on with the healing service. I've got to move on to the next hospital soon," Dyson explained, still standing tall upon his makeshift pedestal. Holding the thick stack of blue sheets in his hand, Dyson pretended to be intently studying the top sheet. He then suddenly began staring around the room as though he might be in some sort of a daze, or maybe some drug-induced trance. In front of his astonished congregation, he began to violently jerk his arms and twitch his facial muscles. He threw all the blue sheets up into the air, and as they fluttered down to the floor, Dyson fell to the floor along with them. He continued to jerk all over. Slobbering now, Dr. DeJarnett wriggled around on the terrazzo floor, getting his immaculate white jacket filthy. *My God he is having a generalized seizure. He's epileptic! I gotta help him!* Mark thought.

Mark was preparing to rush to Dyson's aid when he saw Mose laughing ... and still restraining Jer Bacon. Mark realized the seizure was a fake. Dyson stopped his convincing seizure theatrics a few minutes later. He crawled around the floor on all fours shaking his head. Slowly, he gathered the now widely scattered blue sheets. The hushed "congregation" had quickly backed away, forming a rather distant circle around Reverend Dyson DeJarnett. While still on his knees, he held up the first blue sheet. Pretending to be experiencing extreme difficulty focusing on the blue sheet's words, Dyson loudly called out a name: "Sadie Jones." A few seconds later, with even more volume, he repeated, "Where is Sadie Jones? Please come forward and get healed. Let me lay my healing hands upon you, Sadie. Sadie Jones, where are you?" No reply was heard in the now-silent ER. Dyson then took the Sadie Jones blue sheet and wrote DNA in large letters on the front of the sheet. Out of the corner of his eye, Mark saw a dark female patient quietly walk out of the ER. From Mark's prior experience in the Pit, he knew the DNA acronym stood for Did Not Answer, and when DNA was written on the front of a blue sheet, it was assumed the patient either got tired of waiting, or for some other reason, had voluntarily left the ER.

Dr. DeJarnett continued the calling out of various names, and writing DNA on the front of most of the blue sheets. As Dyson proceeded, Mark could not help but notice a steady and quiet exodus of the "sick" ... those who'd decided not to answer to their name. Finally Dyson managed to stand up, and by then had the sheets sorted: DNA in his left hand, the really-sick-folks in the other.

At the end of the 15-minute singing-and-name-calling show, Dyson approached Jer with a very much smaller stack of blue sheets. He presented them to Dr. Bacon and spoke: "Sorry to waste so much time Jer, but here are the ten folks that are actually sick. The ones that need to be seen." Mark couldn't help but notice: The six stretchers—the gurneys, that should have held the sickest of the lot—were now all *vacant!* Jer had finally managed a sheepish smile. Mose had relaxed his restraining grip on Jer, and all three were now softly chuckling together.

Though obviously relieved, Jer felt obligated to tell Dyson he didn't approve of his methods, even if they were efficient. "Dyson, you and your antics could cost me my residency ... could very well be the final nail in my coffin. I'm already in trouble due to a gun that got in here a while back. Could cost you *your* residency too, if admin ever finds out about this. You can't just come in here pretending you're some kinda singing epileptic faith-healing evangelist!"

"What singin'? What preachin'? I ain't heard no preachin' *or* singin'. Have you?" Mose asked, speaking to Dr. Jerry Bacon in his deep believable voice. "And I bet Dr. DeJarnett and Dr. Telfair here ... well I jus' bet they ain't seen or heard no preachin' or singin' either." Mose turned to look at two winos still slumped over on one of the benches. Pointing at the winos, Mose whispered into Jer's ear. "And I bet them two fellas there didn't see or hear nothin' at all. Heck, they still can't even *feel* nothin' yet! So, when they wakes up, we jus' make 'em a new blue sheet without no DNA on it. Now you can jus' quit your worryin', Dr. Jerry!" Mose concluded with a broad smile that displayed his perfect white teeth.

The threesome was disbanding their ain't-seen-nothing-heard-nothing alibi session when Mark caught Mose by the arm. "Mose, why did all those patients leave when Dr. DeJarnett started calling out their names?"

"Lawd, you still got a heap to learn Dr. Mark," Mose chuckled. "You remember how scared you was that day you had that mojo witch backed up in the elevator? The day she stab you with the ice pick ... remember?"

"Sure I remember that, Mose. How could I ever forget that! But what's the point?" Mark questioned.

"Well, jus' let me say this: Some of them folks that *was* in here, they just as scared of somebody what's got seizures as they is of somebody what's got the mojo. They think peoples with seizures be possessed by the devil, and they flat scared of ev'n bein' *touched* by 'em, 'cause the devil may come into they own body if they ev'n touch! But don't you worry yourself Dr. Mark, 'cause nobody what was *really* sick left from here. I can promise you that."

"Oh, I see," is all Mark Telfair could think of to say, but his mind delivered two blunt questions, then an answer: *Why are many things in the real world so much stranger than I'd thought? Why has my earlier life left me such a narrow view of humanity? It's because I've been so horribly sheltered ... that's why.*

12

COWBOY

The first day of March, 1965, finally arrived ... the date for all interns' rotation to a different service at Grady. Eight months of Mark Telfair's internship year had flown past. His GAC, ER, internal medicine, and the two exhausting months on orthopedic surgery with the legendary Hot Body were now behind him, all ancient history.

The last four months of Mark's straight surgical intern year would all be spent on general surgery wards located on Grady's fourth floor. His first surgical ward assignment had been to 4-A. There he sat. He checked his watch: six forty-five a.m. He waited impatiently for the rest of the crew to show up for the traditional first-day meeting at seven.

In terms of learning about surgery, the Surgical ER and orthopedics had certainly been his best rotations thus far. He only hoped 4-A wouldn't be a comparative disappointment. He knew his schedule would now be more human ... and *humane.* He'd work every day from 7:00 a.m. until around 5:00 p.m. However, every fourth day 4-A's staff would be on "emergency call." Emergency call began at 7:00 a.m. and ended at 7:00 a.m. the next day. This meant dealing with all emergency admissions to general surgery occurring during that 24-hour period. Also, 4-A would be expected to deal with any in-house problems that developed on any of the four general surgical wards between the hours of 5:00 p.m. and 7:00 a.m. the next morning. Mark felt his life would now be similar to what he might experience in private practice, especially if he joined a group having several surgeons who shared emergency call. At night, he'd now be a free man at least three-fourths of the time. *Have I now got time to patch up my ailing love life? I wonder if Carla would even consider having me back?* he thought. An additional member of the new 4-A crew arrived, abruptly terminating Mark's daydreams about his nonexistent love life.

"Well, hello there, Mark," said a surprised Dr. Jerry Bacon, the Senior Assistant Surgical Resident from the ER. "I had no idea I'd find you here."

"Well I'm just as surprised as you are, Jer. I thought you'd be in the Pit forever," Mark commented.

"Just seems that way," Jer said. "When you're SAR you rotate in four-month blocks, instead of the two-month blocks you 'terns rotate in. Just after you left the Pit, the day crew went to nights, and I worked all night last night in the ER before coming up to 4-A this morning. Man, am I glad to get a breather from the ER!"

"Did Mose change to nights too?" Mark asked, knowing he'd recently seen Mose in the ER the night he and "Reverend" DeJarnett lent a helping hand. "Won't that interfere with his activities with his gym children?"

"Yeah, Mose went to nights too, but he sure didn't like it. So he's working with his kids in the daytime now," Jer explained.

Mark noticed that Jer looked unusually tired. Beard stubble attested to the fact that Jer hadn't had time to shave before coming to 4-A.

Jerry Bacon yawned. "So what happened to your intern buddy? That Zack fella? Did he go to general too?" Jer asked.

"Yeah. That bozo went to 4-C, but he may be going back to ortho-pedics in May and June as an elective."

Jer smiled, then spoke. "Even though he's plenty smart, that Zack's definitely a glutton for punishment. I think he may end up specializing in orthopedics. You and I both know how good he is with mechanical things, like drills and cue balls. Right?"

Mark and Jer enjoyed their private laugh which was promptly interrupted by an irritated statement: "Hey, you guys! I know it's Old Home Week and all, but don't I even exist?" The question had been asked by the arriving Dr. Terry Brinson, the Junior Assistant Resident, who'd also rotated to 4-A from the Pit along with Jer. Terry looked almost as bedraggled as Jer.

Jer apologized to Terry for ignoring his arrival, then reached into a pocket to retrieve a bunch of wadded notes. As Jer unwadded one of the notes, Mark realized it was possibly a list of 4-A's new personnel. It had probably been given to Jer by administration at least a week ago. Mark knew Jer could really care less about such insignificant administrative details. Months ago, Mark Telfair had pegged Dr. Bacon: Being punctual, being honest, treating patients effectively, and never cursing in a patient's presence—those were Dr. Jerry Bacon's top priorities. But if a piece of paper couldn't help Jer Bacon treat a patient, he'd just as soon use it for toilet paper.

"Well I'll be dang! Mark, your name is on the 4-A list," Jer managed to say as he finally unwrinkled the list to the point of being legible again. "Says here, we are supposed to have two more interns ... a Dr. Joel Levitz, and a Dr. Adrian Brevard. So where the heck are they?" Jer said, studying his watch.

The words were barely out of Jer's mouth when the two embarrassed tardy interns quickly entered the door slightly out of breath—and five minutes late! Though the pair blamed their tardiness on the slow elevator, politely yet firmly, Jer spoke. "That excuse just don't cut it, guys! On time, *every* time. OK?"

The tardy pair nodded, and Jer made introductions all around. Again checking the battered notes, Jer spoke. "According to this, 4-A will be on emergency call today, so nobody leaves when the whistle blows at five today. OK? And for the first week or so, or until we know all these new patients, nobody can swap night call with guys on the other surgical wards. OK? After we've got the new patients down pat, I'll make out a call schedule for a month at a time, and put it on the bulletin board. OK? And then you guys can swap some call if you want. OK? Just be sure you make a note on the schedule. OK? And Mark, if you'll roll those chart racks in here, we'll all split the patients five ways, but Terry and me will take the most complicated ones. OK?"

"OK on getting the chart racks, Jer," Mark said, "but I think your OK-button is ... well ... it's *sorta stuck, Jer.* OK?"

"Mark, I know I say OK too much ... but it's a lot better than some of that trash that comes outta your roommate's mouth!" Jer said defensively, but still managed a smile.

One of the new interns, Dr. Adrian Brevard, was a Northeast Atlanta native. He had casually known Mark Telfair for a number of years prior to their meeting on 4-A. Hearing Mark and Jer's teasing banter, Adrian couldn't resist asking: "Mark, just who did Dr. Bacon say your trash-mouthed roommate was?"

"Jer didn't say, but his name is Zack Paslaski. He's on 4-C right now," Mark explained.

"You mind looking at something for me?" Dr. Adrian Brevard asked Mark the question while pulling a little notebook from his jacket's pocket. He retrieved one of Mark's DTs spider-test cards pressed between the notebook's pages. "What I want to know is this: Is this *genuine?* Or is it a *fake?*"

Mark accepted the card. He studied the drawing a brief moment, flipped it over, and spotted his own illegible signature on the card's back-side. It was scribbled just below his written instructions for administering the spider-test. The instructions were carefully printed in a block-letter hand, one Mark also recognized as his own.

"Looks perfectly genuine to me Adrian," Mark smiled. "And I wouldn't lie to a guy from my old grammar school and Boy Scout troop, would I?"

"Well, I bought this card from a trashmouth named Zack. Just wanted to be sure I didn't get ripped off. Cost me 15 bucks! He told me it was a *genuine signed original*, but I don't think he actually said who draws these things."

"Adrian, hand me your notebook for a minute."

Puzzled, Dr. Adrian Brevard reluctantly passed to Mark the possession every intern considers his most prized: an intern's pearl book. Such small notebooks contain bits of hand-me-down handwritten clinical wisdom—pearls of wisdom—not found in any of the textbooks. As Mark started thumbing through the private notebook, Adrian was getting a bit nervous. Mark was trying to locate a blank page. When he found an empty one, Mark took out his pen and signed the page, then dated the signature, and returned Adrian's book. Mark's bewildered Atlanta acquaintance was quickly joined by an equally curious Dr. Joel Levitz; the two interns carefully studied Mark's signature in Adrian's book, then compared it to the signature on the back of the DTs spider-test card.

Adrian smiled. "So you're the famous guy who—"

"In the flesh," Mark interrupted without even a hint of modesty. He knew he had just established the pecking order among the 4-A interns!

Jer Bacon and Terry Brinson had patiently waited while their interns went through the spider-test card validation process. Though the humor was appreciated, Jer Bacon, as SAR, knew he needed to get the day going. "Mark, are you going to get the charts in here *so we can get to work?* Or are we going to talk about spiders the rest of the day!" Jer had spoken with minor irritation, and major authority. From his two months' experience with Jer in the ER, Mark knew Jer well enough to realize when he was serious, and when he was not. Jer was dead serious.

Mark promptly rolled the chart racks into the doctors' office, where the five members of 4-A's new crew pored over the records of some 60 new patients. Each team member ended up with about a dozen patients apiece. That dozen would be their individual responsibility to care for, and present on rounds made by the ward's staff twice daily. Mark knew a larger responsibility for the patient's management rested upon Jer Bacon and Terry Brinson, then upon the General Surgery Chief Resident, and ultimately upon the Emory doctors, often professors, who would make rounds with the residents and interns several times a week. Mark also knew the new team was under fire; 4-A was on emergency call, and at any moment their day could be turned upside down. As it was Saturday, Mark prepared for the worst. A number of emergency general surgery admissions were sure to occur, especially during the night ... it always happened on Grady's infamous Saturday nights.

Most of the first day on 4-A had been consumed by learning the details of new patients, late morning rounds, lunch, and late afternoon rounds. It was 5:00 p.m., and the 4-A crew had just seated themselves in the cafeteria for supper when the PA system blared out: "Dr. Bacon ... Dr. Jerry Bacon ... call 3-6-0 please."

"Oh no! Not already!" Jer said, fully aware 3-6-0 was the ER's three-digit extension. "You guys enjoy your meal," Jer added as he headed for the cafeteria's wall phone.

At a distance, Mark observed Jer's animated inaudible conversation. Between words, Jer was taking large bites out of a corn muffin he'd carried with him to the phone. Dr. Bacon hung up and sprinted back to the table, rapidly chewing as he ran, cheeks still puffed out by unswallowed muffin. All eyes were on Jer. He couldn't speak until he gulped half a glass of iced tea.

"They're in deep doo-doo in the Pit! Got two GSWs to bellies, and some dude in shock from a mile-long cut. That's what the new SAR in the Pit said on the phone. And it's his first day on the job, and his JAR ain't never been in the ER before. All their 'terns are green. All from Ivy League schools, and ain't the first one of 'em ever started an IV before. So let's boogie guys! OK?"

Without further words, the 4-A team got up from their table, grabbed any part of their meal that was portable, and rapidly ran from the cafeteria. They headed to the nearest stairwell to avoid the slow elevators. In two minutes flat, the 4-A crew burst into the ER, where Jer Bacon essentially took over.

"Mark, I want you to head up the interns. So you, Brevard, and Levitz all jump on that guy with the mile-long cut. Get what help you can outta those Ivy League 'terns. Me and Terry will take care of the two GSWs!"

Mark led his intern team as they evaluated a black male in his 20s. He was in shock, apparently from massive blood loss. He had a laceration that started in the center of his forehead. Without any visible interruption, the cut spiraled around his entire body, each revolution dropping about two inches lower than the one immediately above. Miraculously, his eyes were located between spirals, and thus spared. The laceration finally terminated at his navel.

"Gosh," said one of the Ivy League interns, in apparent sincerity, "I wonder what his hemoglobin level is?"

"Don't know, don't care!" Mark shot back. "He'll be dead by the time you check it! His BP is forty over zero, so let's get four IV lines and pour in some Ringer's lactate while we're getting him typed and crossmatched for eight units whole blood."

The three Ivy League interns watched in amazement as Mark,

Brevard, and Levitz did their Grady-intern-thing: Four large-bore IV lines placed, fluid flying in, all in less than one minute! After the first three liters of IV fluid, Mark proudly announced: "BP is now 105 over 50, guys!"

With his blood pressure somewhat restored, various points along the seemingly endless laceration resumed bleeding. Mark had the nurse set up six different suture trays; he put everybody to work—Ivy League guys included. Mark instructed: "Try to keep him turned so we can get to the most active bleeders first. For now, just clamp and tie off the bleeders. Get the biggest ones first. Don't worry about closing the skin just yet."

It took about an hour to clamp and tie the active bleeders. The patient was on his seventh unit of blood and his pressure was now normal. He was somewhat responsive, though mentally fogged from having been in shock. Fortunately the patient was not combative, and he didn't smell like he was drunk. *Probably wouldn't be drunk now anyway ... because most of his own blood had been replaced by blood from sober donors,* Mark's mind rationalized. Mark showed the Ivy League fellows how to do the skin closure, using about four or five stitches per inch of laceration. He instructed them to use no local anesthetic; it would take a toxic—possibly fatal—amount of local to deaden a laceration an estimated umpteen feet long. Stepping out of the treatment room to check on Jer and Terry, and their GSWs, a thought popped into Mark's head: *I'm sure glad I've got two months of ER under my belt!*

Mark stuck his head in the single treatment room where both the GSWs had been placed side by side for the convenience of the two residents in attendance. "What's going on, guys?" Mark asked Terry and Jer, who were writing orders on their respective patient's charts.

Terry was first to speak. "Not much. They're both small caliber, both definitely in the peritoneal cavity. Both are stable. From the guesstimated trajectory, I don't think either of these guys will have much injured inside, but we're going to have to do exploratory laparotomies on both of them. Anything to add, Jer?"

"Nope. That's about it for these two. I'm going to give both of these patients to Terry ... and Mark, if you treat Terry real nice, maybe he'll give you one of these exploratories to do as the primary surgeon. So how's the guy with the megacut doin'?"

"Out of shock, Jer. Active bleeding controlled. Just hung the eighth unit of blood, and they're all still stitching like mad," Mark summarized.

"How the heck did he get cut like that?" Jer asked.

"Don't know yet. His brain is still defogging. I'll let you know when I find out. If there's not anything I can help you guys with now, I'll go check on the stitching progress. OK?"

"Yo 'Tern! Just go check on *your* 'terns—but let me know how he got cut, OK?" Jer asked as Mark left.

He returned to the room where the five interns continued suturing. Though the lucky patient was tolerating the stitching without anesthesia, he winced with each stitch placed. His blood pressure remained normal, so Mark administered a healthy shot of Demerol to ease the patient's pain. The patient thanked him for the pain shot. The patient's mind was now obviously clear, and Mark decided now would be the best time to ask him exactly what happened—before the Demerol kicked in and fogged his brain again.

"Say fella, just how did you get cut like this?" Mark asked, though in his own mind he'd already decided it must have been some kind of an industrial accident. He figured the patient must have gotten tightly wrapped with some kind of a small wire. The wire then must have cut into his skin, thus leaving the long continuous spiral laceration, one being almost a perfect quarter-inch depth, from beginning to end.

With obvious embarrassment, the patient finally replied. "Well Doctor, I guess I brought all this on myself. You see, I was messin' 'round with one of Cowboy's womens. Some of *his* poontang, you know. And he caught me right while I was still messin'... and Cowboy he say he were goin' to 'peel me alive with a pocket knife' ... and Doctor, *I think he damn near done it!*"

As sad as the story was, Mark knew he was about to have one of his Telfair mirth moments. He immediately left, found a private laughing place, and let it run its usual course. In a few minutes he'd recovered, but found his mind questioning his actions: *Why do I laugh at stuff like this? Is laughter some kind of bizarre stress indicator? Why is the movie MASH considered funny by most folks? Especially doctors. Is it because horrible things are so painful to the observer ... so bad that some folks use humor as a defense mechanism, a shield to protect their own psyche? I think I'm beginning to figure myself out. Humor will keep me sane through all this,* he concluded.

Feeling comfortable in his mind, Mark stuck his head back into the room where Terry and Jer had their GSWs now ready for transport to the OR. He couldn't resist telling them what he'd found out.

"Hey you guys, the patient says some dude named 'Cowboy' did that to him with a *pocket knife!* You believe that? That someone could just hold somebody down, then inflict such a perfectly symmetrical spiral cut?" Mark asked, now seriously doubting the truth of the patient's story.

"Mark," Jer said, "when and if you ever see Cowboy, you'll understand exactly how it could have happened. When you and I were in the Pit together, Cowboy musta been in jail, 'cause I don't remember him coming in a single time during the two months you were there. But believe me, when Cowboy is out of jail he's a Grady Saturday night regular. If he's already done this much so early on a Saturday, I wouldn't be at all surprised if the cops don't bring him in sometime tonight. But right now, how about getting that megacut fellow admitted and squared away on 4-A. Then I want you to go up to the OR and assist Terry with these two GSW exploratories. OK?"

"Sure boss," Mark said, and immediately returned to Megacut's room. As he entered, one of the Ivy League interns was meticulously counting stitches. The counting intern announced with pride: "Hey everybody, that's 1,068 stitches, if I didn't miss one." Another Ivy Leaguer was recoiling a bloody cloth tape measure: "That's 18 feet and two inches for the cut, so if my math and the stitch count are correct, we averaged about four point nine stitches per inch. Think I should convert that to metric, fellas?" *What useless bullshit information ... but at over 18 feet in length, and well over a 1,000 stitches, it's gotta be a Grady record,* Mark thought.

Mark got the laceration patient admitted to 4-A, then went to the OR where Terry Brinson was already scrubbing for the first of the two exploratory laps. Mark joined in scrub, then asked, "Where's Jer?"

"He's catching some rack time," Terry explained. "I got four hours' sleep last night, and Jer got nothing. So I'm not about to bug him unless we have to. We'll do the next lap as soon as we get this one off the table ... unless something more pressing comes in. OK with you?"

"Sure!" Mark said, feeling the excitement of being the second assistant on an exploratory laparotomy.

And the surgical procedure—or rather *procedures*—went fine; Mark actually did the second one as *the* surgeon, with Terry assisting. Mark's mind was on a high: *I did a laparotomy as an intern! I don't care if Zack did nail six hips!* Both surgeries had largely been exercises in opening and closing the abdomen, and learning how to methodically search for any penetrating injuries to the abdominal cavity's contents. In both GSW patients, only relatively minor small bowel penetrating injuries had been found, then repaired.

As Terry and Mark were changing back into their whites in the OR dressing room, Junior Assistant Resident Terry Brinson sensed Mark's acutely expanding intern's ego. *First his supervising the other interns in getting Megacut out of shock and stitched up ... then next doing his first lap where he was the surgeon ... too much, too soon,* thought Dr. Brinson. Terry remembered well his own previous intern year at Grady, when he'd done his very first exploratory laparotomy with Jer Bacon assisting. It was time to poke a small pinhole in Dr. Mark Telfair's inflated ego.

"Thanks for the help," Terry said, "but what we just did is something a pair of trained monkeys could have done."

Using a defensive tone Mark replied, "Well Terry, there sure must be a lot of smart monkeys out there."

"Yeah," Terry responded, "but for every intelligent monkey, there's a troop of stupid ones. Some of those monkeys even call themselves surgeons, but I certainly don't intend to be among the overconfident stupid ones!"

Mark said nothing, but silently put Terry Brinson on the same level—that same pedestal—with Mr. Mose Mallone, the ER orderly ... especially when it came to real-world perspective, wisdom, and needed ego adjustments.

At 12:30 a.m., Terry Brinson and Mark left the OR after being sure their two patients were doing well in recovery. The pair agreed to go to the cafeteria to see if they could scrounge up a supper they never really had. The minute they stepped into the almost-empty cafeteria, the hospital's PA announced: "Dr. Bacon ... Dr. Jerry Bacon ... 3-6-0 please."

"Oh crap," Terry said. "How do they always know exactly when we try to eat? I'll catch it for Jer. He's still sleeping, I hope."

With Mark at his side Terry went to the phone. After listening a moment Terry said, "We'll be right there!"

Turning to Mark, Terry rapidly explained: "A three-car wreck from I-75. Only one hurt bad. Acute belly from blunt trauma. Possible ruptured spleen. Lets go!"

When Terry and Mark arrived the ER was fairly clear. That in itself was very unusual, considering it was Saturday night, or now actually early Sunday morning. The green ER crew was doing fairly well. The possible ruptured spleen patient already had two IV lines. Appropriate labs and X-rays were in the mill. The patient's blood pressure had been stabilized by IV fluids alone, but free blood was present in the abdominal cavity according to paracentesis (needle tap of the abdominal cavity). Terry was drinking in the initial clinical data, when he turned to Mark and said, "Go call Jer. Tell him I'm going to need him in about 30 minutes in the OR. And Mark, I don't want you to think I'm trying to dump on you, but I need you to stay down here to help these green ER guys deal with all the lacerations and simple fractures that resulted from that three-car wreck. You OK with that?"

"Sure thing Terry," Mark replied, hiding his disappointment about missing the ruptured spleen surgery. "But can I get the 4-A interns back down here if some of these wreck folks have more than the Ivy League 'terns can deal with?"

"Use your own judgment. Just let the new ER SAR know you'll be willing to help his team out, and bring the other 4-A interns back if they're needed. Right now I gotta get up to the OR, and be ready to help Jer when he gets there."

Mark felt left out of the loop by missing the possible ruptured spleen surgery, but felt some consolation knowing that Terry had left him "in charge" of the other 4-A interns, should they again be needed for intern-level work in the ER. Mark found the harried new SAR in charge, introduced himself as an intern from 4-A, then told him he was available to help in the ER. The SAR said, "Yeah, be glad to have you stick around. The ambulances just radioed that they are on the way with another wreck, plus some folks involved in a knife fight. One is coming from Marietta, the other from Norcross, so it'll be a little while before they get here. But in the meantime, look around and see if you can find anybody who's not getting treatment that's immediately needed."

"Sure thing," Mark replied, then proceeded to survey the remaining relatively minor injuries from the I-75 wreck. As Mark moved from treatment room to treatment room, he felt the new ER crew had things under control. While moving about the ER he suddenly noticed a huge man slumped over. He was sitting in a wheelchair backed up to one of the massive tile-covered columns in the ER's common area. No one appeared to be paying any attention to him. At first, Mark thought the guy in the wheelchair might be Mose, the ER orderly, only dressed in his street clothes. *Case of mistaken identity.* On closer inspection, the wheelchair held a man much larger than Mose, even more muscular, but with slightly lighter skin. Shiny handcuffs secured his right wrist to the right wheel of the ancient wooden wheelchair, one that had obviously been brought to the new Grady from the old one. The giant was dressed in a black cowboy hat with a snake skin band, classic western shirt and jeans, and pointed-toe boots, apparently made of lizard or alligator skin. Even in a slumped posture, with his chin resting on his chest, Mark could make out a huge gold chain around his neck. As Mark approached the wheelchair he could detect the now-familiar fragrance—alcohol, blood, urine. *Grady perfume,* he had named it. The giant appeared to be passed out, drunk. At some time he had urinated in his pants, and a large telltale yellow puddle had formed on the terrazzo floor beneath the chair. He had dried blood spattered on his light blue shirt and jeans, but didn't appear to have any wounds of his own. As Mark removed the patient's hat—to check his level of consciousness—a sudden forceful slap to his side sent him sprawling, though unharmed. Surprised, the young doctor found himself on the floor, still holding the hat. The seemingly unconscious patient immediately spoke: "Hey! Gimme my hat back. Don't *nobody* steal Cowboy's hat!"

Cautiously, Mark again approached the wheelchair. Cowboy already had his uncuffed hand extended to receive his hat. As Mark returned it, Cowboy smiled to reveal gold-clad upper central incisors. "Sorry I hit you, Doc. Guess I was kinda sleepin', and jus' forgot where I was at."

"That's OK," Mark said. "Are you all right?"

"All 'cept these handcuffs. They too tight."

Mark checked Cowboy's radial artery pulse at the right wrist below the level of the handcuffs. The cuffed hand's skin was warm. "Cowboy, they're not cutting off your circulation, and besides, I don't have any way to loosen them. You know it takes a special key, and I don't have one."

"Well them po-lices *does!* So go find one of 'em, and you get 'em to loose 'em up."

"I will Cowboy, but first I got to finish checking around and see if anybody is seriously hurt. Then I'll go find the police for you," Mark said.

The words to Cowboy were barely out of Mark's mouth when several ambulances arrived simultaneously. Attendants were rapidly rolling laden gurneys into the Surgical Emergency Room. The many new arrivals were mostly minor injuries but Mark felt the sheer volume might overwhelm the green ER crew. The SAR in charge quickly put Mark to work dealing with the multiple minor lacerations and requested that he also get the other 4-A interns to help; this would free up the new regular ER crew to concentrate on the few major injuries they'd just received.

As Mark dealt with a series of minor problems, he frequently passed Cowboy's wheelchair, and with each pass Cowboy would invariably ask: "Is you found dem po-lices yet?" With each pass Mark would reassure Cowboy he'd get to it as soon as he could. After several hours passed, Cowboy grew quite impatient. In desperation, he finally said, "Well Doctor, I can't wait no longer. I'm just goin' on home and take 'em off myself."

What young Dr. Telfair witnessed next was almost beyond belief. Cowboy stood up. He slowly started walking, dragging the wheelchair sideways. As Cowboy moved the chair, urine continually dribbled from the chair's saturated cushion, creating a trail of urine on the floor. When the massive man had moved to the middle of the ER's central area, he abruptly stopped. Cowboy started swinging the wheelchair around in a head-high circle, as though it might be a mere lightweight toy handcuffed to his wrist. After several revolutions, the wheelchair had gained sufficient velocity to make a loud swishing sound as it circled in the air.

The urine-soaked cushion suddenly separated from the chair's bottom, and flew out, hitting the tile-covered wall with a soggy dull *splat!* After a few more revolutions, Cowboy stepped forward, forcing the chair to violently crash into one of the ER's large support columns. Mark closed his eyes as he heard the loud impact. The earsplitting crash was immediately echoed by a scattering of smaller secondary crashes, as bits and pieces of the chair hit the hard walls and floor. When he opened his eyes Mark saw shards of ceramic tile, fragments of varnished oak wood, and assorted pieces of metal littering the ER floor. Only when he turned away from the crash site, did Mark notice Cowboy ... casually ambling toward the ER's swinging-door exit. The only recognizable part of the destroyed wheelchair—a lone grossly deformed wheel—still dangled from the handcuff around Cowboy's right wrist. *A giant charm on a bracelet,* Mark thought.

"Shorty! Shorty! Help, police! Cowboy's leaving the ER!" Mark yelled, but knew it was about as useless as sending a henhouse chicken to capture the fox. Surprisingly, the stuttering little cop had not been out in the ambulance bay chain-smoking his Camel cigarettes as he usually was. From somewhere *inside* the ER, Shorty immediately appeared—just as Cowboy was stepping through the swinging doors to leave.

"Shorty! Shorty! There he goes, man. Better go catch him!" Mark exclaimed.

"Uh-uh w-w-we k-k-knows where he-he st-tays at, Doctor ... and we-weee go-go get him to-to-tomorrow!" That was Shorty's one and only comment about Cowboy's illegal departure.

In his mind Mark knew one thing for sure: *The useless little stuttering cop was not about to deal with Cowboy ... at least not one-on-one ... not even with a nightstick and .38 revolver on his belt!*

13

THE BUSH HOOK

T he pleasant May morning found intern Telfair daydreaming in the doctors' office on Grady's 4-B general surgical ward. Awaiting the beginning of his first day on 4-B, and still daydreaming, Mark Telfair suddenly realized he would soon be completing the year of straight surgical internship; in two months he'd become a first-year Junior Assistant Resident (JAR). Though elated, Mark knew the end of his formal surgical training was still distant, the storm not yet over. He was merely in a lull. He'd spend another year as a second-year JAR, then another residency year as Senior Assistant Resident (SAR). Finally, if deemed good enough, he'd become a Chief Resident—or "Chief." *If the four residency years pass as quickly as the intern year, I'll be through this shit-storm before I know it!* Mark thought. He yawned, becoming a little more aware of his surroundings, and realized his mind had suddenly tried to race ahead in fast forward. His brain quickly found its pause and rewind buttons.

Though he was now back in the present, myriad thoughts—mostly unanswerable questions—kept sparking in his head: *Would 4-B really be any different from 4-A? In two months, would he actually feel any differently as a first-year Junior Assistant Surgical Resident? Was Cowboy the most treacherous human he'd ever met? Was the 18-foot laceration inflicted by Cowboy really a Grady record? Were mojo and voodoo power real? Would he ever find that beautiful hazel-eyed woman he'd regrettably called a dumb broad?*

Mark's questions were coming faster and faster when Jer Bacon quietly entered the 4-B office. Spotting Mark sitting there with his eyes closed, leaning back in a chair propped at a dangerous angle against the wall, Jer immediately sensed his intern must be sleeping ... or at the very least doing some heavy-duty daydreaming.

"Yo Mark! What planet are you on this morning?" Jer asked in a booming voice.

Startled, Mark jumped and his chair slid down the wall with a loud crash. Wide-eyed, he immediately flushed, though unhurt. "Uh ... don't know! Maybe Venus, Jer. Maybe I'd feel a little better if I were on Venus. Get it?"

"Well get your ass off the floor. Chairs are for sitting, beds are for sleeping ... and uh ... screwing," Jer said, bursting with laughter.

Being thoroughly satisfied with Sylvia Banks, his student-nurse girlfriend, Jerry Bacon was largely unsympathetic regarding his horny intern's comment. Although amused, Jerry Bacon spoke few words of consolation. "Mark, Hot Body does not have a total corner on the market, you know."

Mark quickly righted his chair and sat in it properly before speaking. "Well, the ole Hot Bod sure has a major monopoly going!" Mark shot back, regretting he didn't have a great girlfriend like Jerry Bacon's.

After their initial lighthearted exchange, Jer's expression became somewhat somber. "Mark, do you feel the training program administrators think things through? You know, like, have they got their heads screwed on right? These mandatory rotations through the four *identical* surgical wards don't make any sense to me. SARs are supposed to rotate in four-month blocks, and now they've suddenly decided it'll be two-month rotations. I can't figure out exactly why they'd transfer all of us 4-A guys to 4-B, especially when we had 4-A running so great."

"Beats me, Jer. You've certainly been around here longer than I have. I only know I'm comfortable working with you and Terry Brinson. Brevard and Levitz have also told me they like working with you and Terry. So, at least admin kept the whole 4-A team together when they rotated us to 4-B. Worst case scenario, all we gotta do is familiarize ourselves with 60 or so new patients, and keep working together until July ... when you'll be Chief Surgical Resident!"

Bacon frowned. "Well there's something else about administrative decisions that worries me. In fact, it concerns me a lot more than the way they jerk our rotation schedules around. I haven't told anybody else yet, but I don't think they're going to promote me to Chief Resident."

"What! What do you mean, Jer! You're the best SAR in the bunch. There's no reason you shouldn't be Chief. Heck, except for the GAC, and my internal medicine elective, I've worked directly with you ... or at least often enough to know you're a darn good SAR! I haven't seen you screw up yet. So why all the doubt?"

"Hey 'Tern, I really appreciate the vote of confidence. But it don't have nothing to do with medical judgment or surgical screwups. It has to do with politics!"

"*Politics?*" Mark said with a confused look.

"Yeah, *goddamn politics!* Politics, pure and simple," Jer lamented, using very uncharacteristic profanity. "It seems, or so I hear through the grapevine, that I'm being held fully accountable for that joker who got into the Pit with that gun, and then shot up the place. Seems administration feels a good SAR should have been in full control of his assigned area, or so my inside sources tell me."

"I'll never forget that day. Never. But that certainly wasn't *your* fault!"

Bacon remained distraught. "Mark, It seems admin wants to keep its smooth relationship with the Atlanta Police Department, especially during this integration thing. Ya know, about half the officers at APD are black. They don't want to raise a stink about some sorry ER cop, especially a black one with a speech handicap who's supposed to retire in a coupla years. It appears admin thinks it more racially acceptable to blame the white SAR in charge of the ER. Know what I mean?"

"Jer, it shouldn't be a question of skin color. The real problem is with that inadequate APD cop we have in the Surgical Pit. Shorty just happens to be black. The cops are the ones that are supposed to check for weapons, not the SAR. The City of Atlanta has some great law officers working for them, both black and white, but Shorty just ain't one of 'em! Shorty is the one who should get canned, not you."

"'Tern, you're preachin' to the choir," Jer replied, still despondent.

"Well I'm preaching the truth, Jer!" Mark said, getting a little angry. "Two times I personally hollered for the police in the Pit: The day that mojo witch stabbed me with her ice pick, and the day Cowboy busted his wheelchair, and then just casually left the ER—*while he was still under arrest by APD!* And Shorty was absolutely no help either time. He was either outside on the ambulance ramp smoking, or inside the Pit refusing to do what needed to be done."

"Mark, if you'd been Shorty, would you have tried to stop Cowboy from leaving?"

"Well ... I don't blame him for refusing to go up against Cowboy one-on-one. But in addition to his gun and night stick, Shorty has a radio on his belt, and he could have at least called for assistance!"

"Well Shorty's supposed to retire soon, and—"

"Jer, I know he's supposed to retire soon," Mark interrupted, "and I'm honestly sorry he stutters so badly, but bottom line, he's just not an effective law officer. No matter what his skin color may be, APD should fire his butt, even if it means Shorty might lose his pension. Fortunately, the day that crazy fella started shooting, no one was killed or injured. Your beautiful girlfriend's brain was spared by less than an inch! In my opinion, your getting all of us into the bathroom saved lives among the ER crew. And it was that good APD cop—that Fuzzy McInnis from the Medical Pit—

who subdued the shooter. Remember?"

"Yeah, maybe the Surgical Pit will get one just like Fuzzy after Shorty leaves," Jer said, still depressed.

"Well it looks to me like admin should put some pressure on APD to get us competent police coverage in the Surgical Pit right *now*! Just like the coverage they already have in the Medical Pit," Mark stated, feeling Jer was resigned to accepting the blame for an incident that was all Shorty's fault.

"Dream on, Doctor. Uh ... to be continued later," Jer said, terminating their private conversation. Dr. Terry Brinson, Dr. Adrian Brevard, and Dr. Joel Levitz had all walked into the 4-B office.

"Well, I think it's déjà vu," Terry Brinson said. "Looks like the powers that be have decided to make the A-team the B-team!"

"At least we don't need any introductions here," Jer said. "It's just as well, 'cause I lost the staff list admin sent me. Think it went through the laundry in the pocket of my pants. Or else someone in the laundry don't like me and put a bunch of confetti in my pocket." Jer Bacon chuckled, removed a handful of ragged paper bits from his pants' pocket, and casually placed them in the trash can. "Besides, you guys know exactly what to do, don't you?"

"Sure, Jer," Mark responded for himself as well as the others. Mark headed to the nurses' station so he could get the portable chart racks and roll them into the doctors' office. The team reviewed all the charts. There were only 52 patients. They were able to learn the specifics of their new patients, and quickly finished morning rounds in time for an extremely rare treat—a leisurely lunch.

As Mark was sliding his tray along the cafeteria line, he noticed two nurses seated by themselves in a far corner of the cafeteria. They were in green scrubs, and were obviously among the many nurses who worked in one of Grady's 14 operating rooms. One of them quickly yet discreetly pointed at Mark, then promptly shielded her mouth with a hand. She immediately whispered something to her table companion, who in turn blushed, then covered her lower face with both hands in an attempt to conceal a snicker. It all happened so quickly, the two nurses' actions failed to initially register in Mark's mind.

A few seconds later, as he was dishing up some black-eyed peas from the steam table, the visual image crashed into his off-guard brain: *Oh God! That's THE ONE! The one who pinned my scrub pants back up!* Opening his wallet to retrieve one of his meal tickets, he felt his face flush. In the same wallet compartment where he kept his meal tickets, he still had the large safety pin that she had used on his scrubs that fateful day.

Mark frequently used that same pin as an additional precaution, especially when the drawstrings in some of the older scrubs looked like they might break.

Mark left the safety pin on his lunch tray, and approached the table where the two nurses sat. As he neared their table, both nurses looked down, avoiding eye contact. Mark stopped when he reached their table, placing his tray upon it. The two nurses were now forced to look up at him. Mark immediately confirmed his recognition: *The gal with hazel eyes!* Her name tag stated her name was Anne Hunt, RN. Mark retrieved the pin on his tray, and extended it to her. "I always carry safety pins now, but I believe this particular one belongs to you. Do you want it back?"

"Oh, I don't know," Anne Hunt replied. "I'm just a dumb broad, you know ... but maybe I'll be able to figure out how to operate it again. However, just in case I've forgotten how they work, maybe you could give me some lessons, Dr. Telfair ... Dr. Mark Telfair is it?" she asked, squinting at his name tag.

Mark sensed the heat in his face, and hoped it wasn't as red as it felt. "Look, I'm really sorry for what I said that day. You know ... the dumb-broad thing. Won't you give me a chance to make up for that remark?"

"I'll settle for some lessons on safety pins," Anne said, smiling seductively.

"When?" Mark replied, his eyes still locked on hers, his heart pumping like an engine approaching its design limits.

"Soon," she replied. "I'm going to Orlando for the weekend. I'll be leaving after I get off at three this afternoon, but I'll be back Monday morning."

"Oh? Going by yourself?" Mark feared she might be going off with Hot Body, or some regular boyfriend for the weekend.

Anne Hunt pointed at her lunchmate. "Dr. Telfair, this is Margaret Thompson. She's an OR surgical nurse too. She's also my apartment roommate, and she'll be going with me. I'm just going home to visit my folks for a couple of days. So why don't you call me next week ... about the safety pin lessons?"

"Well I would, but I don't have your number," Mark replied.

"Well now you do," Anne Hunt replied, writing her telephone number on a paper napkin and handing it to him.

"Nice to have met you, Anne. And nice to meet you too, Margaret. Y'all have a good weekend in Florida," Mark said, as he turned to walk back to the table where the 4-B crew was eating lunch.

The moment Mark was out of earshot, Margaret Thompson turned to Anne. "He's precious ... a *really cute little boy!*"

"Margaret, I know he's not very tall—not even as tall as me—but If you'd seen what I saw, I think you'd find the term *little boy* inappropriate. He's ... well he's *all there*, if you know what I mean. Not that I've got all that much experience," Anne added, suddenly realizing she was blushing too, perhaps worse than Dr. Mark Telfair had.

When Mark returned to the 4-B table, he realized the 4-B crew had witnessed his other-side-of-the-cafeteria encounter with Anne Hunt and her roommate. Mark placed his tray on the table to join them, and was promptly greeted by muffled catcalls, smiles, and chuckles.

A grinning Jer Bacon was the first to speak to him. "Mark, you sure they ain't some of Cowboy's women? It's a terrible price to pay if you get caught, you know!"

The entire table erupted in laughter. Even with his reddened face, Mark found himself laughing with them, but their merriment didn't last long. The PA operator's voice echoed in the cafeteria: "Dr. Bacon ... Dr. Jerry Bacon ... 3-6-0, please."

The 4-B crew knew Jer's page was from the ER, and watched Jer sprint to the cafeteria's wall phone. His phone conversation was brief, and he rapidly returned to the table. "They got a young cop with a huge gash in his left side. He's in shock and they can't control the bleeding. Let's boogie, folks!"

They left the cafeteria on the run, and immediately went to the ER using the stairs to save time. The ER crew already had two IV lines in the young unconscious cop, and they were in the process of inserting an endotracheal tube in his windpipe.

When Jer and the ER's SAR made their initial joint assessment, the patient was totally unresponsive, his white skin slightly cyanotic, and his BP only 65 systolic. Soon the patient's color began to improve rapidly, largely due to pure oxygen connected to the Ambu bag. The young cop's light blue summer uniform shirt had been cut off, revealing a 12-inch gash in his thorax. It was located on his left side, diagonally crossing his lower rib margin. With each squeeze of the Ambu bag, frothy blood and air escaped from the large wound with a fluttering sound.

"Obviously he's got a wound that involves the chest cavity, and he probably has a pulmonary laceration too," Jer remarked. "But I just don't believe this much blood is coming from the lung alone. Could be his spleen's involved too!"

"I agree," said the SAR in charge of the ER.

"Well, if you agree," Jer said to the SAR, "I'm going to stick my hand in there right now, and see if I can feel anything. Maybe I can put some pressure on what's bleeding so bad. If we can slow the bleeding, maybe this guy can hold on till we can transfuse him. When's the blood cross-match going to be finished?"

"Should be about another ten minutes, Jer," the SAR said.

Bacon rolled up his jacket's sleeve, quickly donned a sterile glove, and thrust his hand into the deep wound. Jer's eyes immediately grew wide. "God Almighty!" Jer exclaimed, then withdrew his hand from the depths of the wound. *In his palm, Jer held approximately 75 percent of the patient's cleanly amputated spleen!* Jer quickly threw the spleen into the sink, flinging blood droplets on the walls, floor, and ceiling. He quickly plunged his hand back into the depths of the wound. After a few seconds, his eyes tightly closed in concentration, Jer excitedly spoke. "There! ... I got it now. Got that mother! I've got the splenic artery pinched off. I actually felt his blood hitting my palm, fellas! Now it's stopped! How much longer on the bank blood? Terry, could you go check on that please?"

Terry Brinson bolted from the room as though shot from a cannon. All was silent for a few beats while each team member did their job. Moments later, Terry stuck his head back in the door. "Just talked with the blood bank. They're having a real problem with the crossmatch. They even tried a quick cross with O-negative and got massive hemolysis (destruction of blood cells). They think he's got some rare antibodies, and they're trying to cross with other units right now. You still want all eight units, if the bank finds anything that won't kill him with a massive transfusion reaction?"

"Yeah, Terry. I sure do! But looks like we'll have to settle for whatever we can get. I'm afraid to let go of this artery until we have plenty of blood. Then maybe we can open his belly in the OR and substitute a surgical clamp for my fingers. Or chance clamping it blindly through this wound right now.

"On second thought, maybe we shouldn't do that. If we clamp it blindly, we may end up damaging the tail of his pancreas ... or colon, stomach, or something else that ain't already damaged. I'll just keep holding for now, but please go ahead and tell the OR to set up stat. And see if you can speed up the blood bank!"Jer yelled the afterthought to Terry just as he was leaving the treatment room again.

The patient's blood pressure was now a little over 100 systolic. Though pale, he was no longer cyanotic. He remained totally unresponsive.

Jer Bacon feared severe brain damage due to shock. "Hey, somebody—anybody! How about checking this guy's pupils," Jer anxiously requested.

"Midrange, equal, and fully reactive," came the encouraging response from the ER's JAR, who was manually ventilating the patient using the oxygen-filled Ambu bag.

"Great!" Jer exclaimed. "Looks like his brain might not be fried yet. We could even have a save here, *if they'll just get us some blood!* But guys, I'm not sure how much longer I can keep this thing pinched off. It takes real firm pressure to keep it stopped. My arm's beginning to cramp. I'll try to hold on a little longer," Jer said, as beads of perspiration were beginning to form, then run down his neck and face.

The treatment room door burst open again. Dr. Terry Brinson entered, smiling.

"Jer! Blood bank's got six units that look somewhat promising. They think they can possibly find two more compatible units, but here's the bad news: It's going to be at least another 45 minutes before they'll know anything for sure. The OR's ready. You want me to go up and start scrub now?"

"Sure, that would be great, Terry—and tell OR to set up for a thoracotomy too. I think the main problem is in this guy's belly, but I want us to be fully prepared to go into his chest if we gotta."

"Sure thing, Jer. Anything else I can do before I go up?" Terry asked.

"Nah, Terry. I need you upstairs in the OR. But right now, I gotta get someone else to hold this artery. My right hand and forearm are so cramped they're killing me. I won't be able to operate when I do get up there—unless I get some relief. And soon! Where's Telfair?"

"I'm right behind you boss," Mark replied.

"'Tern, think you could hold this artery for a while?"

"Uh, Jer ... I know the anatomy there pretty well, but I'm not sure how we're going to swap places. That's what worries me."

"Mark, just glove-up and slide your right hand in this wound, right on top of mine. I'm pinching off the splenic artery between my index and middle fingers, sorta like a pair of scissors. When I feel your own hand exactly covering the entire back of mine, I'll briefly quit pinching the vessel. But keep your hand *exactly* on top of mine. When I let loose, you'll feel the arterial spurts hitting the space between your own index and middle fingers. Keep your hand *exactly* in that position, and I'll slide my hand out. Then open your index and middle fingers slightly. Just let that spurt go between them, then move in about an inch, and clamp down hard as you can with those two fingers. After you think you've got it, I'll put my hand back in on top of yours, just to be sure you've closed it off. OK?"

"OK, Jer. I'll give it a try, but don't you dare leave until you're sure I've got it!"

The swap of the human "artery-pinchers" went off without a hitch.

Now Mark had his own hand and lower forearm buried deep inside the patient's wound. While a nurse mopped sweat off Jer's neck and face, and out of his eyes, he shook and massaged his badly cramped forearm and hand. "See you in the OR, Mark," Jer commented as he rapidly left the ER treatment room, still rubbing his cramped muscles.

This was a unique experience for Mark Telfair. For the first time in his life he knew he literally had a patient's life in his hands. *Between my fingers,* he thought. Other realities quickly flooded Mark's mind: *Sustained contractions soon lead to very painful muscle cramps, and Jer had been pinching only ten minutes when his hand and arm muscles started doing it. I'm going to have to keep this artery pinched off much longer than Jer did! What if my arm cramps too? How are we going to transport the patient to the OR with me still attached to him?*

Somehow, they managed. The gurney carrying the patient to the OR rolled slowly as Mark walked alongside in an awkward crouch, his hand and lower forearm still buried in the patient's side. The rubberneck gawkers in the ER and foyer were having an absolute field day as the spectacle passed by. Once in the elevator going up to the third-floor operating rooms, Mark began to feel the first arm cramps. Upon entering the OR, Mark was dreading the transfer of the patient to the operating table. He feared he might lose his grip on the artery during the transfer process, but with enough helping hands, the patient was transferred from gurney to operating table without a snag. A stool was brought in for Mark to sit upon, but his position remained awkward. Mark's arm began cramping again. As he looked down, he realized he had on his white clothes and shoes.

"How you doing, Mark?" Jer asked as he stepped into the OR, just finishing a much shorter than normal scrub.

"I'm still holding on, Jer, but I don't know how much longer I can keep this up," Mark replied, now freely perspiring. "And Jer, I'm not supposed to be in here in these regular clothes and shoes. I'm probably contaminating everything. I don't even have on a mask!"

"'Tern, sometimes you gotta break the rules. This is one of those times. We can't treat *death* ... but we can treat the heck out of a *wound infection!* So hold on till me and Terry can get inside his belly, OK?" Jer said.

Dr. Terry Brinson, already scrubbed and gowned, started prepping the patient's entire abdomen and chest with Betadine. Terry smiled behind his mask while he continued painting on the rust-brown antibacterial iodine solution. Terry even continued the prep onto Mark's arm, and, unnecessarily, to a point well above Mark's elbow. Just to aggravate his intern further, Terry put a dab of the dark prep solution on Mark's nose. *Terry, you're a son if a bitch!* Mark thought, while falling into a complete darkness created by the thick surgical drapes being placed over himself and the patient.

Mark's body was now almost completely covered in green surgical linen; only the chrome legs of Mark's stool, his white shoes, and the lower few inches of his white pants remained visible to others in the room. At the patient's left side, Mark's head and torso created a rather ridiculous-looking large "lump" beneath the drapes, making the tense scene seem a bit humorous to everyone there ... except Mark.

Despite the constant 68-degree temperature maintained in the OR, Mark could feel his own body's temperature rapidly rising under the drapes. Sweat continually ran in small rivulets down the middle of his back, and into the crack of his buttocks.

As the midline abdominal incision was being made, Mark could feel someone firmly pushing against him through the drapes. "Still doing OK under there, Mark?" Jer's voice finally asked. "We'll be inside his belly in just a sec, so hold on!"

Mark was now feeling extremely dizzy, his arm severely cramping. *God, please don't let me pass out!* filled his thoughts, until he became startled. He jumped when he first felt the cold steel of a surgical suction tip brushing and slurping against the back of his gloved hand buried deep inside the patient.

"Ah ha! This patient's got a *hand* growing in his belly! That's what's wrong with him, Terry!" Jer Bacon laughed, and intentionally pushed even harder against Mark's back through the drapes.

"Jer, maybe we should just cut that hand out, don't you think?" a laughing Terry Brinson asked.

"Sounds like a great idea to me, Terry. Have 'em get us the bone saw!"

If Mark had felt a little more confident in his ability to remain conscious, he would have joined their laughter, but he was doing well just to feel another cold instrument slide against the inside of his gloved hand. He faintly heard the metallic ratchet's click as the surgical clamp was closed, and locked down tight.

"Hey, Mark! We got it clamped buddy! You can let go now. You can come out from under there. OK? Mark? H-e-l-l-o ... Earth calling Mark, come in please," Jer said.

Beneath the surgical drapes, Mark felt extremely faint, his hand was now almost completely numb, his forearm painfully cramping; nonetheless, he just could not resist doing what he did next: *He flexed his index, ring, and little fingers, leaving his middle finger rigidly extended in the universal sign. He pushed his hand up and out through the midline belly incision and waved it around ... for all in the OR to view, especially Terry Brinson, who'd painted his nose with Betadine!* Mark heard a sudden burst of laughter, then withdrew his hand and forearm from the patient's side. Silently and gently, Mark slid off the stool ... and passed out on the cool OR floor.

Where am I? Mark thought, staring at a strange ceiling. Everything felt so unreal. *Perhaps I've died,* he thought, but the pungent smell of the Betadine Terry had jokingly painted on his nose brought him back toward reality. He wasn't quite sure where he was, but found himself surrounded by two out-of-focus female faces hovering closely over his head. *Hope they're not angels,* he thought.

"Dr. Telfair! Wake up, Doctor!" Mark heard the excited slightly familiar voice speak to him just as a cold wet cloth was being placed on his forehead. The vaguely familiar voice spoke again. "Don't crap out on me now Doctor! I need my safety pin lessons ... remember?"

As Mark's eyes regained their ability to focus, the now well-recognized smiling hazel eyes came into clear view. Their owner spoke to him. "Doctor, you passed out in the OR, so we had to drag you out to the neurosurgery scrub area next door. That way Dr. Bacon wouldn't have to stand on top of you while he finishes the procedure. Anyway, Dr. Bacon ordered us to give you a liter of Ringer's lactate IV. Are you doing OK now?" Anne Hunt asked. Her genuine concern was reflected in both her voice and gorgeous eyes.

"Yeah, I think so ... and you're something else ... for a dumb broad!" Mark heard himself say. He and Anne both burst into tension-relieving laughter.

"*Safety pin lessons? Dumb broads?* Just what's so darn funny?" Anne's companion asked, being at a loss to see any reason for Mark and Anne's joint hilarity.

"Family secret," Anne Hunt replied.

"Y'all related?" asked Anne's puzzled companion, a nurse whom Mark didn't recognize.

"Not yet," Anne said, then burst out in inexplicable laughter.

An hour later, Mark finished the liter of IV fluid Jer had insisted upon. Dr. Bacon had not given Mark the chance to refuse the ordered IV, just ordered that Anne and her companion do it stat. While under the "thermal blanket" of the surgical drapes, Mark knew he'd completely soaked his whites with sweat. He'd become acutely dehydrated. He knew Jer was right, and hadn't argued when Anne had stuck the needle in his vein. After finishing the fluids, and a shower, Mark felt fine. He got into some dry scrubs until he could go back up to his room and change into fresh whites. After completing the three-hour surgical procedure, both Jer and Terry had come to the lounge to check on Mark. They'd told a relieved Mark Telfair the surgery had gone smoothly; they'd stitched a superficial lung laceration, repaired the patient's diaphragm, placed a chest tube, and removed what remained of the patient's spleen.

Mark knew the patient had come close to dying from massive blood loss combined with the collapse of his left lung. The difficult crossmatch had actually delayed blood availability until a few minutes after the splenic artery had been surgically clamped and tied off in the OR. Mark found himself thinking about Jer's quick action in the ER that had saved the patient's life: *The human brain is naturally wired to act now, think later. Jer seems to have rewired himself to think and act at the same time. Will I get that way too? Do all surgeons get that way?* Through his thoughts, Mark finally heard Jer's voice speak the words he most wanted to hear: "The guy's brain is going to be OK."

Barring any significant postoperative complications, Mark thought the patient would be able to resume his normal work routine in a couple of months. He felt proud to have been a small part in the lifesaving process, but he remained utterly embarrassed about passing out in the OR. Once again, Anne Hunt had caught him with his trousers down, so to speak.

After a quick trip to his room to change into fresh whites, Mark went back down to 4-B, where he chatted alone with Dr. Jerry Bacon.

"Jer, just who was that young cop?" Mark asked.

"He's a rookie, only 22. His father is a bigwig with APD, a captain with Internal Affairs. Seems the poor kid went into a bad neighborhood, and some brain-damaged street-doper caught him off guard, then whacked him in the left side with a *bush hook!* That's one of those big sharp hawk-billed blades on the end of a four-foot handle, the kind they use to clear brush by hand," Jer summarized.

"Yeah sure, Jer. I know exactly what a bush hook is. Guess I just never thought of one as a street weapon before." Mark replied. "And Jer ... don't count your chickens before they hatch, but if this kid cop makes it, a captain with the APD should be very grateful to Grady Hospital for saving his son's life, and especially grateful to one Dr. Jerry Bacon—the same Jerry Bacon who is so worried that politics between admin and APD may keep him from becoming Chief Resident in July. Won't you think about that, Jer?"

And if you don't, be assured I will, Mark thought, conjuring a vivid mental image of his own hands strangling Shorty the ER cop.

"Tern, I ain't got time to play their funny little silly-ass political games. I'll just find me another Chief Resident's slot at some other hospital, one outside of the Emory-Grady program, or outside this country if necessary," Jer said, but his despondent tone sent Mark's mind a crystal-clear message: *Jer Bacon is through talking about it. Period.*

Fortunately, the young cop's recovery was uneventful. He continued to show no evidence of brain or other organ damage due to shock. Despite egregious violations of strict surgical aseptic technique, no wound infection developed. Mark had visited the young patient daily during the two weeks of in-hospital recovery. He'd also given the young cop a card for his wallet—one that indicated the several unusual antibodies carried in his blood, thus making most units of type-specific donor blood horribly incompatible with his own.

During the course of several wound dressing changes, and removal of the patient's chest tube and stitches, Mark came to know the young cop fairly well. As he entered the patient's room on the day he was to be discharged, Mark found a gray-headed APD officer visiting the young patient. The distinguished looking APD officer had captain's bars, and a name tag indicating he was with Internal Affairs; the captain's last name matched that of the patient. Mark rapidly determined the captain was the patient's grateful father.

"Captain, sir, I know you don't know me. But I'd like to tell you a little bit about the Grady ER, and about the surgeon who saved your son's life. That doctor's name is Jerry Bacon, and his quick thinking in the ER is actually what saved your son's life. That same doctor now faces problems with administration here, mainly because of a gun incident that occurred in the Grady Surgical Emergency Room several months ago. I'd like to tell you about it. *All off the record,* if I may sir?"

"Sure, go ahead son," the fatherly captain replied.

The captain listened intently as Dr. Telfair explained the details. Mark first described the frightening ER gun incident; then related how he himself had been stabbed by an ice pick while in the ER; next he explained exactly why he felt Shorty was an incompetent ER cop; and finally, Mark revealed the unjust political fallout that apparently settled solely upon Dr. Jerry Bacon ... simply because he'd been in charge of the ER when those things happened. The captain made notes as Mark told the story. When Mark completed his spiel about the ER and Jer's plight, the captain spoke a few simple words as he closed his small note book: "Thank you son. These are my *personal* notes ... for my eyes only. Consider the problem fixed."

Mark had doubts that his concerns would be taken seriously by anyone at APD, but he felt better just getting it off his chest. The next day,

Mark had occasion to go to the Surgical ER—Shorty was gone! *Fired, late yesterday,* Mark quickly learned. Shorty had been replaced by a burly spit-and-polish APD cop who carried a non-issue .357 magnum. The new cop's physical size, and his professional and authoritative look, made a simple unspoken statement: *Don't fuck with me!* Mark thought.

After meeting the new cop, Mark quickly left the ER. He anxiously went up to 4-B to tell Jer the good news about Shorty's dismissal and replacement. When Mark entered the 4-B office, Jer was alone and cheerfully whistling as he did some paperwork at his pig-pen desk.

"Jer, you sure seem happy today," Mark announced.

"Well, I am happy, Mark. Very happy. You'll be the first one in the 4-B crew to know. Admin called me at home last night and told me they had met, and decided that I'd *definitely* be a Chief Resident come July first! I guess I got a little too paranoid about administration and their politics. Maybe I just paid too much attention to the hospital grapevine," Jer admitted.

"Well congratulations anyway, *Chief* ... even if you were a little paranoid," Mark said, as he extended his hand to shake Jer's. "But you know Jer, I just somehow knew admin would eventually get their heads on straight." Mark smiled in thought: *Guess I'll just let him find out about Shorty on his own.* Mark silently left the office, Jer still whistling, and cheerfully doing what doctors hate the most—paperwork!

14

WHERE THE SUN DON'T SHINE

D r. Mark Telfair's milestone date finally arrived: July first, 1965. At 6:45 a.m. he sat in the quiet Surgical ER, waiting to begin his first day's work as Junior Assistant Resident. Sitting alone at the work station, and mostly daydreaming, he glanced at the now-repaired ER ceiling and recalled the day he'd seen electrical sparks and exploding fluorescent light fragments raining down from it to the floor. Unconsciously he rubbed his right shoulder where he'd been stabbed, but there was no pain there now, only a memory. He smiled: *I've made it this far ... I'm a JAR!* Knowing that shedding the lowly title of intern was only the first major waypoint on his long journey, he continued his thoughts: *I'm glad I didn't quit after getting stabbed and shot at ... glad Mose, Jer, and Zack all helped me get over it ... helped me decide to stay here.* In the cool silence of his now-familiar surroundings, he clearly recalled Zack's blunt words and softly spoke them aloud to himself: "Just tough it out, and quit bein' such a candyass!"

By shedding his intern's skin, he knew he'd quickly grow a new thicker one. He knew it would also wrap him in a higher level of responsibility for a patient's care. He'd certainly miss the security of having Jerry Bacon around, especially when it came to split-second decisions. But Jer had moved up to Chief Resident, and would be spending a good part of his final residency year at Emory University Hospital, a rather tranquil academic setting, where he would acquire the polish that would prepare him for private practice. Mark realized he may not run into Jer during the entire year. Despite the new responsibility of being a JAR, Mark felt comfortable. Dr. Terry Brinson had moved up to SAR, and would now be in charge of the Surgical ER. Zack, also a JAR, had decided against going into orthopedics, *or* general surgery. Residency program developers had assigned Zack to the Surgical ER, hoping to prepare him for a specialty still in the early concept-development stage: Emergency Medicine. Then there'd always be Mose. *Thank God for Mose,* his mind told him.

Cheerful words stopped Mark's silent reflections. "Morning, stranger!"

Terry Brinson said pleasantly as he walked by the ER's workstation desk where Mark was sitting. "Doesn't look like we got a lot of new folks," Terry said, pausing as he studied a neatly folded admin personnel list retrieved from his notebook. "So I'll see you in the office at seven when everybody else gets here."

Promptly at seven, Terry started the meeting. Mark immediately noticed a key difference between Terry Brinson and Jerry Bacon: Terry appeared to be Mr. Organization Personified ... on the other hand, Jer Bacon had appeared totally disorganized, but functioned like a finely tuned machine. Mark hoped Terry would be as good a leader—and as good a teacher—as Jer had been. *Oh shit! I'm now a vice-leader!* Mark suddenly thought, losing some of the confidence he'd felt earlier. The reality of his new position in the surgical training hierarchy had just settled in, somewhere deep within his brain.

"Well folks, this will be a short first-day meeting. I'm not going to waste a lot of time with introductions that are not needed," Terry Brinson announced. "The only new folks here today are our three new straight surgical interns, plus a new police officer from the City of Atlanta Police Department. But we do have a familiar face whose presence here today is a Grady first—Dr. Zack Paslaski. Zack, will you tell everybody what's different about your presence here today?"

"Sure thing, Terry," a totally exhausted looking Zack responded. "Folks, I'm a JAR in general surgery, but I'm here on elective. Emory and Grady are in the process of combinin' their two surgical training programs. They are also tryin' to start up a new specialty program called Emergency Medicine, and I've agreed to give it a try. The idea is to create a specialty where a doc can specialize solely in emergency care. That is, he'd work in a hospital emergency room as a career. He wouldn't have an office practice, and he wouldn't have any hospital inpatients. He would deal with both surgical and medical emergencies in an ER, then he'd transfer the patient's care to another specialist for further in-hospital or outpatient care as required. Anything else you want me to say Terry?"

"No Zack, I think you've summed it up. But since this is also a first time for the Grady Surgical ER to have *two* Junior Assistant Residents at the same time, I want to make one thing clear: Even though Dr. Paslaski is here on elective, he is equal in rank with Dr. Telfair, who's our regular general surgery JAR assigned to the ER."

"Dr. Telfair, you have anything you want to say?" Terry asked.

"No Terry, I think Zack—Dr. Paslaski—covered it well. I might add that I'm glad to have someone to share the responsibility of being second in command." *And very glad my brilliant roommate could make even a brief statement without his usual multitude of grammatical errors and foul words!* Mark thought.

Terry looked at his neat notes, then spoke: "And new to all of us is our representative from the City of Atlanta Police Department, Officer Max Bollinger. Anything you want to say, Max?" Terry asked the new APD officer.

Mark marveled at the contrast ... Max versus Shorty. Max was in his late 20s, possibly early 30s. He was well over six feet tall, weighing about 240 pounds. In a way, Max reminded Mark of a much younger white Mose. Maybe even a young Telly Savalas, a.k.a. Kojak, only with blue eyes. He had a shiny white bald pate, having elected to shave his entire head. His uniform appeared impeccable, his black shoes shined to a mirror finish. He did not reek of cigarettes, as had Shorty. His well-muscled frame sent its own authoritative message.

Officer Max Bollinger stood to speak. "Dr. Brinson, I'm a man of few words. All I've got to say is, I've gotten very clear orders from APD: You guys are the docs. You guys do emergency care, and I represent law enforcement. My job is to see that you get to do your job without having to worry about your personal safety, or hassles from some of the lowlife that comes in here." Max promptly sat back down.

Frowning out of concern that Max might be too much of an improvement over Shorty, Terry tactfully spoke to the group at large, though his words were primarily directed to Max. "All you guys— especially police officers—have my sympathy. I've seen you guys get spit on, puked on, kicked and slugged ... all while some unruly patient is yelling 'police brutality' at the top of their lungs. It takes a special kind of cop to work down here, Max.

"Our orderly, Mose Mallone, is great at dealing with some of the unruly blacks. Mose has been around Grady for over 30 years, and you may find him helpful in assisting you with some of the unruly minority patients. I guess what I'm trying to say Max is this: We don't want Hosea Williams, Jesse Jackson, Ralph Abernathy and that bunch around Martin Luther King *rightfully* making Grady's ER the focal point of their agenda ... all because we foolishly overreacted to a problem down here. Those are *my* orders from *my* headquarters. You know what I'm trying to say, Max?"

Max promptly stood again in response to Terry's lengthy comment, making his own equally lengthy one: "Dr. Brinson, sir, I think I understand exactly what you're saying. I've had special training at the Police Academy and the Federal Law Enforcement Training Center ... especially in crowd and riot control. I worked SWAT for two years, and I've dealt with a number of hostage situations. In short, I've been taught how to use what we call a *measured response* when things seem to be getting out of hand. I may carry this .357 magnum on my hip, but I'm black belt in martial arts—both karate and judo—and that's what makes me comfortable in being able to subdue a troublemaker without inflicting any unnecessary injury. I wasn't going to mention this at an open meeting like this one, but I also got specific orders from APD: *No weapons of any type are to be brought in here by staff members, patients, or visitors.* APD already knows about the ice pick and gun that got in here last year, but I'm not at liberty to say exactly how they found out about it.

"At times, Dr. Brinson, sir, I'll need the help from some of your female staff. I'll need them when there is a need to check a female that may be carrying a concealed weapon. And you need not worry that I'm some kinda rogue gunslinger like Wyatt Earp!" Max concluded, hoping he'd resolved any fears Dr. Brinson had regarding an overly responsive APD-gorilla in *his* ER.

Mark looked around the now-silent room. He found it comforting to know Max Bollinger had not publicly connected the Telfair name with information APD had acquired about weapons that had gotten into the Grady ER. Also comforting, Mark saw a smiling Mose, who was obviously happy to finally have effective help in dealing with the occasional rough customers. The three yet-to-be-introduced interns all looked scared shitless—totally shellshocked! *God, what kind of a war zone have we all gotten ourselves into?* Mark thought that was the unspoken question he could clearly read upon each of their pale Ivy League faces. *But you used to feel the same way!* he told himself. Though fighting off sleep during the extended exchange, Zack was obviously impressed with Max. A very good sign also, Mark felt.

"Very well, Max," Terry finally said. "It's good to know we're all on the same page here. Welcome to our team. Welcome to the Pit. I sure hope to God we won't need your services!"

By the time Terry finished introducing the three new interns, Terry's "short" meeting with the new ER staff had stretched to about 45 minutes. Unfortunately, the new interns were all Ivy League and would be of little help the first week or so. Zack was now snoring while sitting up. Mark knew he'd just come off his orthopedic elective, and had worked 36 straight before coming to the ER at seven.

As the meeting was breaking up, Mark turned to Terry and asked, "You want to wake Zack up ... or what?"

"Nah," Terry responded. "Let's let him sleep for awhile. There used to be an extra gurney in that storage closet over there," Terry said. He pointed to a large side door in the office. "If it's still there I'll help you get

Zack on it. We'll put the side rails up and let him sleep till midafternoon."

Mark went to the storage closet and opened the door. "Hey, Terry ... there's only a *piece* of a gurney in here. Well ... no it's actually a *whole* gurney, but it's bent double. Right in the middle. Just like a hairpin. What happened to it?"

Terry just smiled. "I don't know what happened to the good gurney that used to be in there also, but that beat up one—well that's another Cowboy story. I'll tell you about it later. But for now, just go get a couple of blankets and a pillow, and we'll let Zack sleep on the floor here in the office."

Terry and Mark moved a still-snoring Zack from his chair to the makeshift pallet on the office floor. He was totally oblivious to the change in position. As they left Zack sleeping, Mark wanted to ask Terry more about the mangled gurney, and how it related to Cowboy. But patients were accumulating, and Terry and Mark had three green interns to work with.

By noon, it was apparent to both Mark and Terry that this was going to be a long day in the ER. Mark had nothing against the Ivy League schools; it just seemed to him that their graduates were almost always too long on book learning and far too short on any practical experience. Most of the Ivy League folks he'd met thus far didn't seem to have any experience outside their med school classrooms, at least not prior to showing up on Grady's doorstep as an intern. Mark recalled his own insecurities as an intern, and his own relative inexperience, but remained thankful Emory med students got exposure to clinical situations well before their graduation. As the day progressed, he patiently assisted his share of the green interns dealing with their assigned patients.

"Uh ... Dr. Telfair," said Dr. Bill Lebowitz, rapidly approaching Mark at the workstation.

"What can I help you with, Lebowitz?" Mark patiently responded with a smile, but thought, *Here comes another stupid question from that Harvard intern!*

"It won't take but a minute of your time," Lebowitz explained. "It's room six. I've got a problem I need some help with. The patient says he's got a problem with his rectum, and when I did one of those rectal exams with my finger, something feels real funny up there. Could you check and see what you think is wrong?"

"Sure thing, Lebowitz," Mark confidently replied. "You mind giving me the patient's history first, before we go back into his room?"

"Uh, no. Not at all. His name is Bruce LeBlanc. What the patient told me is that he was out at the city dump about seven this morning, just taking some trash out there before going to work. He told me he had this sudden urge to defecate while he was depositing his trash, but there were no restrooms at the city dump. So he built a makeshift toilet using some old boards that he rested on the tops of two adjacent oil drums. While he was defecating, he said the boards suddenly snapped. He fell to the ground on top of a whole lot of trash and stuff, and his rectum just hasn't felt right since. Nor has he finished his bowel movement," intern Lebowitz summarized.

"Very good, Lebowitz," Mark said. "Let's go to the patient's room and have a look."

What Mark saw when he entered room six caused him to switch his brain to maximum smile-suppression mode. The thin effeminate mulatto, with pale blue-green eyes, appeared to be in his mid-20s. He squirmed in obvious discomfort, but remained composed.

"Bruce, Dr. Lebowitz here tells me this happened to you about 7:00 a.m. today ... right?"

"Oh yes, I'm positive of the time. You see I have to be back in town to open my exclusive salon—*Mr. Guystyles*—at eight o'clock, and I never ever open up late. I work strictly by appointment," Bruce explained, using an excessive series of double-jointed wrist movements. Bruce essentially fulfilled all Mark's personal stereotypical requirements: *gay male*.

"Bruce, I'm going to examine you ... do a rectal exam. OK?"

"Oh yes Doctor, by all means. But please be gentle!"

Mark put on a glove, and did a digital rectal exam. What he felt astounded him. About three inches up the guy's rectum was a completely smooth firm mass. *Not another cue ball. Just couldn't be!* Mark's mind raced. "Uh ... Lebowitz, I see what you mean. Let's do a proctoscopic. Just have a quick look."

"Well, I've never done one of those before, Dr. Telfair, but I've read all about them. Think you could give me a hand?"

"Sure, 'Tern," Mark patiently said to Lebowitz while retrieving a proctoscope from one the treatment room's storage drawers. Mark plugged in the transformer that supplied the low voltage current for the scope's light.

Bruce, of *Mr. Guystyles,* was definitely taking in the whole scene. "Oh my! I don't think I've ever seen an electric one of those, at least not a shiny silver one. Is that as big as they get?"

Mark ignored Bruce's comments and question, and quickly inserted the scope. The findings were puzzling, but Mark was almost sure it was *not* a cue ball. "There's a complete obstruction up there Lebowitz ... sorta looks like some whitish opaque object, kinda like the wax of a paraffin candle, but way too big for a candle. Wanna have a look?"

"Yeah, sure," Lebowitz responded, then eagerly put one of his dark eyes to the scope's lens. Lebowitz slowly and carefully studied the obstructing object through the eyepiece. "Hey Dr. Telfair! There's some writing on that thing! Only thing I can make out is '60-W.' You wanna have a look?"

Mark then put his eye back to the scope. Sure enough, sharp-eyed little Lebowitz had been right. The object not only had "60-W" written on it , but also had "Westinghouse" written on it in barely legible letters. *Light bulb!* Mark's embarrassingly slow brain finally told him.

Mark found it humiliating to realize he'd just been scooped by a sharp-eyed Ivy League intern—one who'd never looked up someone's butt before. Even more embarrassing, Mark had to admit to himself he had no idea how to get the light bulb out. They certainly didn't teach that kinda stuff in *any* med school, Ivy League or otherwise. As a short-term solution—mostly to buy more time to think—Mark finally spoke. "Lebowitz, go ahead and order X-rays of the pelvis, AP and lateral views, and let me know when you have the films. OK?" Mark knew he'd bought about 30 minutes of thinking time.

"Well now, how did that bulb really get in there?" Lebowitz asked, rubbing his neat little black moustache.

"Not our problem, Doctor," Mark heard himself say to Lebowitz. "Our problem is how do we get it *out,*" Mark said, recalling almost identical words spoken by Jer Bacon regarding the patient with a cue ball jammed in his mouth. *At Grady, what goes around, comes back around,* Mark thought as he quickly left the room to search for the SAR, Dr. Terry Brinson.

Twenty-five minutes later Mark, Terry, and Lebowitz were studying the X-rays on a view box in the patient's room. Intern Lebowitz was flipping his dark-haired head back and forth like a windshield wiper, as he tried to follow the conversation between Dr. Terry Brinson and Dr. Mark Telfair.

"Well the bulb's intact, threaded end pointed upward," Terry said, as he looked at the X-rays on the view box.

"Wouldn't be a problem if the threaded end was pointed down," Mark commented. "Then we could just grab the metal threaded end with some ring forceps, pull it out, and not worry about breaking the glass and lacerating his rectum."

"Maybe we could get some small obstetrical forceps, like they use on premature babies, and pull the sucker out that way," Terry countered.

"Nah, you'd break it for sure that way Terry, but something like a suction cup might grab onto the smooth glass surface. Yeah that's it! *Suction cup.* If we could just get a small suction cup with a really high vacuum, we could stick it on the glass, then pull it out that way."

"Mark, I hate to say this, but I think it's time we woke up Zack ... that impossible roommate of yours. Or else it's time I called the attending professor."

"Let's try Zack first if you don't mind," Mark replied.

Mark and Terry both abandoned the squirming patient—and bewildered intern Lebowitz—to go wake up Zack. True to his usual form, once they had shaken Zack from his deep sleep on the office floor pallet, his mind was instantly engaged, ready to attack any conceivable problem.

"Hey thanks for the nap fellas," Zack said as he looked at his watch to discover it was now two o'clock in the afternoon. "What's the problem?"

In the privacy of the office, Mark and Terry explained the entire situation as concisely as possible. Zack absorbed every detail. "OK. You guys got a fag with an intact 60-watt bulb up his butt, glass end down. Busting the bulb ain't an option. Grabbing the bulb's glass with steel forceps of any kind is risky. The suction cup principle will work."

"Zack, are you talking about hooking onto the bulb's glass with a suction cup, then hooking up some kinda traction ... like with the cue ball?" Mark asked with suspicion.

"Nah. Ain't necessary. That faggot's probably got such a stretched and lax anal sphincter, traction won't be necessary. Heck, he'd probably shit it out if we just gave him a good double-dose of Ex-Lax and waited several days. 'Course his belly would cramp so bad he'd be better off havin' labor pains. But let's make this look like a *professional extraction!*"

Zack, Mark, and Terry walked in silence back to the light bulb room. Mark and Terry weren't quite sure what a professional extraction was, but listened intently to one side of the conversation while Zack talked to the maintenance department over the exam room phone: "Hey, it's Dr. Zack Paslaski here ... What's the max negative pressure I can get outta the wall suction ports here in the Surgical ER? ... Sure?... That's all?... Well that ain't near enough! So do you guys got a portable high-vacuum pump down there? ... Waddaya mean, 'No!' ... Well then do you have a small air compressor that'll run on a hundred twenty volts?... Up to 200 psi? ... Great! Now I'll need six feet of some fairly rigid rubber tubing that I can connect to the compressor's intake, say about three-quarter-inch inside diameter ... Yeah, that heater hose tubing you use to run from the engine block to the heater core on the ambulances should work fine. Some real heavy-duty garden hose would work too, but not any of that flimsy vinyl Kmart stuff, know what I mean? ... Great man! Oh, and bring the gauges that you check the air conditioning units with, and a T-fitting that'll fit the I.D. of whatever hose you bring ... No man, I ain't goin' to need no Freon! I just need that stuff in the Surgical ER stat. Room six, OK? Bye." Zack hung up and laughed momentarily, then stopped. He realized four people were intently staring at him like he was totally nuts!

The now-agitated patient continued squirming as he sat on the edge of the treatment room table. He'd heard the entire conversation among his doctors; Zack's end of the phone conversation with maintenance had been clearly heard as well. "Uh, look fellas," the patient said, "perhaps this is much more complicated than I thought. I absolutely insist on seeing your head supervisor before you do anything!"

"Our *head* supervisor?" Zack said, smiling slightly.

"Yes! You know, the *head motherfucker what's in complete charge* down here!" Bruce exclaimed, now both frightened and overtly belligerent.

"Ohhhh," Zack responded, as an acronym bolted into his brain. "You must be talking about our H.M.F.W.I.C.C.! (Head MotherFucker What's In Complete Charge). "Sure, Brucie, we'll run it past him, even get him to come in here and talk to you before we go to work on you. OK?"

Mark could see Terry Brinson's dismay fade into an anger that was rising by the second. Terry stared at Zack and simply said, *"Outside!"*

Terry and Zack rapidly exited the treatment room, then headed straight to the office. Terry lit into Zack. "Doctor, you're an absolute disgrace to the profession! I'm not a fag-lover either, but at least I fully respect their freedom to choose their own lifestyle. You don't do that kinda stuff in front of *any* patient. Zack, have I made that clear!"

"Hey man, I'm sorry if I pissed you off, but did you hear me say one single cuss word in front of that patient? Do you want that bulb out, or not? Or do you want to cave in and call the attending who'll probably first laugh his ass off, then be pissed that we couldn't solve a simple little problem without bugging him?"

Terry cooled off while considering Zack's questions before speaking. "Zack, you promised that guy he could see the ... what did you call it again?"

"H.M.F.W.I.C.C.," Zack responded.

"Before we did anything, you promised him. Now just how do you plan to solve *that* problem, Zack?"

"Terry let's don't create problems we ain't really got. All we gotta do is have that new cop—that Max what's-his-name—come into the room, talk with the little fag and tell him *he's* the H.M.F.W.I.C.C. I promise you that will fly, and if it don't, I'll take full blame for the situation. OK?"

126

After a full 30 seconds of deliberation, Terry finally responded. "Zack, against my better judgment, but hearing about the cue ball incident and your success with that problem, all I can say is I hope it works."

"O ye of little faith. Let us proceed!" Zack beamed.

Max, the new cop, was a little reluctant to go along with the scheme at first. He finally agreed to put on an XL green scrub top over his APD uniform, and at least go into the room. As Zack, Max, and Terry re-entered the treatment room, Zack was first to speak to the patient.

"Bruce, this is our H.M.F.W.I.C.C. His name is Max. We've filled him in on your problem. Bruce, do you have any questions you'd like to ask Max about what we plan to do?"

Bruce's eyes locked onto Max's sky-blues like white on rice. Then he nervously started grooming his eyebrows with the moistened tips of his baby fingers, finally speaking to the Aryan hunk from APD: "It's so nice to meet you, Max," Bruce said as he extended a limp-wristed hand to the scrub-clad APD officer. "I'd be glad to do your hair anytime, for free ... if you had any. But, Max ... do you concur with what these other doctors have in mind to solve my ... uh ... little problem?"

"Bruce, I think these doctors have thoroughly considered your problem, and I don't have any better suggestions regarding a solution. I highly suggest you let these doctors do what is needed," Max said convincingly, though he was truly leery about the entire situation.

As Max excused himself from the uncomfortable scene, the man from maintenance arrived with all the paraphernalia Zack had requested. Zack checked it over, surprised to find he had all the essential elements for his homemade bulb-sucker. He was also pleased to see that the maintenance man had brought assorted sizes of hose clamps, something he'd failed to request on the phone.

"I need a piece of paper," Zack announced to his worried observers. Mark handed Zack a blank page out of his pearl notebook. Zack started writing madly. Mark recognized the formula for the area of a circle, then another formula or two he didn't recognize. About a minute later, Zack proudly made an announcement to an audience that now questioned his sanity: "Don't know the exact internal diameter of this hose, but I should be able to get a vacuum seal on the bulb that will allow us to pull with at least ten pounds of tension. That's enough to pull it out."

Zack quickly constructed his jury-rig device, complete with in-line vacuum gauge to monitor the level of suction. He lubricated the end of the thick-walled rubber tubing with some KY Jelly, then gently inserted it into the patient's rectum until the end of the rubber tube lightly bumped against the light bulb's glass dome.

"OK! Plug in the compressor, and hit the switch," Zack directed as he pointed to the compressor's on-off switch.

"Ready?" Mark asked uneasily.

"Ready!" Zack confirmed.

The noise from the compressor was deafening in the small hard-surfaced room, but Zack ignored the noise and watched the in-line gauge intently as the vacuum level quickly climbed. The red rubber automotive heater hose tubing was trying to collapse, but was rigid enough that it didn't.

"OFF!" Zack yelled over the compressor's racket.

The room immediately fell silent. Zack gave the rubber hose a tug. *It was firmly attached to the bulb.* With a little additional steady tugging the frosted SoftWhite 60-watt Westinghouse was delivered intact!

Every eye in the room was now staring at the light bulb ... as though it might have been the very first one Tommy Edison ever made.

"Thank God!" Bruce exclaimed. "But I gotta shit, fellas!"

Mark quickly handed Bruce a trash can, which Bruce promptly sat upon. The expression of relief reflected in Bruce's face defied description.

While holding the bulb securely in his left hand, Zack expertly released the bulb by disconnecting the other end of the hose from the compressor's intake port, thus breaking the strong vacuum. Zack next took the freed bulb to the sink. There he washed it with antibacterial soap, then thoroughly dried it. He shook the bulb next to his ear, then removed a bulb from one of the smaller exam lights, and screwed the just-retrieved bulb in: *It burned brightly!*

"Uh, Bruce," Zack said, "do you mind if I ask you a question while you're sittin' on that can there?"

"No, go ahead," Bruce said, his voice distorted as he strained to continue his bowel movement.

"Bruce, why do you think someone would take a perfectly good light bulb and throw it away at the city dump?" Zack asked, succeeding in his struggle to appear serious.

"Uh, somebody just made a mistake ... I guess ... maybe?" Bruce replied lamely, his mulatto skin failing to hide the flush of his embarrassment.

Mark had already left the room to go find himself a laughing place. Bruce had finally gotten off the makeshift toilet. Lebowitz looked at Zack in total awe. Terry Brinson, who had remained silent during the whole debacle, smiled and shook his head while looking at his Polish JAR.

"Zack," Terry said, "how did you know that an air compressor could create such a strong vacuum?"

With a nod of his head, Zack indicated they should step outside of the treatment room. Once outside, Zack whispered in Terry's ear: "Terry, most compressors are sorta queer ... *they can suck just as hard as they can blow!*"

A usually reserved Dr. Terry Brinson burst out laughing, but when he noticed some of the ER staff staring at him, he promptly moved himself into the privacy of his office. Upon entering, Terry found Mark, who moments ago had also isolated himself there. Mark had almost fully recovered from his own laughing fit, but upon seeing Terry, the laughter began anew.

But that would not be the end of rectal problems that day. Poor Ivy League intern Bill Lebowitz drew the other two rectal patients: One, a redneck, had acquired a massive impaction of chicken bones in his lower rectum. This occurred two days after betting one of his buddies he could eat a whole roasted chicken—bones and all—at a single sitting. The X-ray, showing all the impacted chicken bones encircled by a human pelvic bone, was indeed a strange sight. That problem had been solved by digitally breaking up the impaction, and manually removing the chicken's skeleton a few bones at a time.

Lebowitz's other rectal patient had been an embarrassed Emory undergraduate chemistry major. At an SAE beer party the night before, he had agreed to remove his underwear and fart upon the open flame of a Bic lighter ... to prove or disprove a statement he'd recently read in a chemistry book: "The hydrogen sulfide and methane gases present in human intestinal tract are highly flammable, explosively so." In the process, the chem major had acquired substantial second degree anal, perianal, and rectal burns. Painfully, the Emory undergrad had validated the chemistry book's statement for himself, as well as for his inebriated fraternity brothers.

Near the end of the shift, the doctors gathered in the office to finish paperwork. Indeed, it had been an exhausting day.

"Hey, fellas?" Lebowitz asked. "Is it *always* this way down here?"

Feeling sorry for the haggard-looking intern, Zack said, "Nah. You just had a bad day, Lebowitz. You probably won't get three assholes in a row for a long time!"

Mark saw Terry look up from his paperwork when he'd heard Zack's crude comment to Lebowitz. *Terry's probably wishing he could stuff a sock in Zack's mouth,* Mark thought. Terry just smiled, slowly shook his head, then returned to his papers without saying a word.

The room slowly emptied, leaving only Mark and Terry.

"Terry, it's really been quite a day. At least we got another Grady acronym out of it ... H.M.F.W.I.C.C. Don't believe I've heard that one before. And we've got a prototype for a new vacuum-operated foreign body removal device," Mark said, making small talk, just waiting to ask Terry about the "folded-up" gurney in the closet ... and exactly how it related to Cowboy.

Terry smiled, "You want to know about that gurney, don't you?"

"Read my mind, Terry."

"Well, it was about two years ago. The cops brought Cowboy in, dead drunk. Passed out. We put him face down on that gurney, then restrained both his wrists and ankles, spread eagle, using padded leather restraints."

Terry got up, went to a closet and got something off the top shelf. He tossed it to Mark. Mark caught, then studied the thick leather four-inch-wide restraint cuff. *Impossible for a human to break one of these,* Mark thought upon examining it.

"So Cowboy *broke* the restraints when he sobered up, then somehow bent up the gurney like that?"

"Nope. When he sobered up he started rocking the gurney side to side until he finally turned it over. While on his side, Cowboy bent over double so he could reach his restrained ankles with his hands, folding the gurney along with his body. He unbuckled both ankle restraints from the gurney's foot-end restraint rings, and began walking around desperately trying to figure some way to get his hands free. So, Mark, Cowboy had to have used only his abdominal and thigh flexor muscles to fold the gurney's steel tubing like that. Engineers for the company that made the gurney said it was impossible for a human body to bend the tempered steel that way, but they never sent a factory rep down here to look at it."

"Did Cowboy get away?"

"No ... but it took six men to get him in leg irons and handcuffs, and into a paddy wagon. I heard later that Cowboy was shifting his weight so violently in the back of the wagon, he darn near turned them over a couple of times before they got him to jail."

"Out of curiosity, Terry ... where was Shorty during that episode?"

"I have no idea, but it wouldn't have been any different if he had been there ... would it? I think we should call it a day," Terry said, looking tired.

As Terry left the ER, Mark was a few moments behind. *I sure hope Officer Max Black-Belt Bollinger doesn't have to tangle with Cowboy. Either one of them could end up getting the surprise of their lives,* Mark thought as he headed to his room on Grady's 14th floor.

15

MISS FRANCES

In mid-September, 1965, Dr. Mark Telfair had been at Grady well over a year. Strangely, his current rotation as JAR in the Surgical Emergency Room seemed less hectic than the previous one he'd done there as an intern. A quiet moment alone in his room at the hospital allowed him time for casual reflection: *I'm changing ... less of a chickenshit, becoming a bit more worldly, beginning to see things as they really are, becoming more capable of dealing with chaos,* his mind concluded. Yet Mark knew Grady's building—its mortar and tan brick—were not directly responsible for what he perceived as self-change. It was Grady's people, the patients, the characters he'd met there. Mark felt sure all large teaching hospitals had their share of such characters; Grady just seemed to harbor an abnormally generous collection. Mark's head carried a mental list of those persons who had somehow influenced his emerging real-world thinking. Miss Lucifer the witch, Jerry Bacon, Zack, Mose, Cowboy, and Hot Body were certainly on his list. Mark wasn't sure who else he'd put on his mental Grady character list, nor did he know how long that list would ultimately become. He knew only one thing for certain: He'd never forget any of the characters he'd placed there—not for the rest of his life.

Nor did he plan to forget Anne Hunt, RN. After he'd finally found her in the cafeteria several months earlier, it seemed Anne was more or less constantly on his mind unless his thoughts were occupied by some surgical issue. He'd gotten over the embarrassing way they'd met, and dated her regularly. At first, Mark was concerned about their relationship getting too heavy too soon, but ignored the warning signs, as did she. Neither Mark nor Anne seemed ready for a formal commitment, but their circle of close friends could already see it: Their relationship was a serious one. Mark soon found himself "trading call" with some of the Grady surgical JARs who were qualified to fill in for him in the ER. Occasionally, he'd been able to work out an entire weekend off. On one such weekend, Mark and Anne left Atlanta around 11 in the evening, then drove through the night to Orlando to visit her family. Mark immediately liked Anne's mother, Betty; she seemed not the least bit unhinged by their unannounced arrival at 6:30 that morning. Anne's dad had already left for work and he missed their arrival, but Mark found Betty just as attractive and outgoing as her daughter, Anne. Undeniably, Betty was quite comfortable in the presence of a stranger. When Anne introduced Mark to her mom, Betty promptly gave him a big boob-squashing hug, and then planted a kiss on his cheek. After seating the pair at the breakfast table in the Florida room, she served hot coffee in mismatched mugs that looked like souvenirs from the yet-to-be-completed Disney World.

While sipping their coffee, Betty Hunt asked an uncomfortable question: "Mark, Anne has certainly said a lot about you on the phone. I know you two met at Grady shortly after she graduated from nursing school, but she still flatly refuses to tell me exactly how you two met. Do *you* mind telling me?"

Mark could feel his face flush. He turned and looked at Anne, who was now also crimson. Anne's mom rapidly surveyed both their faces.

"That bad, huh guys?" Betty asked, wearing a curious smile.

Mark looked at Anne. In their mutual embarrassment, they continued to smile at one another. Anne finally turned her hands palm up, resting the back of them on the table. Mark did the same, hunting for the right words. He decided on the truth.

"Betty, your daughter first met me in an operating room at Grady ... when I was naked from the waist down," Mark answered, becoming a deeper crimson.

After an awkward silence, a smiling, yet pensive Betty finally spoke. "Well, Anne's the only one of my kids that always knew exactly what she wanted to be ... knew exactly what she wanted in life ... so Mark, I guess when she first met you, she saw exactly what she wanted!"

The three laughed at length. In the process, Mark clumsily spilled his coffee on the table, some of it ending up in his lap. Undeterred, Betty continued to laugh and smile as she cleaned up the spill with a series of paper towels. Not the lest bit shy, Betty dabbed gently at areas of his pants normally reserved for his touch only. While putting the finishing touches on the cleanup, Betty asked how he came to be half-naked in an operating room in the first place. The pair then shamelessly recounted all details of their first meeting.

They next volunteered uncensored specifics of their second meeting, one that had occurred in the Grady cafeteria when Mark had returned Anne's safety pin. The pair went on to reveal their third meeting, when Mark had passed out while pinching off a splenic artery in the OR. Betty, a humor-loving and pleasant person, was not the least bit perturbed by the highly unusual circumstances under which her eldest daughter had met her current beau. This left Mark somewhat confused: Betty Hunt just did not fit the stereotype his mind associated with a mother-in-law. *Somehow I think Betty Hunt wouldn't be a bad one,* he thought, wishing he could deny his own conclusion.

The remainder of their Orlando weekend flew by. In the process, Mark had met Anne's very friendly but straight-laced dad, Thomas, when he'd returned from a Saturday half-day's work at Martin-Marietta. Anne's long-haired early-teen brother, Tommy, was perhaps best described as rebellious but polite. Tommy's shoulder-length bleached hair reflected the "surfing scene," his current full-time preoccupation. Mark learned that Anne's younger sister, Susan, was married and living out of state with her Air Force husband, a pilot with the rank of captain. The next day, after meeting neighborhood friends and enjoying a relaxing family lunch, Mark and Anne politely declined her dad's offer of a quick tour of the Disney World construction site; it was now after three on a Sunday afternoon, and Mark had to be back at Grady for work early Monday morning.

On the long drive back to Atlanta, Anne napped while Mark drove his old Volvo. The monotonous interstate allowed his thoughts to wander to several previous weekends when he and Anne had gone to the North Georgia mountains. In the mountains they'd usually rent a simple cabin in a quiet state park. Such weekend retreats had allowed them to spend unhurried hours just talking. When not talking, they were luxuriating in their strong physical attraction for one another, a process they often repeated every few hours.

During the few weekends they'd spent alone together, Mark recalled being amazed at Anne's ability to talk shop. He felt glad to have a companion to share both the professional and the physical aspects of his life. During their long talks, Anne shared many stories about what it was like to be a Grady student nurse. She told him how controlled the student nurses' lives were. During their three years of training, they lived in dormitories adjacent to the mammoth Grady Hospital. Evening curfews severely cramped their social lives. The curfew hours became slightly less restrictive as a student nurse advanced through the three-year program; however, all student nurses, even the third-year ones, most of whom were in their early 20s, still had to sign in and out of the dorm. A housemother, usually an elderly nurse, lived in each dorm and enforced curfews. Punishment for being late resulted in "grounding," or a one-month total loss of the privilege to leave the dorm in the evenings. Mark had thought

Ms. Costellanos, who ran the GAC, was overbearing with new interns. He soon realized Ms. C's discipline was nil, when compared to what the poor student nurses had endured.

Many of Anne's favorite stories had revolved around a Miss Frances, a Grady legend that he'd personally seen only in passing ... but after hearing Anne's stories, he knew he'd have to add Miss Frances to his own mental list of Grady characters.

Miss Frances was in her 60s. She carried the name and title: Miss Frances Hartman, RN, Director, Grady Memorial Hospital School of Nursing. Mark had encountered Miss Frances personally on only a few occasions in Grady's corridors. He recalled first *hearing* rather than seeing Miss Frances's approach. Her skirts hovered mere inches above the floor, and were so stiffly starched they made a peculiar sound when she walked—like a trapped flying animal batting around inside a cardboard box. On the few occasions Mark had seen Miss Frances up close, she was always pale as paper, with veins visible beneath her translucent skin. She rarely used makeup of any kind, but her hair was dyed so black it actually looked like blued gun metal.

As Mark continued the long drive back to Atlanta, Anne remained asleep. His mind wandered next to Anne's favorite Miss Frances story, one she'd told him during a long weekend six weeks ago. The Volvo's radio didn't work, so for entertainment Mark mentally replayed Anne's story as if he were hearing it again:

"Mark, you wouldn't believe what that woman was really like! Miss Frances didn't totally trust the strict dorm housemothers, you know. She frequently patrolled the dorms *herself*. She inspected all rooms, and even made the girls turn their boyfriends' pictures toward the wall while they were getting dressed, or undressed. Miss Frances would confiscate any alcohol she found in our rooms, so that's when we all learned that we could inject substantial amounts of vodka into oranges and other fruits she'd allow us to keep in the rooms."

"Well, I'd heard she was strict, but I had no idea she was *that* strict! She still that way?" Mark asked.

"Yep, afraid so. Apparently Miss Frances hasn't changed one iota since I was a student nurse. All the Grady student nurses I work with now still complain about her strictness. Heck, one of the students recently told me, 'What Miss Frances needs is a boyfriend, a gigolo!' We'd all had exactly the same thought when I was a student nurse, and my class actually tried to make it happen," Anne explained.

"*Tried* to make it happen?" Mark questioned.

"Yeah. We all took up a collection—raised about 50 dollars in all—to be given to a fairly good-looking young wino we'd talked into trying to seduce her, have sex with her. If he was successful, he would get the full 50 bucks, but it didn't work out very well."

"What went wrong?" Mark asked, to keep Anne talking.

"Well, we were never quite sure, but about 11 o'clock one night, the wino approached Miss Frances as she entered the parking lot. It was only slightly misting that night, but she'd carried a closed umbrella when she'd gone to the parking lot to get into her car. We were all watching from the third-floor windows in the dorm, and making bets about the fella's chances of success. Anyway, she and the wino had chatted for a few minutes, and she finally allowed him to walk her the rest of the way to her car. Both then got in her car, and stayed in it about five minutes before popping back out. The wino had her old-lady drawers in his hand, Miss Frances had the umbrella in hers. We all figured he'd lost his nerve ... or appetite!"

"I couldn't blame the fellow," Mark allowed. "But what happened next?"

"Miss Frances proceeded to beat the crap out him with her umbrella, then chased him across the street, and down the sidewalk. The wino finally ran out of Miss Frances's sight. We later learned the fellow had run into the ER's ambulance entrance. One of the student nurses working in the ER that night said it took about 50 or 60 stitches to repair all the umbrella wounds! Fortunately, they were minor."

"My God, Anne! I thought the men were devilish," Mark replied, laughing. "What did you gals ever do with the money you'd collected?"

"Some of it, about 30 dollars I think, was given back to the contributors," Anne replied.

"Well why not *all* of it? Sounds like the fella actually failed."

"He did, and admitted he didn't actually get to first base, if you know what I mean. But, because we all felt so sorry for the beat-up wino, we agreed to give the poor fellow ten dollars for Miss Frances's underwear, which he'd somehow managed to keep while eluding her umbrella-beating. We gave him another ten just to be sure he'd have enough to buy some wine before he went into DTs. But the poor fellow flatly declined to have another go at it ... 'Not even for a million dollars,' he'd said!"

Amid laughter Mark finally asked a question. "Well, what happened to her underwear?"

"Well, I'm not real sure where her undies reside today. Next to the last time I saw her old-lady drawers, they were thumbtacked to a bulletin board in the dorm. We used the bulletin board as a makeshift dartboard. A dart in the center of the crotch panel counted the same as a bull's-eye!"

"God, Anne. You ladies are *bad, bad, bad!*" Mark exclaimed, repressing laughter. "You said 'next to the last time you saw her old-lady drawers,' but when was the *last* time you personally saw them?"

"The very last time I saw her drawers, they had been put on an articulated human teaching skeleton that we'd borrowed from the classroom in the dorm basement."

"Why on Earth would you gals do that?" Mark questioned, feeling this was getting totally bizarre.

"It's a long story ... and something I'll never forget. It's also a story that told all of us student nurses we'd stepped over the line, at least as far as pranks are concerned."

"Well don't stop now!" Mark said. "You've got me curious."

"Promise me it won't go any further?"

"Sure," Mark replied, feeling it strange she wanted the story kept secret.

"Well, as I said, one night we borrowed the teaching skeleton from the classroom in the dorm basement. We had to post lookouts so we didn't get caught with the thing in the elevator. We took it to the dorm's third floor about 11 o'clock that night, and put it in the community bathroom."

"Why the bathroom?" Mark asked, feeling that was strange.

"We did it because we knew Miss Frances *always* personally checked the bathrooms around midnight ... just to be sure none of her precious students were in there smoking, or having stand-up sex with a boyfriend in one of the stalls. She'd walk through the restroom and shine her flashlight under the stall panels, checking to see if someone was standing in one of 'em."

"You mean some of the gals had their guys do it to them in the bathroom? Like stand-up sex?" Mark asked.

"Well *I* certainly never did anything like that, Mark Telfair!" Anne replied, incensed. "But I do know for a fact that a certain orthopedic resident has visited our dorm bathrooms on more than one occasion. And he certainly wasn't alone in that stall!"

"Unbelievable," Mark smiled. "You must be talking about Dr. DeJarnett ... the one we call Hot Body. Is that who you're talking about?"

Anne paused, then said, "I'm sorry, but that's all I'm going to say about bathroom sex."

"Well then how about getting back to the other story ... the one about Miss Frances's drawers," Mark pleaded.

"OK. Well, anyway, we sat the skeleton on a toilet seat, just like a live person would sit there. We'd put Miss Frances's drawers—the ones we got from the wino—on the skeleton. We put some white shoes on the skeleton's feet, put a lit cigarette between the fingers of one of its hands, and had a sign in the other hand that said: THIS IS WHAT CONSTIPATION WILL DO FOR YOU! We all knew she'd smell the cigarette smoke, see the white shoes with her flashlight, and open the stall's door latch with a nail file she carried just for that purpose. Many times before, purely to aggravate her, we'd latch all the stall doors, then crawl out the space at the bottom of the panels. After she'd made her midnight rounds the stalls would all be unlatched!"

"Well, getting back to your story Anne, did Miss Frances ever find the skeleton?"

"Sure did! You could hear her screams all over the building. It scared her so badly she had a heart attack, and she had to be admitted to the hospital. The whole dorm got grounded, because no one would admit to having a part in the prank."

"Heart attack ... a real heart attack?" Mark asked.

"Yes, a *real* heart attack! Fortunately she recovered, but it sure scared all of us. That's why I said we stepped over the line, and that's why I don't want this story repeated. Ever. OK?"

"Ah, lass! Your tale is perfectly safe with me," Mark said with mock chivalry.

"How do you spell that, Doctor?" Anne asked with a naughty grin.

"Spell what?" Mark asked.

"Is it spelled t-a-l-e ... or is that *t-a-i-l?*" Anne asked with a smile.

"*Both,*" Mark replied, a devilish grin on his face.

"Mark, did you guys ever do anything that crazy ... something that may have put a life in danger?" Anne asked.

"Well, I've done some dumb things too, Anne. The most stupid that comes to mind is when I was a senior medical student. Me and another medical student went to one of those pharmaceutical company open houses, where they'd try to brainwash you into prescribing their products once you finally become a bona fide doctor."

"Brainwash?" Anne asked.

"Yeah, that's really what it was. They'd have these open-bar presentations in fancy downtown Atlanta hotels, and would give us all sorts of trinkets: doctor bags, stethoscopes, penlights, notebooks, reflex hammers, and all sorts of other stuff ... including more free booze than any of us could handle. And the whole time they'd be telling us how their drugs were so much better that their competitors' products."

"And?"

"And, we'd all leave the presentation so drunk none of us had any business driving. I remember one I went to with Duncan Prather. We were both seniors in med school at the time. We both were so drunk, I told Duncan neither of us should drive. Duncan said he could. It was about two in the morning. I remember telling him I'd let him drive on one condition: I expected him to go *real slow*—and he did. About 15 miles an hour all the way toward home, using the Northeast Expressway."

"That doesn't sound all that bad, though really not smart," Anne summarized.

"Well there wasn't hardly any traffic on the expressway at that hour, but every time Duncan came to one of those light poles that arched over the expressway, he'd just casually drive off the expressway onto the grass, then go around the light pole's base, then back onto the expressway again, still not exceeding 15 miles an hour!"

"He musta been really blitzed," Anne said.

"He was. I was actually more worried about us getting rear-ended, but there was so little traffic at that hour it probably was not a significant threat. Anyway, we'd finally gotten as far as the North Avenue exit ... where the Varsity is, you know. The cops came off the North Avenue ramp and pulled us over there."

"So now Duncan has an Atlanta DUI record?"

"Nope. When the cop pulled us over, Duncan rolled his window down, and politely said 'Evening, Officer.' The cop then responded, 'Are you drunk, sir,' and Duncan promptly replied, 'Hell yes, Officer! You don't think I drive like this ordinarily, do you?' "

Anne first laughed, then said, "You're kidding, aren't you?"

"Afraid not, but upon hearing Duncan's statement, the cop started uncontrollably laughing. He was forced to sit down on the expressway pavement as he desperately tried to write Duncan's citation. He finally gave up, and motioned for his partner to get out of the police car. The partner promptly got out, and strode over to his buddy sitting on the emergency lane's concrete."

"Well?" Anne prompted.

"Well the partner cop, who'd just gotten out of the car, noticed we were dressed in whites, and he asked if we were doctors. Then he asked if we were *Grady* doctors. Fortunately, Duncan had the presence of mind to lie, and say 'yes' to both questions. Duncan's car was promptly put in the Varsity parking lot for the night, and we were both driven home in an APD patrol car. At six the next morning, another APD car picked us up, and drove us back to get Duncan's car."

Mark's mind returned to the present. Flashing blue lights and a siren's wail prompted Mark to immediately stop reminiscing about Anne's student nurse days and his senior year during med school. He looked down at the Volvo's speedometer which, unlike the radio, still worked. He was 20 miles over the speed limit, and 80 miles south of Atlanta. As he pulled the Volvo into the emergency lane, Anne woke up to be greeted by bright flashing blue lights that disturbed her sleepy hazel eyes.

"Evening, Officer," Mark boldly said as he presented the required credentials to the Georgia State Patrol Officer.

"You realize how fast you were going, son?" the patrolman asked, as he studied Mark's license and registration with a flashlight.

"Uh ... yes sir, once you called my attention to it," Mark replied.

"Well, Doctor ... Telfair is it? Just where are you going in such a hurry at this relatively early hour of the night?"

"Well, officer," Mark said, "I've got to get this young lady to the hospital."

The patrolman shined his light at Anne, obviously checking to see if she might have a big belly indicating a late stage of pregnancy. "She don't look pregnant to me," the officer said.

"I better not be pregnant, Officer!" Anne chimed in. "I'm an *unmarried* Registered Nurse, and I've gotta be at work in the operating room at Grady in Atlanta by 11 o'clock tonight. Doctor Telfair and I both work there."

"No shit! Grady? You guys work at *Grady?* Hey, y'all really done a fine job on patching up Luke, my APD fishing buddy ... you know the one that got shot all to hell when apprehending a DUI on Northeast Expressway about two months ago?"

Anne had a memory like an elephant. "Oh yes Officer, I remember him well. You're talking about Officer Luke Burkheart, shot five times with a .38 at the North Avenue Exit of the Northeast Expressway. Nice fellow, glad we could help him out. But how about just giving Dr. Telfair his speeding ticket, and let us be on our way. We're already running late, and I really do have to be there at 11 o'clock," Anne said.

"Doc, how fast does this old Volvo run?" the patrolman asked.

"Don't know," Mark replied. "I keep good tires and brakes on it, but I've sorta let the nonessentials slide till my finances get a little better."

"Follow me, Doc. I'm your personal escort to Grady. Just stay right on my butt. I'll try to keep it under 90, and we'll have you at Grady in time for that pretty nurse to be there at 11 o'clock ... maybe even a little before."

Mark was uncomfortable with the situation, but it sure beat getting a speeding ticket he couldn't afford. For a long while, Anne said nothing as they frequently ran 85 to 95, safely slicing through increasingly heavy traffic while approaching Atlanta.

At their current driving speed Anne did not want to be a distraction, but finally spoke. "This old bomb runs pretty good."

"Yeah it does, thanks to my roommate, Zack," Mark said. That's what he calls it too. 'The Bomb.' Zack's a whiz with mechanical things. He completely rebuilt the transmission a few months back ... just did that in the Grady parking lot! I just can't believe how smart that guy is."

"So Zack's the one who keeps it all patched up?" Anne asked, becoming impressed by Zack's hidden talents.

"And he helps me with the payments. In turn, I let him use it anytime he needs a car."

They arrived on the Grady ambulance ramp at 10:45. Anne promptly got out of the Volvo and disappeared into the hospital, her overnight bag in tow. Mark did the math: 80 miles covered in a little less than one hour. Mark thanked the patrolman for the escort service, and the patrolman again thanked Mark for the good care Grady had given Luke, his fishing buddy.

As Mark parked his car in the Grady lot, a thought suddenly struck him: *Anne is not even scheduled to work tonight!*

Mark quickly walked back to the hospital, entering through the ER, and found the nearest phone. He had the operator page Anne Hunt. About a minute later the phone rang at Mark's location. He was in the residents' office in the Surgical ER.

"Hi. Where are you?" Anne asked, as though nothing unusual had happened.

"I'm in the Surgical ER! Where the heck are you?" Mark asked, a little unsettled.

"Up in the cafeteria, enjoying a cup of coffee. Want to join me?" she said.

"Be there in a minute," Mark replied.

Mark quickly located Anne in the largely empty cafeteria. He quickly approached her table and sat down. "You're not even scheduled to work tonight!" Mark blurted out.

"I know ... but that patrolman didn't know that. He didn't give you a ticket, did he?"

"Well ... no," Mark allowed.

"Well you look after my tail ... that's spelled t-a-i-l ... and I'll look after yours. Same spelling. OK? Now, how about getting your car back out of the lot and drive me to my apartment. That way I can get a good night's sleep before coming back here to work for real ... at seven in the morning."

16

A STRANGE SOUND AND DOIN' THINGS RIGHT

A little after midnight, Mark dropped Anne off at her apartment in Northeast Atlanta. They'd resisted the temptation to spend the rest of the night together. Neither Mark nor Anne were exactly "quiet lovemakers," so the fact that Anne's roommate was in the apartment sleeping created a certain awkwardness. Another factor was the long weekend they'd already spent together in Florida. The whirlwind pace of meeting Anne's Orlando friends and family, combined with the driving pace during the last 80 miles of the return trip, had left them both bushed. For once, a quick and quiet goodnight kiss seemed adequate for both.

Mark quickly drove back to Grady through Atlanta streets that were largely deserted. He parked the trusty old Volvo in the Grady lot, then headed for his room on the 14th floor. There, he planned to catch a much-needed full night's sleep. As Mark approached his room's door he had a strange feeling that something was not quite right—a strange low frequency vibration, a sound that seemed to be coming from *his* room, the one he shared with Zack. Determined not to be surprised by anything, Mark put his key in the lock, then barely cracked the door. The slow rhythmic mellow sound ... *whoom-pa-ta* ...*whoom-pa-ta* ... *whoom-pa-ta* ... repetitively spilled out into hallway. *Stereo. That's it! Zack's bought a sound system. Excellent bass response,* Mark thought. Feeling confident that he had correctly diagnosed the sound, he opened the door—to be greeted by a large K-Model Harley-Davidson! The motorcycle smoothly idled on its kick stand, and filled most of the floor space between their beds. Zack was sitting on the floor in his underwear, vision tunneled, carefully adjusting the carburetor's fuel mixture with a screw driver.

"Have you lost your mind, Zack?" Mark yelled over the idling bike's rhythmic noise.

"Do I look nuts?" Zack quickly shot back.

"Well quite frankly, yes ... yes you do, Zack! You look absolutely completely certifiably totally nuts! Just how many guys do you know who just sit on the floor in their underwear at one o'clock in the morning—on the 14th floor of a hospital, for Christ's sake—adjusting something on a running motorcycle?"

Zack turned the bike off. "Well, I've finished working on it now. I wasn't expecting you back tonight anyways. Just figured you'd spend the night with Anne in her apartment. After you guys got back from Florida, you know. How'd the Volvo run?" Zack casually asked.

"It ran just fine, Zack. Transmission quiet as a mouse. And it shifted perfectly. I really appreciate you fixing it ... and helping with selling the spider-cards that gave us the money for the parts. But you're trying to change the subject on me!"

"What subject?" Zack asked, feigning confusion.

"That damn motorcycle! *You are nuts!*"

Zack silently walked to their room's windows and while closing them, he finally spoke. "Mark, if I was really nuts, I wouldn't have opened all these freakin' windows. This bike here was running so rich at idle, this room would have a lethal level of carbon monoxide in a coupla minutes. So crankin' it up in here, with the windows *closed* ... now *that's* what would have really been nuts."

"Zack, I still think you're crazy! Crazy just for having that thing up here in the first place. And speaking of that, just how did you get it up here?"

"Freight elevator," Zack calmly answered.

"You just plan to keep it parked here? In our room? You're not going to be stupid enough to try to ride that thing in Atlanta traffic are you? You've worked in the ER. You've seen how bad the bikers get beat up when they get hit by cars. You given that any thought? Have you Zack?" Mark asked, now shaking with anger.

"You through now?" Zack calmly asked.

"Yeah, I guess so, but you need to know I'm about to give up on you as a roommate. I just can't put up with this shit anymore!" Mark said.

"Pretty good cuss words there, Markie. But on a scale of one to ten, that shit's about a three, the damn you said before that only a two. Didn't think you'd ever learn to cuss at all," Zack teased.

"I normally don't, Zack. At least not out loud, but you just drive me to it!"

With a serious expression on his face, Zack apparently decided he had to respond to Mark's tirade. "Before you get totally bent out of freakin' shape, and get your panties totally in a wad, let me say this: First place, this room was *my* room before it was *our* room, OK? Second place, I'll get paid 50 bucks for fixin' this bike. Or is it that you don't want no help with the car payment this month? And third place, this bike don't even belong to me. It belongs to a rich first-year urology resident way down at the other end of the hall. Room 1404. He brought it up here on the freight elevator, and asked me to fix it. And he's been trying to sell it, because he's seen just how bad busted up folks get when they try to ride these freakin' things in traffic. He's been unable to sell it because it would quit runnin' on potential buyers when they'd take it for a test-drive. It'd quit every time they stopped at a traffic light. So there! You happy now, Mr. Smart-ass?" Zack concluded.

Mark smiled, then burst out laughing. The sight of tall skinny Zack just standing there, with a dead-serious expression, in his Jockey shorts, and pointing his screw driver at Mark while saying "You happy now, Mr. Smartass," had all been too much. Mark just could not find any way to answer his serious diatribe.

"Sorry, Zack," Mark said after he finished laughing. "But you're not going to leave that thing in here tonight ... are you?"

"Hell no! I'm going to return it to 1404, down at the far end of the hall," Zack responded.

"Good! I'll help you push it down there. It must be a good 100 yards to 1404," Mark offered.

"Nah. I'll get it," Zack said as he put a room key under the waistband of his Jockey shorts, then started pushing the heavy bike out into the hall by himself. Mark couldn't help but notice the vanity GA motorcycle tag on the urology resident's bike: DIC-DOC. Zack proceeded to crank the bike with one kick, hopped on, and instantly roared off down the long hall. Mark was almost afraid to look. Zack opened the throttle fully as he went into second gear about half way down the hall, and did a wheelie for about 50 feet. Mark saw the closed steel fire door at the far end of the long hall, and prepared to hear a loud crash. Instead there was the screech of the bike's tires as Zack skidded to a perfect stop in front of 1404. Zack promptly dismounted, retrieved the key from his Jockey shorts, opened the door, and pushed the big bike inside the owner's room. All in less than ten seconds!

Zack was now walking casually back to their room. Several doors were beginning to open along the long hallway. Half-asleep residents and interns poked their heads out various doorways. All were obviously curious about the loud rumble that had rudely jarred them awake at 1:30 a.m. Mark heard Zack explain to one curious 14th-floor resident: "Just that damn police chopper buzzing the hospital again, fellas. Ya know, we really need to report that prick to the FAA!"

Casually entering their room, Zack remained clad only in his underwear. Mark felt absolutely determined to be serious, continue his lecture, and let Zack know he totally disapproved of his actions. But a serious reprimand would not come out. Every time Mark tried to formulate serious words in his mind, he found the urge to laugh too overpowering; he could not even speak. Mark finally caved in, started laughing, and was unable to stop. All the while Zack was strutting around in his underwear, just staring at Mark with his intense green eyes—like *Mark* was the crazy one!

When Mark's laughter reached five minutes and had not slowed the least, Zack was obviously becoming concerned about his hysterical roommate. "Hey, Mark! Knock it off, will ya? Are you OK? We gotta get up and go to work in four hours, you know."

"I know ... it's just ... it's," Mark tried to speak again, but failed. He had vaguely and unintentionally pointed at Zack's lower body through tear-filled eyes as he desperately tried to speak.

"Hey man. My fly's shut! So what's so freakin' funny?"

"No it's ... well it's just ... it's just ... it's..." Mark could not even finish the sentence.

"... it's my freakin' bird legs?" Zack finished for him. "That's it, isn't it? My legs. Hey, I know they look like freakin' toothpicks, man. But that's just the way I'm made. I don't make fun of *your* body. Do I?"

"No," Mark finally got out, then blew his nose and wiped his eyes. "Let's go to sleep, Zack."

"Most sensible thing you've said since you got back from Orlando. I've been a little worried about you, Mark. Started back when you was drawing them spiders on those cards—and it seems to be getting a little worse, especially since you started dating Anne Hunt so regular. But we ain't goin' to talk about that now. So I'll see ya at six," Zack concluded, as he prepared for bed.

Without a word, Mark undressed, arranged his covers, and turned out the light. He was sure he'd finally purged the laughter from his system, and would now be able to sleep. But on the edge of sleep, Mark took a deep sighing breath. His olfactory senses detected the faint lingering odor of oil and gasoline in the room's air, and that brought the whole episode back to the forefront of his sleep-seeking mind. Without warning, he again burst out laughing in the darkened room.

Zack immediately snapped the light back on. "What *now*? What's with you? You some kinda freakin' laugh-aholic or somethin'? How about going somewheres else to laugh. Jeez, Mark. I need some sleep ... even if you don't!"

Zack got out of bed, went to his closet, and got a thick blanket off the shelf. Zack folded the blanket into a pillow, which he promptly put under his head, then put his regular bed pillow on top of his head, in an attempt to block out any of Mark's further laughter. As Zack sequestered his soundproofed head, Mark turned the light off, and told his mind to think only of Anne. Finally, sleep came.

The 6:00 a.m. wake-up call came way too soon for Mark's liking, but he and Zack had gotten up without difficulty, showered, shaved, dressed, and walked together down to the elevator at the far end of the 14th-floor hall. Mark couldn't help but notice the black marks on the highly polished tan vinyl floor. A two-foot black mark, about midway down, marked the beginning site of Zack's wheelie; farther down the hall, an additional 40-foot pair of closely spaced black marks were literally burned into the tan tile. The skid marks stopped exactly at room 1404. Mark made no comment to Zack regarding the motorcycle's tire marks. He didn't want to get started on another attempted reprimand ... or another laughing episode. But the silent message of the hallway's "floor-tile-evidence" told Mark Telfair's mind one thing for sure: *It wasn't all just a dream!* Without mention of the motorcycle, Zack and Mark boarded the elevator, headed down to the second-floor cafeteria for breakfast, and then on to the Surgical ER to start work at seven.

When Zack and Mark walked into the ER, it was essentially empty. Their superior, Dr. Terry Brinson, apparently had arrived early, and was doing some paperwork at his always-neat desk. Terry looked up and spoke when he heard Mark and Zack enter the office.

"Morning, you guys. The ambulance radioed about ten minutes ago. They're bringing in a GSW to the head. He's apparently stable. But admin is really on my butt about getting the ICD code numbers on these ER charts ... so do you think you fellas can evaluate the GSW when he gets here, then get neurosurgery to admit him, if he isn't DOA?"

"Sure, glad to," Mark replied, knowing that looking up International Classification of Diseases code to match the patient's diagnosis was a pain in the butt, even if it was essential to good medical record keeping.

"Yeah, Terry, you just keep working on your codes there. Me and Mark will get everything evaluated, then we'll give you the straight skinny," Zack added.

"*Straight skinny?*" Mark asked, turning to look at his roommate. "Is that some kind of Polish terminology?"

"No, man! That's a *real-world term*. Probably one that never got used in your fancy Northeast Atlanta Buckhead neighborhood," Zack chided, seemingly jealous of Mark's comparatively affluent background.

"Translation please," Mark said.

"Well the *straight* part means accurate and truthful ... and the *skinny* part means condensed. Understand?" Zack explained.

"Hey, could you guys conduct your Polish grammar lesson—or whatever it is—somewhere else?" Terry sighed, obviously annoyed, since he was trying to concentrate on the codes listed in the oppressively thick ICD Manual.

"Dr. Zack! Dr. Telfair! Gunshot patient's here," Mose said as he stuck his head in the office door.

Without further words, Mark and Zack left Terry with his paperwork, and followed Mose into the treatment room. The young white male patient appeared to be about their own ages, late 20s. Sure enough, the motionless patient had a bullet wound ... *right between his eyes.* Dried blood was on his upper lip and inside his nostrils. The wound itself was not bleeding. He was breathing well on his own. Zack checked the patient's pulse while Mark checked blood pressure.

"BP's normal," Mark announced.

"Pulse 88 and regular," Zack added.

Mark looked at the patient's pupils with a penlight. "Pupils equal, mid-range ... but *not* reactive to light."

Zack got an ophthalmoscope and began studying the interior of the patient's eyes. After a few moments, he spoke. "Mark, the retinas look fine. The optic disc is sharp bilaterally, not swollen."

Mose, standing silently by, cleared his throat. "Either one of you doctors see anything funny 'bout that bullet wound?" Mose asked softly, not wanting to disrupt the doctors' evaluation.

Mark was the one to respond to Mose. "Well no, Mose. I don't think it's funny at all. It's not funny one bit. It's a dead-serious wound!"

"You missed my meaning, Dr. Mark. What I mean is, do you see anything *peculiar* 'bout that wound?"

Mark and Zack both now looked closely at the gunshot wound, the GSW between the eyes. Zack was the one who finally spoke up. "Well Mose, is does look a little funny—that is *peculiar*—around the edges. Looks like pepper, sorta dark, or somethin'."

Two seconds later, Zack and Mark spoke in unison: *"Powder burns!"*

Mose smiled, nodded his head, and said, "I got somethin' I needs to go check on, so see y'all later ... if that's OK?"

"OK with us," Mark replied, answering for both himself and Zack.

Mark and Zack knew they had both completely missed an important observation: This was a close-range gunshot wound, possibly self-inflicted. The pair went through a whole litany of shoulda-noticed, and finally decided to start an IV. They personally wheeled the patient to X-ray for a full series of skull films. When the images finally started coming out of the

Kodak processor, Zack caught each film at the machine's exit slot. They immediately put the half-dozen images on a view box, and found a radiology resident to look at the films with them.

"Well, fellas," the Chief Radiology Resident said, speaking to both Mark and Zack, "looks like you got a .22 cal hard jacket in the middle of the optic chiasm. Should have clipped both his optic nerves where they cross at the base of the brain. Don't think the bullet went far enough to get the pituitary gland. How's the patient doing clinically?"

Zack responded first. "He's got good vital signs. Optic discs look OK. Retinas look fine."

"Can he *see?*" the radiologist inquired.

"Don't know," Zack responded. "Pupils don't respond to light though."

"Can he move his extremities? Any motor impairment?" the Chief Radiology Resident asked.

"Don't know," Zack heard himself say again.

"Is he conscious?" the radiologist asked.

"Don't know," Mark replied.

"Well," the radiology resident continued, "based on where that bullet is situated, I don't see any reason why your patient should be anything worse than *blind.*"

Mark was 50 percent of the GSW-to-the-head evaluation team ... the team that was supposed to be getting the straight skinny to report to Dr. Terry Brinson. Mark had to admit that both he and Zack didn't seem to be doing too good a job thus far. The questions asked by the Chief Radiology Resident were indeed pertinent. Mark's mind clearly recalled Zack's strongly opinionated recent comments about X-ray docs: *They ain't nothin' but freakin' pussies that look at shadows all day long and don't never look at a real patient. They don't know jackshit about what's really goin' on!* Mark smiled at Zack, who was usually objective when confronted with reality. Mark said nothing, but knew Zack was now choking on a very large slice of humble pie.

Mark and Zack took their patient, and his films, back to the ER to finish their evaluation. Mark was the first to touch the patient again. He took a safety pin out of his wallet. He opened it, then lightly pricked the patient on the sole of one of his feet. The patient promptly drew his foot away from the painful stimulus. Mark checked the other foot. Same response.

Zack loudly yelled in the patient's ear. "You hear me fella?"

The patient promptly responded. "You don't need to yell, Doctor. I can hear you just fine, and please quit sticking my feet, unless it's necessary."

"Well, why didn't you say somethin' earlier?" Zack asked.

"Because I thought you might not let me die if you knew that I'm only blind," the patient sadly explained.

Zack and Mark then did a complete neurological exam. Their only net finding: *total blindness!*

"How did this happen to you?" Mark asked the patient.

"I did it to myself. I just didn't do it right, did I?" the patient responded, tears now forming in his non-seeing eyes.

"Why did you do it?" Mark asked.

The patient patted a pocket on his neatly ironed clean shirt, then reached in and pulled out a folded note written on white tablet paper with blue lines. Several sheets were folded together. The patient extended his note toward the sound of Mark's voice, then spoke. "It's all in there. Read it, if you have to know why. Maybe you doctors will understand. I hope God will too."

Mark took the note and unfolded it. It was six pages long, written in pencil, presumably in the patient's own hand, and possibly his suicide note. The message was neatly printed, surprisingly well written, and chronologically organized by date and time. Mark and Zack simultaneously read the pages in silence. The detailed note started off, *"Dear God, friends, and family ..."* The message that followed painted a sad picture that covered the last six months of the patient's troubled life.

He had gotten laid off at the carpet mill where he'd worked as a shift manager for eight years. Following that, his only vehicle, a late model pickup, had been repossessed. He had since bought an old clunker pickup truck with money he made doing odd jobs around his rural neighborhood. At least the truck allowed him to get to and from whatever work he could find outside his own community. Two months earlier, his wife of ten years had told him how much she still loved him, despite their bad economic times. Two days later she'd run off with the lead gospel singer at their church, and hadn't been heard from since. Their only child, a four-year-old boy, seemed to be dearly loved by the father, and apparently well cared for in the mother's absence. The patient had gotten his son a dog—actually an unclaimed stray chow—which seemed to help the child feel less pain about his momma's sudden disappearance. The boy and the chow played together and became inseparable. Two weeks ago, without apparent provocation, the dog turned on the little boy. The child had been fatally mauled in minutes. Using his son's toy baseball bat, the patient had beat the killer chow to death.

When the patient had returned from his little boy's funeral, he'd parked the clunker truck next to his trailer. That night, only hours after the funeral, an apparent electrical short in the old truck started a fire in the vehicle, and it had quickly spread to his mobile home. Both vehicle and home had been a total loss by the time the volunteer fire department arrived. After the fire he went to his brother's home in Atlanta, and had stayed there for the last ten days. Only a few hours ago, the patient had secretly borrowed his brother's .22 pistol and shot himself between the eyes. The last sentence of the note read: *"God, friends, and family, please forgive me if you can."*

Upon reading the note in its entirety, Mark and Zack looked at each other in silence. They both remained composed but had tears in their eyes. Mark's own reaction to the note didn't surprise him. He'd developed tears before, especially when dealing with some of the tragically mangled and horribly burned kids he'd seen in the ER. He just never thought he'd see the day when street-tough Dr. Zack Paslaski would shed a tear for any person ... for any reason.

Zack cleared his throat, blew his nose, wiped his eyes, then spoke to the patient. "Buddy, is there *anything* we can do for you? You just let us know, and we'll do it."

"I think my brother followed the ambulance here. If he's out in the waiting area, I'd like to talk to him if that's allowed," the patient politely requested.

"You got it," Zack said as he left the room, still rubbing his eyes, and carrying the refolded note with him.

Zack soon located the patient's brother in the foyer outside the ER. After Officer Max Bollinger checked the patient's brother for concealed weapons, he was allowed to enter the ER common area. Zack waited five minutes in silence while the brother read the patient's note. Zack retrieved the note, then escorted the man to the ER treatment room where his wounded brother lay.

Upon entering the room, and speaking to both Mark and Zack, the patient's brother said, "Fellas ... I mean doctors ... is he going to be all right?"

Mark summarized: "We don't know for sure yet. The only thing we can find wrong so far is that your brother is completely blind."

The patient's older brother just stood there. His lips started quivering, his eyes filled with tears, he shook his head side to side. His face distorted in a grimace as he made his sad summary statement: "You know that poor boy ... my own baby brother ... he just ain't never done nothin' right!"

Comfortable that their patient was stable, and feeling that the two brothers might want to talk privately, Mark and Zack went into Terry Brinson's office carrying the patient's X-rays. Terry was still doing paperwork, but looked up as Zack and Mark entered. Terry Brinson got the straight skinny on the GSW from Mark, and Zack gave him the suicide note to read. Terry, too, shed a few tears, then called the neurosurgery admitting resident and relayed the straight skinny.

After several days of intense neurosurgical conferences at Grady, and multiple expert and experienced opinions, a decision was made to attempt to remove the bullet. The patient had developed a slow leak of cerebrospinal fluid through his nose; infection involving the brain would soon follow. Two weeks after successful removal of the bullet, and a repair that stopped the fluid leak, the still-blind patient suddenly died from a massive blood clot that went to his lungs.

Mark felt guilty; he had admitted to himself that he was actually relieved by the news of the patient's death. The patient had finally gotten his wish. He'd finally escaped the hell his life had become ... he'd finally done something right. For the first time in Mark's life he realized mental depression is a real disease, a potential killer, and not just a mere figment in some psychiatrist's mind. He felt he may one day see some humor in the statement made by the patient's brother—the "he ain't never done nothin' right" statement—but it would be a long, long, time ... if ever.

17

A STAR IN THE EAST

With Christmas only two weeks away, a cold December night in 1965 found Dr. Mark Telfair in his room at Grady Hospital. Now 10:00 p.m., he was reading the *Annals of Surgery*—a journal largely devoted to the field of general surgery. As the Junior Assistant Resident assigned to Grady's 4-C, he was not on call that evening. He was merely sitting there reading ... but mostly he was lonely and missing Anne, who'd again gone to visit her family in Florida for the weekend. He'd been unable to swap one critical night of call, and couldn't go with her. His roommate, JAR Zack Paslaski, was working that night in the Grady Medical Emergency Room—the Medical Pit. The phone rang.

"Telfair here," Mark answered, expecting a call from Anne.

"Hi! It's me ... Carla. So, how has it been going for you lately?"

Mark instantly recognized the voice: Carla Lay. He froze in thought: *We haven't spoken a single word since the breakup ... so exactly why is she calling me now?*

"Mark? You still there?"

"Uh ... yeah. You just surprised me, that's all."

"Are you doing OK?"

"I can't complain, Carla. At least my work schedule is a lot more human now. I've got more time off."

"Mark ... you gotta minute to talk?"

"Well uh ... sure. About what?

"Do you have a new girlfriend yet?"

"Yes."

"Well I'm happy for you. Are you in love with her?

"Yes," Mark replied again, not knowing where their conversation was headed. "She's a surgical RN who works here at Grady. So how's it been going with you?" Mark asked, wanting to steer their conversation in a different direction.

"Well, I'm dating a guy from the office at Frito-Lay. It's sorta against company rules, but he's OK, I guess. I'm really not in love with him, and

I think his main interest in me relates to both money and sex, but I'm not sure in which order." Carla laughed uneasily.

"Well, I'm sure that's one of the hazards of having a father who is a multimillionaire. But at least you still have a living father. Unfortunately, mine died trying to get rich like your dad."

"I know. And I'm so sorry you got cheated out of having a dad so early in life. But Mark, you don't know the half of it ... I mean what it's really like to have an excessively rich father. I now know I've been very pampered and sheltered. I now realize how impatient and selfish I was at the last of our relationship. I couldn't help it. I felt you were more in love with surgery than you were with me. But I never felt you were in love with me for my money. Have you forgiven me for walking out on you?"

"Yes, I have ... but it was partly my fault too. And for me our relationship was never about your family money. It was never a case of marry well and live happily ever after. I'm still in love with surgery, and I think I always will be. I think trying to become a surgeon has caused me to grow a little. The intern year has definitely shown me another side of life. A side where poverty, ignorance, and brutality openly reign."

"Mark, you know me. I'm allergic to conflict of any kind. Thankfully, I've never seen that part of life ... and I probably never will. All I had to worry about was which one of our airplanes or yachts we'd take to the next Riviera vacation ... or which of the 15 family cars I'd get to drive to Northside High or college at Agnes Scott."

"Carla, those kinds of decisions were never a problem for me. People in my part of Buckhead certainly weren't poor, but they didn't have that kind of money either—or the problems that go with it. Seems they had only little problems. Seems nobody would ever admit they got pregnant out of wedlock ... or became a drug addict or an alcoholic ... or caught VD. I guess I grew up expecting people to be better than they actually are. I'm sure the bad stuff was there all along. In the Buckhead I know, the folks simply *denied* it."

"I think you are absolutely right. About denial, I mean. So how are you coping with that now? I'm talking about the bad stuff they can't hide at Grady."

"I'm coping the best I know how. Dark humor sometimes ... tears at others. Laughing at some of the tragedies I see here seems to insulate my mind from things ... horrible things like neither of us ever saw while growing up. Crying over some of the sad stuff seems to wash them out of my mind. That's what allows me to keep functioning without going crazy."

"Mark, you're a strong person ... and you're gonna make a fine surgeon. You'll make some lucky gal a great husband. Deep down I'll always care about you as a friend. And if I can ever get out of Daddy's shadow, and Buckhead's shadow, maybe I'll grow up too someday. Should you ever need me, just call Frito-Lay. They'll know how to get in touch. Thanks for talking to a hopelessly spoiled little bitch. Bye." Carla clicked off, not giving Mark a final word. *Wow! That took guts. I'll always think of her as a friend ... but never again as a girlfriend,* his mind concluded.

Mark had just hung up when the phone rang again. It was Mom—just checking on her little boy. Mark knew he was on Mom's shit list in indelible ink—all because he didn't call her often enough. But every time they had a conversation, she tried to pry into details of his love life, or praised him for dumping Carla, the girlfriend Mom called hussy and trailer-park trash. To simplify his life, he had absolutely no intention of even mentioning Anne to Mom—not until it became completely unavoidable. Finally, just to get Mom quickly off the line, he lied and told her he had to go to the ER and check on something urgent.

He'd been off the phone only seconds when it rang again. *Carla again? Mom calling again just to be sure he'd actually gone to the ER? No, it's Anne. Better answer it,* he thought.

"Hi, Honey," Mark answered sweetly, fully expecting the call to be from Anne.

"Well, hello Markie Baby," Zack said, with poor attempt at feminine voice. "Sorry to fuck up your wet dreams, but you guys who went to Emory got a lotta OB experience when you were students ... ain't that right?"

"All the Emory students got a good bit of OB, Zack. I think I delivered about 100 babies by the time I was a senior student. Of course there were OB residents lookin' over our shoulders and—"

"Hey, Mark!" Zack interrupted. "I don't need your entire OB history, man. I just need to know if you've got time to look at a female patient I've got down here in the Medical Pit. She's got a belly problem."

"Well sure, Zack ... but are you in a real big hurry? I'm sorta waiting on a call from Anne. She went to Orlando this weekend. I couldn't arrange to be off and go with her. She should be calling any time now, and I want to be sure she got there OK."

"Well Mark, what I got down here ain't no real emergency. She's got normal vitals. She's in no acute distress. It's just that I'm a little too embarrassed to call OB. You know ... to call an OB resident until I'm a little more sure about what's wrong with this gal's belly. She's refused to give us urine and blood samples for a pregnancy test. I've had the medical SAR down here look at her, but when it comes to belly problems of any kind, he's about as useless as wings on a penguin. So I'd really appreciate your opinion before I holler for help—and make myself look real stupid in front of the OB guy. Know what I mean?"

"Sure Zack, but it might be an hour or so before I get down there. That OK?" Mark asked.

"Sure. Come when you can. Bye," Zack said, and hung up.

Mark closed the surgical journal he was reading. His mind first wandered to Anne. Was she OK? Had she gotten to Orlando safely? Then his mind slipped back to the OB experiences he'd had at Grady when he was a junior and senior medical student.

The first experience that came to mind was one night when he had a 30-year-old female in labor with her 16th child. Mark had done a pelvic examination while she was in her labor room bed. He had determined that the patient's cervix was fully dilated and effaced, and the baby's head was already well into the upper birth canal. She had strong contractions only a minute or so apart. In other words, in his opinion (based on about 40 deliveries at that point in his junior med student career), birth was imminent. Mark recalled instructing the OB nurse to take the patient back to the delivery room. The patient had heard his orders to the nurse. His mind shot back to that moment in time:

"Doctor, I ain't ready to have no baby jus' yet!" the patient authoritatively announced.

"Ma'am," Mark said, "your examination indicates you are fully dilated and effaced. The baby is coming down. I can feel about half the head. Your water's already ruptured, you know."

"I knows all about busted water! Jus' how many babies is you had, Mr. Doctor ... jus' how many has *you* had?"

"Well ... be serious! You know I haven't had any babies," Mark responded.

"Well I's had 15 befo' this'n ... and if I say I ain't ready yet, then *I ain't ready yet!*" the seasoned mother emphatically stated.

Mark was a little irritated by the patient's attitude. *OK lady, you just stay right here in this regular hospital bed and have your baby,* he thought. The patient seemed to sense Mark's displeasure at her refusing transfer to a delivery room table, where things would be a lot easier for both the patient and the student doctor.

"Say, Mr. Doctor? Ain't they got a little room back there where you doctors sleep at? You know, where you can rest till I really is ready?"

"Yes ma'am, we got a room like that," Mark said, still feeling a little annoyed with her, but liking the fact she was calling him "Mr. Doctor," instead of "Mr. Med Student."

"Well jus' go rest yo' head down in that room, and when I's ready, I'll ax the nurse to come get you—but you better come quick when I say I *is* ready!" the patient instructed.

Mark went to the call room conveniently located nearby within the OB area. It was just a simple lounge with a couple of beds and a few chairs. Mark pulled his shoes off, stretched out, and while falling asleep had a final thought: *Lady, it's your own damn fault if you have that baby in your hospital bed.*

Two hours later Mark was jarred from sleep by an OB nurse. She was shaking Mark as she spoke. "That woman having her 16th says she's now ready for you Mr. Telfair. You want to check her in bed before I take her on back to the delivery room?"

"Yeah sure," Mark said, sleepily.

Mark approached the patient's labor room bed, then did an exam assisted by the nurse who had just jolted him from sleep. Mark couldn't believe his exam findings. She was no longer significantly dilated and effaced. He could feel only a dime-sized area of the infant's skull. No palpable contractions occurred over a five-minute period. Fetal heart tone and rate were normal.

Junior med student Mark Telfair hated to retreat from his previous pronouncement that she was ready, but the present exam gave him no option. "Ma'am, I'm sorry to tell you, but it looks like your labor has stopped. You're not ready just yet."

"I is so, Mr. Doctor! Jus' take me on back there and let me have dis baby!" the patient demanded.

"OK," Mark condescended, "we'll do it *your* way ma'am. But you'll be back there hanging up in those cold stirrups for hours."

The patient was taken to the delivery room, placed in stirrups, and draped on the delivery table. The patient had declined any sedation or anesthesia, and was wide awake. Mark sat gloved and gowned on a stool, waiting for what he knew was impossible.

"You ready down there Mr. Doctor?" the patient asked, as she craned her neck to peep over the obstetrical drapes.

Mark yawned, then stretched before he answered. "Yeah, I'm ready." *But you're not,* he thought.

"OK, here it come," she said, and took in a deep breath, then began emitting a loud groan as she strained down. Mark saw the baby's head crown in three seconds! He did his best to restrain the uncontrolled descent. The baby actually popped out—like a chicken laying an egg! He didn't exactly drop the baby, but sorta gently juggled it all the way to the floor. In short, the baby ended up in the stainless-steel floor bucket used to catch amniotic fluid. Fortunately the umbilical cord was very long. Upon contact with the cold stainless-steel bucket, the baby instantly sucked its first breath, then screamed. It certainly didn't need the traditional smack on the bottom to stimulate the first breath of life; the juggling fall and the cold steel had done the job.

Sensing something might be amiss, the mother apprehensively said, "Mr. Doctor! Mr. Doctor! What's wrong down there?"

"Oh nothing, ma'am," Mark said, trying to ignore the big lump of crow he felt in his throat. "Yours is the first baby I've delivered that needed to be put in a cold bucket to stimulate its breathing. Sometimes, I'm told, you gotta put 'em in there *two* or *three* times before they start breathing right. But your little boy, he's breathing just great now! So, do you wanna hold him as soon as I get the cord cut?" Mark asked, trying to sound both confident and professional.

"Sho does, Mr. Doctor. And I sho thanks you and the Gradies. Lawd, ain't he cute, Mr. Doctor?" the proud mother asked, as she snuggled her newly born seven-pound infant to her breast.

"Oh, yes ma'am. Pretty baby. Sure is cute," Mark answered with an embarrassed smile.

"What you think his name should be?" the experienced mother asked.

"Ma'am, I think you should just call him *Lucky,* no middle name," Mark said.

Almost immediately Mark recalled stories where real doctors—and even student doctors—had named babies for some of Grady's most prolific mothers ... mothers who had simply run out of names from their own repertoire: Girl's names like *Syphilis* (*Psy*-fill-is), *Gonorrhea* (Gone-*nor*-ra), *Vulva,* and *Placenta* came to mind. Boys names like *Scrotum, Meatus*, and *Mandible* were among the most popular, but Mark was happy with his more sensible name selection for the appreciative mother: *Lucky*. Lucky was indeed lucky he had not been seriously dropped by overly confident medical student Mark Telfair ... and Lucky's mother was lucky her bottom had not been torn to shreds by the precipitous delivery ... all because Mark had ignored the sage advice from a patient with over 15 years of birthing experience she'd acquired while having her 16 babies.

The phone's loud ring startled Mark. He stopped his reminiscing about things that had happened while he was a medical student. The phone had to be either Anne, or an impatient Zack Paslaski. It was Anne, who had arrived safely in Orlando. After five minutes of lovey-dovey talk, they hung up. Mark headed down to the Medical Pit to lend Zack the inexperienced help he'd promised earlier.

Mark waded through a zoo of patients: emphysema, heart attacks, catatonics, strokes, psychotics, and overdoses. He finally found Zack in one corner of the Medical Pit's common area; he was in the process of placing a gastric lavage tube to remove the stomach contents of a young girl stretched out on a gurney. She'd just swallowed a whole bottleful of unidentified tranquilizers.

"Jilted by her boyfriend," Zack explained, as he poked a tube the size of a garden hose down the unfortunate girl's esophagus.

"God, Zack!" Mark exclaimed. "Is it *always* this way down here?"

"Pretty much, man ... Surgical Pit's definitely a cooler place to be," Zack replied.

He was recovering a number of identical tranquilizer tablets as he continued with the lavage. From the returned lavage fluid, Zack picked out several of the tablets, then issued an order: "Hey somebody! Anybody! Please take these tablets to the pharmacy, and see if we can get a definite ID on 'em. All the writing is dissolved-off, so I ain't sure what they are."

"Zack," Mark said, "I know you've got your hands full right now with this overdose, but where is that patient you wanted me to look at? The one with some kind of belly problem?"

"Mark, I really don't know where the patient is at the moment. But if you can find Sylvia Banks ... you know Jer Bacon's girlfriend, the senior student nurse with the really big boobs? She'll know where the patient is. OK?"

"I get the message, Zack," Mark said, and left Zack with his OD patient to search for Sylvia Banks.

It didn't take long to find Sylvia, who took Mark to the doctors' office in the Medical Pit. They had put the patient in there to insulate her from the bedlam going on outside in the Medical ER. Sylvia introduced Mark to Zack's problem patient, a Miss Nancy Brigham.

"Nice to meet you, Nancy," Mark said, as he observed the attractive 18-year-old. She was impeccably dressed, well groomed, and obviously out of place in an inner-city hospital. Mark was still trying to fine-tune his definition of a Rooter, but Nancy Brigham didn't seen to fit the profile.

Nancy extended her soft well-manicured hand to Mark. "So nice to meet you too, Dr. Telfair. I do hope you can diagnose the problem within my abdomen. The first doctor I saw—a Dr. Paslaski—said he thought I was pregnant, or 'knocked up,' as he so crudely put it!"

"Well are you?" Mark responded.

"Absolutely *not,* Doctor! You see ... I don't even have a boyfriend."

"So you've never had sex with anyone? Is that what you're telling me?"

"Yes Doctor, that's *exactly* what I'm saying."

"Do you mind if I examine you?" Mark asked.

"No, not at all," Nancy said.

Sylvia Banks escorted the patient and Mark to the only vacant exam room left in the Medical ER. The patient was set up for a pelvic exam. As Mark did his examination, he questioned her regarding menstrual history. Using the fruit-system, her uterus was the size of an early June watermelon. This watermelon had the telltale *tic-tic-tic-tic-tic* sound of rapid fetal heart tones clearly audible through the stethoscope he pressed tightly to her abdomen. *Seven to eight months' pregnant,* Mark thought.

"Nancy," Mark said, "please wait here with the nurse, and I'll be back in just a few minutes to talk with you." Mark left the pregnant teen in the treatment room, and shortly found Zack, who'd retreated to the privacy of the doctors' office to make notes on the OD patient's ER form.

Zack looked up as Mark approached the desk. "You get a chance to examine that Nancy Brigham chick yet? Knocked up, or not? Whatcha think?"

"Zack, Miss Brigham is knocked up, as you say ... but telling her she's pregnant would be a much nicer way to put it. Even got fetal heart tones. So are you going to call the OB resident, or what?" Mark asked.

"Yeah, I'll call OB, just for an official confirmation. I really appreciate you lookin' at her. I thought she was knocked ... uh, I mean impregnated up too. But I got so little experience in that area I wasn't absolutely sure." Zack immediately reached for the phone.

Minutes later the Chief Obstetric Resident, Dr. Barry Goldstein, appeared in the Medical ER to examine the patient in question. Both Zack and Mark related the patient's history: no periods for eight months, and no boyfriend or sex ... ever. The OB resident introduced himself to Nancy Brigham, and again questioned and examined her. Upon completion of his exam, Goldstein requested that SN Sylvia Banks return the patient to the doctors' office.

In the modicum of privacy afforded by the residents' office in the Medical Pit, Dr. Barry Goldstein would deliver his professional opinion regarding her "abdominal problem." Zack, Mark, and Sylvia Banks were at the patient's side when the fatherly looking 32-year-old Goldstein addressed the anxious young patient.

"Nancy, are you sure you're being completely honest with us? You can be, you know. Any information you give us here is completely confidential, and because of your age we're not obligated to tell your parents anything."

"I'm not some kind of teenage Jezebel, Dr. Goldstein! I've been completely honest with you doctors. Now how about you fellows being honest with me. What's wrong with my abdomen?" she demanded.

"Well, Nancy," Goldstein said, "you're pregnant ... about eight months' worth. Either you're not telling us the truth, or you are a very sound sleeper ... or someone drugged you about eight months ago."

"I don't do drugs! You're *all* wrong about my being pregnant too. Can't be! That would mess up my plans for college next fall. I've already been accepted at Agnes Scott!" she yelled, then started crying. Sylvia tenderly comforted the patient while handing her a Kleenex.

Except for the patient's soft sobs, the room went completely silent. Dr. Goldstein anxiously started pacing around the room. He finally went to one of the room's windows, which were covered by closed Venetian blinds. He separated two of the blinds' slats with his fingers, and peered out into the dark night. He went to another window and did the same. He then went to a third window, again separated the slats, and peered out. Everyone, including the patient, watched Dr. Goldstein's rather ridiculous-looking actions. Finally Miss Nancy Brigham broke the silence.

"Dr. Goldstein, what on Earth are you doing?"

"Looking," Goldstein replied.

"Looking at *what?*" the young patient asked, now with definite irritation in her voice.

"Well Nancy, it's like this. I'm a Jew. But I've heard the last time something like this allegedly happened, a very bright star appeared in the east ... and should it happen again, I just don't want to miss it!"

Mark later heard rumors that Nancy Brigham had returned to Grady about a month later and delivered a healthy male infant. To satisfy his own curiosity, one night he had the Grady medical records librarian pull Nancy Brigham's inpatient chart. He became appalled by what he read: The chart clearly indicated Nancy had been sexually abused by her own father (a physician!), who had drugged her for his own sexual pleasures. He'd done so since she was 12 years old. The doctor, a respected name Mark recognized, had lived in Buckhead; he'd committed suicide shortly before his daughter's baby boy was born. He recalled reading the flowery obituary in the *Atlanta Journal,* indicating the doctor had "... died unexpectedly at home." *God, what bad shit happens even in my Buckhead, too ... it just all gets hidden from public view. How could I have ever been so damn blind all these years?* Mark only hoped that some doctor, or a student doctor, hadn't read Nancy's outpatient ER record alone ... and cruelly suggest that she name the baby *Jesus.*

18

ZACK GOES TO MEDICINE

D r. Mark Telfair and Dr. Zack Paslaski continued to room together at Grady. They'd even begun to have a hint of a normal social life. Mark and Anne dated each other exclusively; Zack dated around.

On the first day of July, the young doctors had become second-year Junior Assistant Residents. In the general surgery program, Mark would now spend all his time serving on Grady's various surgical services. In this way his schedule of rotation for the second residency year was cast in concrete. On the other hand, Zack's time would be split between surgical and medical services, but the exact schedule for Zack's second residency year remained highly speculative. It seems the program developers were still having difficulty deciding how much of this or that training was appropriate for Zack's newly evolving Emergency Medicine specialty.

In any event, Zack was currently on 5-C, the same internal medicine ward where Mark had done his internal medicine elective as an intern. Fortunately, Dr. Thomas E. Wellington—the Chief Medical Resident Mark had encountered on 5-C—was no longer at Grady. Reportedly, he had crawled off into the bowels of some obscure cardiology research facility at an Ivy League school. *Great place for him,* Mark had thought, when he'd heard the news. As a bit of good fortune for Zack, Dr. Charles Cromwell— the visiting Professor of Internal Medicine from the UK—had again returned to the USA. Dr. Cromwell would be conducting Grand Rounds the entire time Zack would be on the 5-C medical service; that alone, Mark knew, should make Zack's internal medicine rotation a great learning experience.

Since Zack and Mark now had work schedules more in sync than at any previous time since they'd been roommates, they had more time off at the same time, and therefore more time for bull sessions. They spent time together socially as well. Mark's Volvo remained their only car so they frequently took their dates out together. Though Zack rarely had a date with the same woman twice, his dates, or at least the ones Mark had met when they doubled, all seemed to be very nice gals. Almost without exception, Zack had selected dates from the pool of Grady student nurses. In candid comments to Mark, even Anne seemed positively impressed with Zack and his dates: "Despite his trash-mouthed reputation, he selects very nice dates. Zack is really bright, and he can be a very courteous entertaining fellow. Someday he'll find the right one, and settle down ... or the right one will find him, and she'll settle him down." *I'm not too sure about that,* Mark had thought at the time, but he didn't argue with Anne. He'd already learned she was invariably right about those kinds of things.

Following a quick trip to the cafeteria for coffee, Zack and Mark had just returned to their room on the 14th floor. It was 10:00 p.m. They were trying to catch up on their journal reading, but Zack said he first wanted to talk to Mark about something before they got started.

"Mark, you ever do anything you felt really guilty about?" Zack asked.

"Well sure, Zack. Who hasn't?"

"Well let me say this up front: It don't have nothin' to do with no freakin' woman ... if that's what you're thinkin'. It has to do with something I did with a *man*," Zack admitted.

Wheels were wildly spinning in Mark's mind without traction: *God, please don't let me have an in-the-closet gay or bisexual roommate!* Zack's next statement stopped Mark's mind-spin.

"Has to do with something I did to a stethoscope ... a real nice doctor's stethoscope. A joke that sorta backfired. I ain't told nobody about it yet. If I tell you, it won't go no further, will it?"

"Well Zack, I can keep a secret. So exactly what's bugging you?"

"You remember that British professor—that Dr. Cromwell—who's visiting here, and does Grand Rounds on internal medicine?"

"Sure I remember him. Real sharp fellow. So ...?"

"So he's been trying to teach us guys on 5-C how to use a stethoscope, to listen to the heart valves and stuff. You know, to teach us to hear way more than they teach us to hear in med school. Cromwell seems to hear things in my patients' hearts that I can't hear. It ain't like my hearing's bad, man, 'cause I had mine checked out when I had my deferred-entry Army physical, same as you had yours checked out when you signed up for the Air Force. Remember?"

"Sure, Zack. They checked everything I owned, including my ears. Even took my fingerprints."

"Well anyways, the Chief Medical Resident *swears* Cromwell can hear a heart murmur through a brick wall. I thought that was total bullshit. So I decided to do an experiment, and—" Zack stopped, looked down, as though he might not continue.

"And what?" Mark prodded.

"And I got this patient who has a faint murmur of A.I. Faint, but I could definitely hear it," Zack said, referring to a cardiac murmur produced by aortic valvular insufficiency. "Everybody on Grand Rounds could hear it too ... except Dr. Cromwell. The reason he couldn't hear it was because I put some little wads of cotton in the earpieces of his stethoscope. He'd left his scope on the desktop in the doctors' office while he went into the head for a whiz. That was right before Grand Rounds, ya see. So I unscrewed the earpieces, poked a little cotton ball in each one, then screwed 'em back on again—all while he was still in the head."

Mark had one of his laughing jags. As it resolved, Mark decided he should at least say something to comfort Zack in his state of guilt. Mark felt the cotton-in-the-stethoscope-thing was not all that bad, but apparently it was significant to Zack, and against the dictates of what little conscience he might possess.

"I know you feel bad about it Zack, but Cromwell's got a good sense of humor. Actually, he has a *great* sense of humor. And he can take a joke. He didn't really get bent out of shape when we put that live goldfish in a patient's IV bottle. Heck, I'd just tell him you did it, and take the cotton back out. End of story."

"Well it ain't quite that simple, Mark. I've made a clusterfuck here. Ya see, that poor old British fart went and had a full ENT evaluation—right after Grand Rounds that day. I mean like really complete ... with audiograms, the whole nine yards. And when I saw him on the next Grand Rounds, he'd went out and bought himself one of them fancy stethoscopes. Paid $1,500 for it! You know, the kind that has some kinda high-tech electronic amplifier?"

Mark had another laughing spell while long-faced Zack just sat there, fully consumed by self-reproach. Zack seriously wanted some help. Mark felt determined to control himself. Somehow just knowing that his roommate's big guilty secret had nothing to do with closet gay or bisexuality made self-control more difficult, but control eventually returned.

"Zack," Mark finally said, "I think you've just got a simple case of *pedal-phallic* syndrome."

"You don't need to be fancy with that Latin shit for me. I know when I've stepped on my own dick. What I need is a cure, man ... a goddamn solution!"

An idea popped into Mark's head: "Zack, where did Dr. Cromwell have his ENT tests done, his audiograms and stuff?"

"Right here at Grady. Down on the eighth floor at the ENT clinic.

Why'd you ask?"

"Well I think it might be a good idea to look at Dr. Cromwell's audiogram. Maybe the old fella really needed a stethoscope with a built-in hearing aid." Mark paused. "But come to think of it, he seemed to hear conversation quite well when I did my medical elective on 5-C. Anyway, I'm sure the ENT clinic door is locked up at night, and they probably keep the medical staffs' records in a separate file. And I bet that file is locked up," Mark added.

"Well that ain't no problem, at least not in *this* hospital. These institutional locks are a piece of cake," Zack said.

"Zack! Are you suggesting what I think you are ... that we break into the ENT clinic, and steal Cromwell's ENT records?"

"Heck no! First place we ain't got to break nothing. Second, we ain't going to take nothing. All we are goin' to do is *look* at something."

"Hey wait a minute, Zack! What's this *we* stuff? I'm not about to have any part of entering locked doors around here at night, so you're on your own, buddy."

"No problem," Zack said. He then removed something from the back of the drawer where he kept his socks and underwear. It looked like a bunch of bobby pins tied together with a string.

"What's *that* ... or is it *those*?" Mark asked, puzzled.

"*Those.* You ain't never seen no lock picks before?"

"Well no Zack, actually I haven't. I've tried to live on the right side of the law most of my life. And I'm extremely sorry I even suggested we look at Dr. Cromwell's records from his Ear Nose & Throat Clinic exam. Like I just said, you're on your own."

"No problem. One-man job anyways," Zack said, as he reached for the phone and dialed the operator. "Uh, operator, could you report something to Hospital Security for me? This is Dr. Paslaski. I think a mugging is goin' down in the parking lot next to the Glynn Building—right across the street from the hospital here!"

After Zack hung up, he went to their room's window, and when he saw multiple "flashlights" frantically running through the Glynn Building's dark parking lot, he smiled. "See ya in ten minutes." Zack instantly disappeared through their room's door, lock picks in hand.

Mark was too stunned to say anything. He'd really tried to help his guilt-ridden roommate, but now felt he'd compounded the problem instead. He waited the longest ten minutes in recent recollection. Finally, Zack suddenly burst back into their room. He was carrying handwritten notes about Dr. Cromwell's ENT evaluation.

"Take a look at this shit!" Zack said, a little out of breath from running down, then back up, six floors in the fire stairwell. Mark noted Zack was now wearing latex examination gloves.

"Zack, anybody see you?" Mark asked, whispering.

"Nah. I looked out the ENT clinic's window. The whole damn security squad was still in the parking lot—just running around like somebody pissed on an anthill. Man they was looking in and under every car in that lot. But I may have made one screwup."

"*Screwup?*" Mark asked, prepared for the worse.

"Yeah. I couldn't relock the deadbolt from the outside without a key, though I was able to turn it with the picks from the outside when I went in. I was able to relock the file drawer and the passage lock when I left though. They'll probably think they just forgot to lock the deadbolt when they closed up the clinic for the day."

"Let's see what you've got, Zack," Mark said, relieved, and now anxious to look at the data. A few minutes passed in silence while both quickly reviewed Zack's handwritten notes. Unusual for a doctor, Zack's hand was highly legible.

Mark was first to speak. He pointed to a particular line in the notes. "Zack, you say here they first removed bilateral cerumen impactions."

"Yeah, they did," Zack responded. "So the old geezer had wax packed in his ears, but look at the audiogram numbers. Seems he could hear pretty good after they got the freakin' wax out. Especially out of the left ear."

"That's what I'm looking at now, Zack ... the audiogram numbers you wrote down. I can't remember exactly what the normal numbers are, but I don't think Cromwell's numbers look too good, especially for the right ear. Let's look up the normal numbers in *Harrison's*," Mark said, referring to an American standard regarding internal medical textbooks.

"Yeah, great idea, Mark. I just bought the latest edition last week. Figured I'd need it, since I decided to do the new Emergency Medicine specialty. Let's see what *Harrison's* has to say."

Zack slid the new four-inch-thick book from beneath his bed. In the section on hearing disorders, he found an illustration which depicted the average normal human audiogram in graph form. It included sound frequencies from 250 to 8000 hertz. It indicated a person's threshold, in decibels, for standard pure tones within the frequency ranges. Zack quickly transferred the numbers he'd stolen from the ENT clinic to a hand-drawn graph of his own, then studied his graph a brief moment before saying excitedly, "Wow! You know Mark, this audiogram shit is pretty friggin' neat! It ain't nothin' but a logarithmic representation of the sound energy needed to achieve threshold! Ya see?"

Zack was eagerly pointing to his hand-drawn graph. Mark didn't reply. He only thought: *Zack's quick mind simply does not fit his exterior image. Zack's brilliant brain shouldn't be in his obnoxious skinny red-headed body, yet it was that skinny freckled body that went to both college and med school on a full academic scholarship. Maybe looks are only skin deep, but ugly and scholarships go all the way to the bone. It just shouldn't be, but that same body has just broken into Grady's ENT clinic ... and stolen information from a professor's medical record!*

"Shit, Mark! That delightful old fart couldn't hear crap in the lower frequency ranges ... much less a faint A.I. cardiac murmur through a brick wall."

Feeling like a mental midget, and somewhat defensively, Mark spoke: "Let's not be too quick to assume he couldn't hear the A.I. murmur, even if he did have a bunch of earwax, plus the cotton you put into his stethoscope. As I said before, Cromwell could hear conversation very well." Though Mark felt intellectually inferior to Zack, he still hoped he could find some way to relieve his roommate's guilt regarding a prank run amok. "Let's see what that textbook says about the audio frequency range of aortic insufficiency murmurs."

"Good idea," Zack responded, as he quickly went to the cardiac section of the book where aortic insufficiency was described. Details of the audible murmurs created by such a condition were clearly presented.

Zack and Mark read the text in silence. After a few minutes, Mark was the first to speak.

"Zack, I'm looking at the audio frequency range of A.I., and it is the same frequency range where Cromwell's audiogram indicates a severe hearing deficit in *both* ears. I don't think he could have heard that particular murmur with either ear, even after they'd cleaned the wax out ... even if you had not stuffed the cotton in his stethoscope's earpieces. His left ear is very good for hearing ordinary conversational sound frequencies, and that's probably why he didn't appear to be hard of hearing on rounds. So the straight skinny—you Polacks would say—is this: Cromwell's ability to hear a murmur through a brick wall is a total myth, and he truly needed the expensive stethoscope you prompted him to buy!"

A broad smile appeared on Zack's face. "Makes me feel a lot better, Mark ... really does, man. But should I confess to him what I've done?"

"Only if you're crazy—and you are—but for now, I'd keep my Polish mouth shut if I were you!" Mark exclaimed, then laughed.

The phone rang. Mark and Zack jumped, both fearing the Hospital Security Department may have somehow discovered Zack's "visit" to the

ENT clinic. They stared at each other, wondering if they should avoid answering the phone altogether. On the fifth ring, Zack finally grabbed the phone.

"Paslaski here ... Uh, yeah I was the one that called the operator about the muggin'. So?"

Mark felt his own pulse quicken, and was dreading what Zack's side of the phone conversation might reveal.

"Was two black dudes muggin' an old white lady ... That's right ... Yeah, I'm sure ... Well I really appreciate you guys checkin' it out anyways, and I'm sorry you couldn't catch nobody, but still appreciate you guys checkin' ... Yeah you guys have a good evening too," Zack said, then hung up.

"Mark, what say we get back to readin' our journals. Sorry for the interruption." Zack spoke as though absolutely nothing unusual had transpired.

"Sure, Zack. Good idea. But you'd look a little less ridiculous if you took those latex gloves off ... and less suspicious if you took those lock picks off your bed, and hid them back in your drawer," Mark commented, while tearing the stolen ENT notes into very small bits in preparation for flushing the "evidence" down the toilet.

The pair read their respective journals for about an hour before taking a quick trip to the cafeteria for a coffee break. Both agreed they'd promptly return to the room and continue their reading by midnight.

Sipping a hot cup of coffee in the cafeteria, Zack peered over his steaming mug and saw one of the security guards sitting at a nearby table. He was also sipping steaming brew.

"Hey, Mark," Zack whispered, wearing a smile, "wonder if that security guy over there was involved in that Chinese fire drill out in Glynn Building parking lot?"

Zack started to rise from their table, with obvious intentions of going over to the guard's table. Mark quickly caught Zack's coat sleeve, and discreetly jerked him back to his chair. "Zack, you just don't know when to leave it alone, do you?" Mark whispered, now both serious and irritated.

"You're right, Mark. I don't know when to leave it alone. Guess that's why I don't ever gamble, and maybe that's why I'm afraid of gettin' too involved with one woman. Just might find my butt broke and married ... with a buncha little linoleum lizards runnin' around the house."

"Zack, I haven't figured you out. Never will. I've done all the psychotherapy I plan on doing this evening, so let's change the subject, finish our coffee, and get back to our reading. OK?"

"Sure. I really appreciate your help about what I did to Cromwell. I feel better about that now. So let me tell you about a strange pair of stroke patients I had on 5-C. They both died at the same time last week."

"Is this a long story?" Mark asked, looking at his watch. "It's quarter till 12 now."

"Nah. This is a short story. Only a one-cup-of-coffee story."

"OK, but I'm going back to my reading at 12 sharp. Shoot."

"Well like I said, two elderly black female patients were admitted the same day with strokes. Bad ones. They was both my patients, and put in the same semiprivate room. The first one, in the A bed, I named her Oh Lawdy. The second one, in the B bed, I named her I Hear You Jesus."

"Why'd you pick such weird names?"

"Well, it was easy. The only thing Oh Lawdy could say was, Oh Lawdy ... and the only thing I Hear You Jesus could say was, I Hear You Jesus."

"Zack, I can't see where that's really all that funny. Kinda sick if you ask me."

"Well Mark, it ain't so much the names I give 'em. It's the way they was sorta mentally bonded. It's like some little pieces of their brains—some parts that wasn't destroyed by the strokes—was hooked together. Oh Lawdy was the dominant one though. Every time after Oh Lawdy said her name, three seconds later—just like an atomic clock—I Hear You Jesus would say, 'I Hear You Jesus.' So it constantly went on like that day and night: 'Oh Lawdy' ... *one, two, three* ... 'I Hear You Jesus.' 'Oh Lawdy'... *one, two, three* ... 'I Hear You Jesus.' "

"Zack, I agree that's strange. But you said they both died at the same time?"

"Yeah, they did. Well *almost* exactly the same time. Both were no-codes (no CPR to be done) anyways. Oh Lawdy actually died first, ya see, but about a week before they both died, I did this little experiment trying to figure out how their brains hooked together, and—"

"*Experiment?*" Mark abruptly interrupted, frowning, almost afraid to ask his clearly certifiable roommate any further details.

"Hey man, don't gimme that look! Not like Hitler experiments. Not nothin' like that. I simply found that if you'd pinch Oh Lawdy's lips together—so she couldn't speak—I Hear You Jesus would *not* respond. In fact, I Hear You Jesus would even quit taking a breath in, because the only time she would actually take a breath *in*, was immediately *after* she'd said 'I Hear You Jesus!' You could also stop I Hear You Jesus from breathing if you put your hands over her ears, so she could not *hear* Oh Lawdy say 'Oh Lawdy.' I even tried saying 'Oh Lawdy' to her myself, just to see if I Hear You Jesus would respond to *my* voice ... but she wouldn't. It had to be *Oh Lawdy* who said 'Oh Lawdy.' Nobody else saying Oh Lawdy mattered!"

"God, what a weird thing," Mark said. "Did Dr. Cromwell see these stroke twins?"

"Sure did. Cromwell called them the 'Oh-Lawdy-I-Hear-You-Jesus-Duet.' 'Course I didn't tell him about my breathin' experiments, and how their breathin' related to their talkin', but he was fascinated—especially about the perfect three-second interval between their speech and breaths. But even Cromwell couldn't explain it. Neurologists couldn't explain it, and of course I couldn't explain it either, the perfect timing thing, you know. But now here's the funny part: About a week after I done the experiments, we was all gathered around her the moment Oh Lawdy died, and without thinking, I told all the fellas, *I Hear You Jesus will quit breathing in exactly three seconds, then die.* And she did. And died! Now everybody on 5-C thinks I'm psychic!"

"Psychic and nuts are two different things, Zack. Time to go read," Mark said, containing his laughter as best he could. Mark left the cafeteria with Zack tagging along. *A genius, trash-mouthed, streetwise, crazy, psychic Polack, with a conscience—what an impossible combination!* Mark thought, as they boarded the elevator, heading for their room to resume reading.

19

A COP AND DOCS MAKE A NEW ROOTER'S DAY

little before seven in the morning, on the first day of July, 1967, downtown Atlanta was already headed for another oppressively hot day—unusual in Atlanta for that time of the year. But Dr. Mark Telfair didn't care about the heat and humidity outside; he'd sequestered himself within the cool confines of Grady's Surgical Emergency Room—the Surgical Pit. Sitting there, Mark felt slightly insecure, though really not for any good reason. The foundation for his new level of responsibility had been adequate. He was now Senior Assistant Resident, the SAR in charge of Grady's Surgical Emergency Room. With the SAR title came the same level of responsibility that Dr. Jerry Bacon had shouldered there only three years ago—but three years ago, Mark Telfair had been a lowly ER surgical intern. He now began to fully appreciate the weight of accountability Jer Bacon must have also felt when he was in charge of the Pit. Being the Senior Assistant Resident in charge of one of Grady's ERs was possibly worse than being on the staff of Air Traffic Control at Atlanta's Hartsfield, or at least Mark Telfair felt that way. With ATC, your mistakes killed the passengers and crew all at once ... but they'd all be people you'd never seen eye to eye. As the ER's SAR, your mistakes would simply kill patients one at a time: folks you'd seen up close, even touched, and possibly spoken to before they died. Mark's macabre train of thought was abruptly interrupted by a familiar voice.

"Good morning, Chief," Dr. Adrian Brevard said, wearing a smile as he walked into the ER. Adrian, like Mark, was an Atlanta Buckhead native. Their paths had occasionally crossed in earlier life—grammar school, Boy Scouts, high school, a few college classes at Emory. At their most recent crossing, Mark and Adrian had come to know one another a little more closely; they had been straight surgical interns together on Grady's 4-A surgical ward. But a couple of months after their time together on 4-A, Adrian had suddenly lost three years in his surgical training sequence. First, his beautiful wife had been killed in a car crash on I-75 near Atlanta.

Two weeks later Adrian faced a second tragedy: His affluent father had suddenly dropped dead from a massive stroke while at work. His dad had owned Brevard Imports, an Atlanta-based business he'd built from the ground up. Adrian had dropped out of the Grady surgical training program to take care of personal grief and the family's business.

"God, it's good to see you, Adrian!" Mark said, looking up at the familiar smiling face. "Man, I haven't seen you since the, uh—"

"Funerals," Adrian finished. "I'm glad to be back in surgical training ... just happy Grady could find a slot to get me back in their program, and hopefully on with my life."

"How's your mom doing, Adrian?"

"Mom's doing OK, Chief. Mentally and physically. Financially she's in good shape, too."

"Adrian, all I can say is I'm glad you're back. But don't call me Chief yet. I won't be that till next year—assuming I don't screw up this year. So we're still equals as far as I'm concerned. You're just getting back from an unavoidable three-year leave of absence."

"Mark, you need to know I didn't have much time to read surgical journals while I was away. I hope I won't disappoint you by being too rusty. When are you going to do the first-day meeting for the new ER staff?"

"In ten minutes ... at seven," Mark replied, checking his watch.

Mark tried to emulate the traditional first-day meeting that Jer Bacon and Terry Brinson had held when they were SARs in charge in the ER. Mark explained the ER's chain of command, and introduced himself to the new crew. Though Dr. Adrian Brevard had been about three months short of fully completing the intern year, program administrators had allowed him to re-enter training at the first-year Junior Assistant Resident level. Two new straight surgical interns were the only new ER doctors. Fortunately the new interns were homegrown—both Emory-trained—and already possessed some practical experience and familiarity with Grady. They would be immediately useful and wouldn't require the extensive spoonfeeding Ivy League interns needed. ER clerks and RNs remained the same. Officer Max Bollinger from APD had replaced Shorty, the inadequate ER cop. Fortunately, Mose Mallone, the muscular 65-year-old ER orderly (a.k.a. Mr. Clean), remained a permanent piece of black ER granite. *They just don't make folks like that anymore,* Mark thought.

SAR Telfair had a genuine appreciation for Mose. He was both soft-spoken and streetwise. Mark knew Mose had literally seen hundreds of young doctors pass through the ER during their training. By osmosis, Mose probably deserved an honorary medical degree of some sort, or at least some kind of special recognition. Mark knew Mose would never be offered or receive any accolades. Humble almost to a fault, Mose was fully content with both his lowly ER position and the black color of his skin. It had often been Mose who'd quietly managed to keep many young ER doctors out of trouble, or helped them when they were in trouble, and he'd tactfully done so for more years than Mark Telfair had been alive. Mark admired him greatly.

After the first-day meeting of the staff in Mark's office, most members left to face their day. The ER was still relatively tranquil, so following the meeting, Adrian had remained with Mark in the office.

"Mose never changes, does he?" Adrian asked, breaking the silence.

"Man, I hope he never changes. Every new SAR needs Mose. I'm really counting on Mose—and on you, Adrian—to keep my butt out of trouble while I get my feet on the ground."

Sensing Adrian wanted to do more than talk about Mose, Mark risked asking him a pointed question: "So how's it really been goin' for you these last few years? You look OK. Look healthy to me. You've even put on a little weight."

Adrian took a deep breath, exhaled through tight lips, then responded. "Looks can be very deceptive, Mark. At first, with everything happening so fast, it was an absolute and total hell ... at least emotionally. My brain was in complete chemical chaos. At one point I even considered taking my own life. In fact, I even considered seeing a spook, and probably should have," Adrian said, using the Grady slang word for a psychiatrist.

"My own dad died when I was in med school, and it took me a while to adjust," Mark said with empathy. "But what you had to deal with was a triple whammy. I don't know how you did it, Adrian. Maybe your tough Italian genes, you think?"

"I'll never know, but I do know no woman will ever replace the wife I had, and I'm really glad we didn't have kids. And taking over Dad's import business—now that was a real stress! The last three years kept my butt at a desk about 16 hours a day, just trying to talk on the phone to foreigners from all over the world. Hell, I could barely understand half of 'em—especially the ones from those countries that end in s-t-a-n.

"After Dad died, the VP of Dad's corporation jumped ship and opened his own import business. Everything fell in my lap. I ordered millions of dollars worth of shit, not even knowing what some of the stuff was. Out of frustration, I've done nothing but stuff myself with fast food for two years. And put on 15 pounds! On my little five-six frame that's a lot. But finally I found some great people—ones who know the import business and markets—to run Dad's business. So maybe now I can get back to catching up on surgery. And I'm sure the pace down here will help me get this weight off."

Mark knew he could never fully appreciate the man's agony; despite the stress, Adrian still looked like the same old Adrian he'd been acquainted with for years. He retained that same warm smile, same dark shining eyes and neatly styled black hair. Adrian had an olive complexion that made him look perpetually suntanned—not what you'd expect of someone tied to a desk for the last few years.

Apparently wanting to steer the conversation away from his recent three-year nightmare, Adrian changed the subject. "What ever happened to old Jer Bacon? Did he do his chief residency? When I left Grady, it was rumored he was going to be dropped from the Grady program. Wouldn't make Chief because of an incident where some crazy guy shot up the ER when Jer was the Pit's SAR."

"I was in the Pit the day that happened! Scared the heck out of all of us. But to answer your question, Jer was not dropped from the program." *And I'd like to think I had a part in that,* Mark thought smugly. "Jer did most of his Chief year at Emory, some time at the VA, and a month or so here at Grady. He married Sylvia Banks, the really good-looking blond from the nursing school. Remember her?"

"Remember her? Yeah sure! Who at Grady doesn't? She's the one with the really big pumpkins on her front porch," Adrian smiled, gesturing with cupped hands, each placed about ten inches from his chest.

"Yep, she's the one! Anyway, they're married now," Mark explained. "Jer went in the Army after he completed his Chief year—assigned to Brook Army Hospital. Talked to him about two weeks ago on the phone. Sometime this month he'll be out of the Army and moving back to Georgia. He'll be joining a five-man surgical practice just north of Atlanta ... in Gainesville, he said. He wants a few of us Grady guys to come up and visit him and Sylvia, once they get settled in. Jer told me Sylvia's about seven months pregnant. He said he'd give us a call after the baby comes and they're all squared away."

"Dr. Mark! Dr. Brevard!" Mose said, as he poked his head into the office. "We got a fella out here that says he got a real bad headache. He just walked in. No ambulance. No nothin'. He won't tell me or them new interns what happen ... jus' say he wants to talk to the head doctor. He got a small hole in his head, 'tween his eyes! Think you fellas needs to look at him," Mose said, then dropped his voice to a whisper. "And he sho ain't no Rooter, I can tell y'all that!"

As much as they would have liked to continue, Adrian and Mark immediately terminated their catch-up conversation and hurried to the treatment room. Upon entering the room they surveyed the dignified middle-aged white male sitting on the edge of the examining table. Midway between his eyebrows, he had a small nonbleeding hole in his skin. The diameter of the hole was about that of a small English pea. It was surrounded by a narrow rim of purplish bruising. Though he appeared to be in no life-threatening distress, he kept both hands pressed to his temples. He seemed extremely anxious—nervous as the proverbial long-tailed cat in a room full of rocking chairs. With the exception of a moderately elevated pulse rate, vital signs on his ER sheet were normal. His clothes were a bit rumpled, but the dark blue blazer, light blue oxford shirt, tasteful tie, tan slacks, and expensive-looking shoes all led Mark's mind to the same basic conclusion reached by Mose: *This guy is not your typical Grady Rooter.*

"Good morning, Mr. Smith," Mark said, extending his hand to the patient. "I'm in charge down here. I'm Dr. Telfair, and this fellow here with me is Dr. Brevard. He's second in command here." Adrian nodded, but did not shake the patient's hand. "What seems to be your problem, sir?" Mark asked.

"Well doctors, I'm not positive. I think I've been hit in the head. All I know is I have one hell of a headache, a hole between my eyebrows, and possibly another hole in the center of the back of my head too."

"You say you *think* you've been hit in the head? You mean you don't *know?*" Adrian asked.

The patient started fidgeting, then reddened as he spoke. "Is this conversation off the record?"

"Yes," Mark replied. "But if you've actually been assaulted, Mr. Smith, the law requires that we doctors report it to the police. Any detail you elect to tell the police is your own business."

"But this conversation we're having right now is all off the record ... right?"

"Absolutely," Mark said. "So tell us what happened, or at least what you think happened."

"I guess I should start with the truth," the patient replied. "My name is *not* John Smith as stated on that record you're holding in your hand." The patient reached inside his blazer and pulled out a pin-on plastic-covered convention name tag. He handed it to Mark.

"Says here you're Thomas Torrington, Vice President - Sales, Oxford Floor Covering Products, Inc. Dalton, GA. This name tag has the Atlanta Convention Center logo on it. Is all this correct?" Mark asked.

"Yes, and Tom Torrington is my real name."

"So what actually happened, Mr. Torrington?" Mark asked.

"You guys are single ... right?" Torrington asked. Mark replied "yes"; Adrian looked down at the floor.

"Well, that'll make it a little easier for me to tell you guys, but I'm still very embarrassed."

"Embarrassed?" Adrian inquired, now looking up.

"Very ashamed and embarrassed," Torrington said, staring down at his lap. "That's why I didn't go to one of Atlanta's upscale private hospitals, even though I could easily afford to."

Feeling a little insulted, Mark said, "Well maybe you don't consider Grady upscale, Mr. Torrington, and I'll be the first to admit we don't try to be fancy here, but you will get excellent care here at Grady. So let's get on with your story."

Torrington looked up, finally met Mark's eyes, but continued to press his temples. "Well you see, doctors, after the convention closed down last night, a bunch of us guys went to a bar and proceeded to get very intoxicated. Several of us picked up some hookers. Using my Hertz rental car, I took my date to a motel out near the airport. There she did all the sexual things my wife of 15 years refuses to do. Between sex sessions we drank some more. I was pretty much out of it when I caught her leaving the motel room, just slipping out the door, you know. She was fully dressed and carrying her purse. I vaguely remember following after her in my underwear.

"When she caught me following her, she reached in her purse, and pulled out a very small silver object. I believed she somehow punched me in the head with the object—maybe even threw it at me—from several feet away. Drunk as I was, I do remember some sudden pain between my eyes. I remember falling forward on the carpet in the motel hallway. And after I fell, I think she hit me in the back of my head too, but I'm not sure. Then I must have passed out completely."

"No ambulance brought you to Grady, so how did you get here?" Mark asked, feeling certain Adrian was wondering the same thing.

"I drove," Torrington replied. "But I don't even remember how I got back into the motel room, and when I finally did wake up this morning, I had a very severe headache. It hurt so bad I didn't think I'd even be able to drive over here. In addition to the headache, I discovered I had a small hole in my forehead, possibly *another* hole in the back of my head ... and no wallet!"

Neither Mark nor Adrian were all that naive, but both were left a little slack-jawed by the patient's confession.

Mark closed his mouth, cleared his throat and spoke. "We'll need to examine you further, Mr. Torrington. Then we'll get some X-rays to see if something has damaged or penetrated your skull."

"Am I going to be all right?" Torrington asked, trembling from fright.

"We don't know for sure yet. We don't know if you have any damage to your skull, or if there's any damage to something inside your skull," Mark said with complete professional honesty.

Mark and Adrian did a full neurological exam. No deficit. While doing the exam, Mark couldn't help but recall the ER patient he'd seen over three years earlier ... a young depressed patient who had shot himself between his eyes using his brother's .22 pistol. That patient had been permanently blinded, and subsequently died from blood clots that lodged in his lungs after surgery. Mark felt comfort in knowing the present patient—Mr. Tom Torrington—could see just fine.

The pair then closely checked the head wounds. Other than one being in the front, the other in back, they looked *identical.* They weren't bleeding, so the doctors elected not to probe them. There was no stippling from powder burns indicating a very close range gunshot wound. They rechecked the patient's vitals, then wrapped a gauze dressing around his head. Mark and Adrian transferred the patient to a gurney, then started a just-in-case IV. As Adrian and Mark left the ER, they casually told Mose to keep the interns out of trouble while they went up to X-ray with their "headache" patient.

Waiting in X-ray while technicians made the films, Mark was deep in thought. Finally, he spoke: "I just don't see how that could be a through-and-through wound. Do you Adrian?"

"No I don't. If it is a through-and-through, he's the luckiest guy I've ever seen. The one in the back doesn't look like an exit wound. Both look like entry wounds. I'm sorry I don't remember my neuroanatomy well enough, but I guess it's at least theoretically possible to have a small object, a spike, or something else, pass all the way through your head and not hit anything vitally important."

"Guess that depends a lot on what you've got inside there in the first place," Mark joked, just as he heard his own name called.

"Dr. Telfair!" a radiology resident yelled, poking his head out a door in the X-ray department. "Could you come into the viewing room for a minute?"

Without a word, Mark and Adrian went into the radiology viewing room. The patient's multiple skull films were displayed on a large array of lighted view boxes. The radiology resident finally spoke: "Your patient, your Mr. John Smith here, is one lucky son of a bitch! Give me his history," he said, as his eyes intently studied the series of films.

Adrian eagerly replied. "Well, his name is actually—"

"*John Smith,*" Mark instantly interrupted, as he gave Adrian a forceful elbow poke to the ribs, one that went unnoticed by the X-ray doctor.

"Yeah, your Mr. Smith here has *two* bullets that have penetrated only the outer table of the skull," explained the radiologist. "One in front, one in the back—look like soft .22 cal to me. Apparently neither had enough kinetic energy to actually go inside!" the excited little radiologist exclaimed, while pointing at the films with his pencil. "Musta been shot from quite a distance ... or maybe these are low-velocity ricochet slugs, but they don't look deformed enough to be ricochet. You guys know any details of the shooting?"

"We're working on that as we speak," Mark lied.

"Yeah, we'll let you know what we find out," Adrian said, joining Mark in the deception, still rubbing his ribs where Mark had so forcefully poked him.

Drs. Brevard and Telfair quickly gathered the patient's films after the radiologist's reading, then left the X-ray viewing room. Carrying the films, they rapidly wheeled their patient out of X-ray. Once they returned to the privacy of the ER's treatment room, the patient was growing extremely anxious, and moved himself to a sitting position on the foot-end of the gurney. Mark and Adrian then maneuvered the patient's gurney so the patient was sitting directly in front of the treatment room's small X-ray view box. In preparation for showing the patient his own films, Mark and Adrian took positions on either side of their distraught patient.

"Well, what's the verdict? What do the X-rays show?" patient Torrington asked apprehensively, hands visibly trembling as he pressed his temples.

Knowing a picture is worth many words, Mark selected the patient's lateral-view skull X-ray to display first. The patient, Mark, and Adrian were all intently focused on the skull film before them on the view box. Even a layman would have absolutely no problem identifying the two clearly defined bullets lodged in the patient's skull. Using a pen as a pointer, Mark was in the process of explaining to the patient that the bullets had not fully pierced the skull—only the outer table (layer) had been penetrated. Mark's detailed explanation was interrupted by a loud thud—*Tom Torrington had fallen back on the gurney. He was unconscious!*

Mark and Adrian feared the worst and were preparing to call a code for CPR. When Mark detected a full slow steady pulse, Adrian aborted the code and hung up the treatment room's phone. After a few whiffs of ammonia, and the passage of several minutes, Torrington was again fully conscious.

"Have I died?" Torrington asked, blankly staring at the treatment room ceiling.

"Uh... no sir!" Mark reassured, as his own pulse slowly returned to normal. "You just passed out on us for a minute or two."

"Might have been better if I'd died though," Torrington flatly stated. "How am I ever going to explain this to my wife and kids? Just tell me, doctors! How?" a very frightened Tom Torrington asked.

"Well you'll have several days to come up with the answer to that question on your own," Mark offered. "I'm very sorry we're not upscale enough here at Grady to do marital counseling just yet."

"What do you mean *several days!* I've got to be back in Dalton, Georgia tonight. My wife and kids are expecting me!"

"Mr. Torrington, we are going to remove those bullets down here in the ER, and then admit you to the hospital for a few days of observation," Mark explained.

"Absolutely not! My wife would find out for sure. There'd even be a hospital record. I just can't do that!" Torrington emphatically announced.

Mark was thinking rapidly. Adrian was apparently thinking even harder and faster.

"Mark, is it mandatory that he be admitted?"

"Well not mandatory but highly recommended!" Mark shot back.

Adrian immediately replied, "Why don't we just take the bullets out, debride and suture the wounds, give him a tetanus shot and some antibiotics, and let John Smith here sign out AMA?"

"AMA?" Torrington inquired.

Mark explained: "That stands for Against Medical Advice. If you sign out AMA, that relieves us of legal liability. Especially should you walk outside the hospital, then fall over dead!" Mark had just finished the scare-tactic words to Torrington, when another thought immediately popped into his head.

"Adrian, can you see if Max will come in here for a minute?"

Adrian left the treatment room. Almost immediately, he returned with Max Bollinger, the ER's spit-and-polish APD officer. Upon seeing the towering cop's hulk, the large gun on his hip, and the snappy blue APD uniform, Torrington became emotional and began to cry like a baby.

"Do I need a lawyer? Am I under arrest?" Torrington asked, now sitting on the gurney and sobbing.

Mark and Adrian politely ignored the patient's questions and tears as they explained the entire situation to Max. They even re-explained the X-rays showing the two bullets lodged in the patient's skull. Max rubbed his chin, scratched his cleanly shaven head, then turned to the patient and spoke to him.

"Sir, do you wish to file robbery and assault charges against the perp—uh, the lady—who shot you?"

"No! Definitely not. I just simply want to get the hell out of here! And try to preserve what little dignity I've got left," Torrington replied, still distraught, still pressing his temples.

Max addressed the patient again. "Sir, you are not under arrest. Retain a lawyer if you wish. But please, before you leave, allow me to suggest the following: First, allow these doctors to remove the bullets and repair the wounds ... and give you what medications and instructions they deem appropriate. Second, they will give me the removed bullets, and I'll put them in APD evidence vials. They will be placed in our evidence retention facility over at APD's headquarters. The vials will indicate that they were removed by Drs. Telfair and Brevard from one John Smith, on this date, as indicated on Grady ER record number such and such. Third, I'll file APD armed robbery and assault reports indicating one John Smith was indeed robbed and shot by an unknown female assailant, but John Smith declined to file charges. Fourth, cancel all your credit cards, take a taxi back home to Dalton ... and get a new driver's license before you drive any car. Call Hertz and report their rental car stolen. I'll see that it is found, and they will get their car back. Fifth, I'd recommend you take your wife to all future conventions. Any questions, sir?"

Torrington was dumbfounded but obviously relieved. He even smiled, and finally removed his hands from his temples as he started to speak. "Officer, why didn't those two bullets go completely through my skull?"

"Because you were probably shot with one of these," Max said, as he hiked his left trousers' leg, and removed a small .22 Derringer from an ankle holster. Max removed one of the bullets from the tiny gun. "These are what we call 'light-loads,' even lighter than the standard .22 shorts. They don't make much more noise than a kid's cap pistol. They are designed to intimidate, to frighten, or—pardon my language, sir—to piss off somebody. But, if you really intend to kill somebody, you use one of these," Max said as he patted the large silver .357 magnum holstered on his right hip.

After the gun show, Max excused himself from the room. Mark and Adrian quickly removed the bullets under local anesthesia. They used special technique and padded forceps that would not scratch the bullets, thus preserving them for ballistics. But both young doctors knew the bullets would never see the light of day—they'd simply stay in the APD evidence room forever. The patient's two skin wounds were debrided (elliptically excised), then neatly closed with a few sutures. This converted the round bullet holes to "straight lines," each about an inch long, and thus indistinguishable from simple lacerations that had been properly sutured.

"Want to take a look?" Mark asked as they finished. He reached into a drawer for a mirror. *Hope he doesn't faint again,* Mark's mind worried.

Inspecting his forehead in the mirror Torrington said, "Hey, that's really neat, fellas! Just looks like a small straight cut that's been closed up with four or five stitches."

"Sir, the one in the back looks just like the one between your eyes, but we had to shave off a small patch of hair back there so we could work," Mark explained.

"Mr. Torrington, sir," Adrian said with a faint smile, sending a non-verbal message.

"What is it, Dr. Brevard ?"

"I just thought you might like to know that when I was an intern down here, a few years ago, I had a male patient that had actually been mugged. He had two cuts on his head *exactly* like yours in the same locations. They looked exactly like your sutured wounds do now—and that fella lost his wallet too!"

As Torrington was preparing to leave the ER, he signed the AMA disclaimer statement as John Smith. Smiling warmly, he shook the young doctors' hands and handed both Mark and Adrian business cards retrieved from inside his blazer. "If you doctors ever need any free carpet, including installation and pad, please give me a call. Same goes for that fine police officer too. And I think Grady's pretty damn upscale! Do you guys ever accept private patients here?"

"Oh I don't know if we could do that. We're pretty selective ... but if you've been referred by someone really influential, I guess we'd occasionally have to make an exception," Mark said, wearing a poker face that hid his deep sense of satisfaction.

Adrian was standing behind the patient's back during Mark's comment to Torrington. Mark could see Adrian was about to explode with laughter, but somehow Adrian managed to contain himself.

The ER clerk called a taxi for Torrington, Max took care of the "stolen" rental car parked somewhere close by, and the patient left the ER ... singing a Grady Rooter's praise all the way out!

Mark and Adrian quickly went to the privacy of the office where they immediately stripped off their professionalism and had a rib-jarring laugh together.

Adrian was still holding his left side when he finally quit laughing. "Man, I really needed that. But not right after you poked me so damn hard in the ribs—the way you did up in X-ray! I think you may have cracked one of 'em, but I could care less. I haven't laughed like that in several years. God, what a great way to get going again ... with the first patient. And on my very first day back, no less!"

After Mark's own laughter dissipated he spoke. "Adrian, I thought you said you hoped you hadn't gotten too rusty during your several lost years. In my book you sure haven't. Welcome back to the Gradies, brother!" Mark said, giving Adrian a gentle Grady-guy hug, keeping in mind he may have indeed cracked one of Adrian's ribs.

Mark knew there couldn't have been a better patient to welcome Adrian back to Grady. Mark also knew they'd both gladly forfeit a full month's pay just to be a fly on the wall while Tom Torrington explained his Atlanta "mugging" to his wife in Dalton, Georgia.

20

ANOTHER AMA AND A NEW ROOF

"No suh! Ain't no way I can go in no hospital ... not even the Gradies!" the patient had yelled at Dr. Mark Telfair in the ER treatment room.

Regarding difficult situations, the patient's statement placed Mark in the worst position he'd experienced thus far as the ER's Senior Assistant Resident. He'd exhausted his own thinking, and had called upon his consultants: Dr. Adrian Brevard, his JAR; Mose, the orderly; and Max, the cop. Eventually his roommate, Dr. Zack Paslaski, became involved too.

The October day in ER had started simply enough. The usual scrapes, cuts, and simple fractures had filled the first two hours of the day. With only minimal guidance, the interns were capable of dealing with the trivial injuries as they trickled in. Dr. Mark Telfair and Dr. Adrian Brevard were in the ER office reading, and catching up on ever-present paperwork. Mose suddenly burst through the office door, turning their quiet day upside down.

"Y'all come quick. It's one of my boys. I think he's hurt real bad!"

Mark and Adrian speedily followed Mose to the treatment room. A small clean-cut muscular male lay on the treatment room table. He appeared to be in his late teens. The patient rapidly panted; beads of sweat glistened on his dark face and scalp. His torso was covered by a snug white T-shirt worn inside his jeans. The shirt's entire abdominal area appeared to sport a large pink "flower," perhaps an impressionistic rose, printed on the shirt's white background. Initially, Mark thought the shirt might be a tie-dyed hippie creation, but then realized the white T-shirt's pink rose was an unintentional adornment concealing an underlying mass the size of a seven-month pregnancy.

"Take a look Dr. Mark!" Mose said, obviously shaken.

Mark and Adrian quickly donned sterile gloves, then untucked and slid the shirt up a bit. They were shocked: The patient's entire small intestine was outside his abdominal cavity! His bowel had apparently herniated through a fresh six-inch laceration, and now rested on the skin of his upper abdomen. There his guts formed a heap, contained only by the shirt. The entire pile jiggled in perfect rhythm with the boy's rapid panting.

"Oh my God!" Adrian and Mark said in unison. Manually they contained the pile, while quickly pulling the T-shirt back down and tucking it back in. They did so to keep the patient's intestines from sliding off the surface of his abdomen onto the treatment table, or to some point beyond.

"Adrian, please start the IV," Mark said. "I'm going to the office and call the general surgery admitting resident. Mose, you stay here with Dr. Brevard and help him if he needs any."

"Yes sir, Dr. Mark," Mose said, shaking his head in disbelief regarding the injured boy. Mose quickly retrieved the IV supplies from a wall cabinet, then turned to speak to Adrian. "Dr. Brevard, I thought I had my boy here straighten' out. Really did. He been comin' to my gym for two year straight. He ain't never miss' a single night. I were ev'n able to get him a job, working over at the Rich's warehouse, you know. They tell me he the hardest worker they got, and say he don't miss no time on the job for no reason."

"Mose, is this young man one of your children?" Adrian asked, while adjusting the quickly started IV's flow rate.

"No. I ain't got no real chile that I knows of ... might have a few 'yard chillen' from my earlier days, if you get my meaning, Doctor. But I do considers ev'r last one of them boys what comes to my gym to be my own."

"Yeah, Mose, Dr. Mark was telling me about your gym. He said you've done a lot to get kids off the streets, off drugs, and out of gangs. Even more than all those government programs combined. That's what Dr. Mark told me."

The patient had obviously been listening intently to all that had been said. He finally spoke. "I ... don't know ... who my ... real father is," the patient said between his puffing breaths. He struggled to explain that if he ever did find his real father, he hoped the man would be "just like Mose." Adrian noted unshed tears in the corners of Mose's eyes. He felt some forming in his own too.

Adrian cleared his throat, dabbed his eyes on his white coat sleeve, then spoke to the patient. "Son, please don't waste your breath trying to talk to us now. We're going to give you some pain medicine in your IV, and some antibiotics too. We're going to put some wet stuff on your T-shirt that will help kill germs. Soon as we get some more IV fluid in, and the pain medicine starts working, you'll feel better. We'll talk then. Ask you a lot of questions. OK?"

"OK," the patient nodded.

Adrian rechecked his vital signs, which were passable. The rapid breathing had already started slowing, apparently due to the small incremental doses of IV morphine Adrian administered. Adrian had just finished injecting another two milligrams in the patient's IV line when the treatment room door burst opened. Mark and Dr. Zack Paslaski entered, immediately going to the patient's side.

"You've met Zack, my roommate here, haven't you?" Mark asked Adrian.

"Yeah, I think so. A while back," Adrian said. "He's the one I bought one of your DTs spider-test cards from. But what's *he* doing in here now? I though you said you were going to call the general surgery admitting resident."

"I did. Zack is actually a resident in Grady's new Emergency Medicine Program, but he's presently rotating on 4-C. Today, he's serving as their admitting resident, and their crew's on call today," Mark explained. "So let's help Zack get the patient admitted to the hospital, and up to OR."

The wary young patient was still intently watching and listening to all. Somewhere, deep within his morphine-laced brain, the words "admitted to the hospital" apparently struck a very sour note: *"No suh. Ain't no way I can go in no hospital ... not even the Gradies!"* the patient yelled loudly enough for all to hear, but his words had primarily been for Dr. Mark Telfair's ears.

"God Almighty, man!" Mark screamed. "What do you mean! Don't you know you guts are hanging out under that shirt?"

"Sure I know! I ain't as dumb as I look. I tried to put 'em back in myself, but they won't stay in ... jus' kept poppin' back out. I even opened up a whole box of brand new small T-shirts over at the warehouse, to see if a more-tighter shirt would hold 'em in. But it wouldn't, so I walked over here. So please help me get 'em back in. I can't be admitted to no hospital. Can't miss no work!"

The room fell silent. Mose, Mark, Adrian, and Zack stared at one another in utter disbelief. Mark's mind was on fire: *Somehow this young man has gotten disemboweled while working at the department store's warehouse. In an attempt at self-help, he stole a small-sized T-shirt to act as a makeshift girdle. The T-shirt has picked up the "pink rose tie-dye" from the seepage of his own blood and serum while walking some ten blocks to Grady!*

"Mose, please say something to this boy. He's got to be admitted. Period!" Mark shouted, shattering the room's silence.

Mose moved closer to the patient's side. "Son, Doctor Mark here is right. You need to be admitted. Mose wouldn't tell you wrong. Won't you please listen to the doctor?"

"Mose, I'm sorry man. I can't do that. Can't miss no work. Can't lose my job," the patient said, squinting through half-open eyes.

"Roddy Green, you're a hardheaded young man!" Mose said, using the name the patient had given Mose when he first started doing workouts at the gym.

"Mose, I don't mean no disrespect man, but you know what them signs over at the gym say, don't you?"

"Roddy, *I'm* the one that put them signs up over there!" Mose said, mentally recalling the gym's signs: IT TAKES GUTS, NOT DRUGS, TO BE A MAN, and A HEALTHY BODY HEALS ITSELF.

"Mose, you respect what them signs say? What *your* signs say?" Roddy asked, now breathing normally.

"Roddy, I respect what they say, but—"

"Well, you please respect what *I* say Mose," the patient interrupted. "I can't be admitted to no hospital!"

The room fell silent for what seemed an eternity. For the first time since Mark had known Mose, the ER orderly seemed at a total loss for words. Finally some found their way to his lips.

"Roddy, you remember me talkin' to all you boys about niggers and black peoples, and how I say they wasn't the same thing? Unless the black person act wrong ... and make it be the same. You remember that? Remember what I say?" Mose asked in desperation.

"I remember exactly what you said, Mose, and I respects that ... but I guess I jus' gonna have to be a nigger for a little while. *I ain't goin' in no hospital!*"

"You one hardheaded little nigger, Roddy Green!" Mose said with overt anger, as he rapidly left the room, obviously upset, disappointed, and struggling to avoid saying something far worse.

Mark, Adrian, and Zack just stared at one another ... and Roddy Green. The strikeout Mose had with the patient was very discouraging. Zack decided to have a go at the reluctant patient. Time was critical.

"Say, Roddy my man, just how old are you?" Zack casually asked.

"I'm 18, goin' on 19. Why you ask? What's that got to do with my guts?" Roddy asked, his speech slurred from the morphine.

"Well, to tell you the truth Roddy, I was hoping you was a minor, so there'd maybe be some legal way we could make you come into the hospital," Zack said, unaware his words had just sparked an idea in Mark's head.

"You guys keep talking to Roddy," Mark said. "I'm going to talk to Max a minute, and see if he has any ideas." *Legal way,* Mark thought, as he left the treatment room, not only to find Max, but also to be sure Mose was OK after being so sorely disappointed by one of his gym children.

Adrian and Zack kept trying to change Roddy's mind, but made no progress. They tried to explain to Roddy that time was of the essence. Infection was increasing, germs were growing on his exposed gut, and would get worse every second they wasted in talking. In despair, Adrian even resorted to asking Roddy which funeral home he wanted to pick up his body. Roddy stubbornly declined to budge from his position of flatly refusing hospital admission.

Ten minutes later Mark returned to the treatment room. "Sorry to be so long fellas, but I waited while Max talked to a judge he knows about getting us a court order. The judge said only if he was legally a minor, or mentally incompetent, or arrived unconscious, or was not oriented as to time, place, and person ... only under those circumstances would he give us a court order."

"Well," Zack said, "let's fix him up right here in the ER."

"Have you lost your mind, Zack!" Mark fired back.

"Well people was havin' their guts put back in long before ORs even existed ... and they was workin' with a lot less stuff than we've got right here in this ER. You guys ever hear of the Civil War, or do you Southern folk still call it that Period of Unpleasantness?" Zack said.

"Zack," Mark angrily shot back, "we need to talk in the office *NOW!*"

In the confines of the office Mark lit into Zack. "Well you've finally flipped! This is *not* somewhere on a battlefield during the Civil War. This is a goddamn hospital, for Christ's sake! There must be a terrible short circuit in that brilliant brain of yours. You have gone totally bonkers! I know you think this is all funny, but the only 'fun' I see here is your dys*funct*ional thinking!"

"Well, Mr. Mouth of the South, just what do *you* suggest we do?" Zack calmly asked in an insulting way.

"Call the attending," Mark replied, referencing the Emory surgery professor on call for the ER.

"Here, be my guest," Zack said as he abruptly slid the desk phone to a position directly in front of Mark.

A few minutes later Mark was talking to Dr. Ettinger, an Emory Associate Professor of Surgery. Mark gave the professor an initial brief summary regarding Roddy Green's injury and refusal of admission. Zack slouched back in his chair, his eyes closed, intently listening to Mark's side of the remaining conversation.

"Yes sir, that's correct, Dr. Ettinger ... Well, he's been in the ER for over an hour now ... Yeah, and he was probably injured about an hour before that ... Yes sir, he's been getting antibiotics in his IV ... Yes, we've already tried a court order, but the judge declined ... Yes sir ... No sir, we didn't see any wounds to the bowel itself, but the abdominal wall is cut transversely ... It's about two inches above his navel, and about six inches long ... Yes sir, the bowel itself looks pink, has good peristalsis ... No, not dirty with soil, sir, but he's got a lot of excelsior, or some kind of straw-like packing material, stuck all over his bowel surfaces."

Zack could hear only snatches of the professor's voice radiating from the phone receiver. After a long pause on Mark's end, Zack opened his eyes to see his wide-eyed roommate finally reply: "Are you sure, sir? ... Well, OK! ... Yeah, we'll get him to sign ... Thanks. Bye sir." Mark quietly hung up, appearing completely shaken.

"And?" Zack calmly asked.

"And Dr. Ettinger says we have him sign out against medical advice, and—"

"Wow! Ettinger's flipped!" Zack interrupted, obviously disappointed.

"If you'd just allow me to finish ... sign out AMA, *after* we fix it down here *without* admitting him to the hospital," Mark said with a crimson face.

"You get sunburned or something? Your face is red," Zack replied.

"Kiss my grits, you Polack!" Mark smiled, while patting his own butt.

"Well at least I now know where you Southern Bubbas stash your grits!" Zack shot back.

"Sorry I blew up," Mark said as they both left the office smiling.

Mark and Zack returned to the treatment room. Mark explained to Adrian and the patient what Dr. Ettinger had said. In essence, the professor had said it may take days to get a court order to admit a mentally competent patient against his will, especially one that was at age majority, therefore legally an adult. Getting the patient's gut cleaned off and quickly back inside was far more important than dealing with the slow legal process. Time was especially important since the delay of two hours had already allowed significant bacterial growth to occur on the surfaces of the exposed bowel. After delivering Dr. Ettinger's message, Mark couldn't help but think: *Sometimes it may be better to quickly do the right thing under the wrong conditions ... as opposed to doing the right thing far too late under more ideal conditions.*

In the ER Mark and Zack quickly changed into scrub clothes, put on masks, then did a brief surgical scrub. They donned surgical gowns which had been quickly brought down from OR, then slipped on sterile gloves.

An extra RN and student nurse were brought in to assist with the attempt to make the ER procedure "somewhat sterile," and more like an OR procedure. The student nurse promptly fainted. Despite the diversion of reviving the SN, Mark and Zack put Roddy Green back together again in about 45 minutes. It wouldn't have even taken that long, but picking and washing off all the packing excelsior had been time consuming. There had been no injury to the bowel itself; only the abdominal wall had been cleanly cut. *Like a surgical incision,* Mark thought.

During the procedure, Adrian had been forced to play anesthesiologist. The gruff Chief Anesthesia Resident they'd consulted had emphatically stated: "I just ain't havin' any part in putting an *outpatient* to sleep in the ER!" So Adrian gave muscle relaxants and a larger dose of IV morphine immediately before it was time to stuff Roddy's cleaned-off guts back where they belonged. Roddy was awake enough that he and Adrian were able to chat through most of the procedure. Roddy never once complained of pain.

Finally, Zack and Mark returned to the office; Adrian remained with the patient and arranged Roddy's outpatient follow-up care. Roddy readily agreed to come back to the ER several times a day for pain medication, antibiotics, and possibly IV fluids if needed. In addition to the standard AMA disclaimer, Roddy eagerly signed an after-the-fact surgical consent form.

With Roddy squared away, Adrian did a repeat neuro check on the student nurse who had fainted earlier, then started putting a few stitches in the small scalp laceration she'd sustained when she hit the terrazzo floor. "I think I should probably be a medical nurse, don't you, Dr. Brevard?" she asked. "Definitely," Adrian replied while stitching her up. He didn't know why, but the cute student nurse had been the first woman he'd felt any attraction for in the last three years. He was encouraged, feeling he might someday fully accept his wife's death.

In the office, Zack spoke excitedly to Mark. "Well, my man, you've just seen the wave of the future!"

"Wave of the future?" Mark asked, seeking explanation.

"Yeah, you know ... what's coming down the pike. In 20 years outpatient surgery like we just did will be commonplace, or that's what Dr. Ettinger thinks. You know he's primarily responsible for developing the new Emergency Medicine Program at Grady?"

"No, I didn't know that, Zack. Maybe that's why he allowed us to do what we just did to Roddy Green as an outpatient. But I'm not sure I agree. I can see doing some elective surgical procedures under local anesthesia on an outpatient ... like maybe hernia repairs, or something simple," Mark replied. "But putting somebody's contaminated guts back in their belly is a whole different ballgame."

Zack grinned as he spoke. "Well let me tell you what Ettinger told me when I agreed to be his guinea pig for his Emergency Medicine Program. He even envisions souped-up ERs that he'd call 'Trauma Centers.' He thinks we could do a bunch more than we now do in today's major ERs. Many patients wouldn't have to actually be admitted to the hospital to do certain emergency operations, or selected elective operations. He also says he thinks we're gonna see Urgent Care Centers—UCCs he calls 'em. Sort of a doc-in-a-box-thing, where patients can get quick care for relatively minor emergencies—like small cuts, nosebleeds, migraine headaches, and stuff like that. The UCCs would deal with the insignificant emergencies that clog up today's ERs, which were originally intended to deal only with the true major emergencies."

"I don't know, Zack. I agree some patients are different, some tougher than we think. Maybe those patients could be treated mostly as out-patients."

"You guys from the South are different," Zack replied with a phil-osophical stare.

"Southerners different? How so? What do you mean?" Mark ques-tioned.

"Well some of the dimwitted bubbas I've met down here spell worse than they talk, and others talk like pussies. But it's mainly that a lot of you guys are a whole lot more rugged than you actually look—or talk! I'm even surprised you guys lost the Civil War. Most of you guys just seem tougher than the folks we got up near Harlem. Heck, even your niggers down here are a whole lot tougher than our Harlem niggers!"

"Zack! I wish you wouldn't use that word—it offends me! And a lot of other folks too," Mark said.

"Well I know you don't like my four-letter words. You hear me say any today? Did you? I been working real hard on that, but I still occasionally mess up. And now you tell me a seven-letter word offends you ... but I bet your family had some Negroes that worked for them here in Atlanta. Right?"

"Zack, it's none of your business who worked for my family. But I don't mind telling you, we did have some blacks that worked for us. We respected them; they respected us. Pure and simple. We improved the quality of their lives; they improved the quality of ours. When a member of our family got sick or died, they grieved and helped out. When a member of theirs got sick or died, we grieved and helped out. It's something you Yankee Polacks will never understand!"

Mark and Zack's escalating North-South discussion got sidetracked, as Mose entered the office with a broad smile on his face, then excitedly spoke: "Doctors, let me tell you! That Roddy Green ... he's one tough little nigger, ain't he?"

Zack laughed so hard he almost wet his pants. Mark indeed did. Mose, who failed to see what was so funny, promptly left shaking his bald head, muttering to himself.

But Roddy was indeed a tough little guy. For two weeks, he came back to the ER every day to be checked. He did require some IV fluids during the first two days. He received injectable antibiotics for a week, yet declined all pain medications. Surprisingly, no infection developed. In fact, he never missed a full day's work. In a "supervisory capacity," Roddy had immediately returned to the warehouse to be sure the other workers were doing their jobs. The coworker that had cut his belly had fled after the incident. Roddy didn't even miss a single night at Mose's gym. Mose later said Roddy was a "little upset" about just walking around the gym, and not being allowed to lift weights for a full six weeks following his ER surgery.

The week following Roddy's injury, Mose learned that a black coworker at the warehouse had inflicted the wound. It had been done with a hawk-billed knife—the type used to open shipping boxes. Roddy had apparently gotten into a fight defending his best friend's honor. That friend was Mose. It seems the fight erupted shortly after Roddy's coworker made a statement: "Mose ain't nothin' but an old honkey-lovin' Uncle Tom fag-nigger, who tries to get them sweet little young boys to come to his gym."

About a month after the incident at the warehouse, Mose came to work one morning beaming. He had received a check for 10,000 dollars, a donation to his gym to be used to replace the gym's ancient leaky roof. The check was enclosed in a letter from the owner of Rich's Department Store. The letter indicated the employee who assaulted Roddy had been fired, apprehended by APD, and jailed. Roddy Green would be promoted to Assistant Warehouse Inventory Manager, the first black to hold that position. *Times are indeed changing,* Mark Telfair thought, as he recalled Martin Luther King's getting jailed for participating in a 1960 student sit-in ... at the Atlanta Rich's Department Store!

21

UNDER HOUSE ARREST

"Well you almost got me convinced the South is better than the North," Zack said to Mark. The two were having a full-blown Grady bull session in their room. They were already an hour into it.

"You'll have to make up your own mind, Zack. I know if I had to live the rest of my life in Harlem or Atlanta, I'd certainly choose Atlanta."

"The longer I stay here the better I like it," Zack admitted. "I've been here three years and, what? Eight months? No, make that three years and *ten* months, since it's now April, 1968."

"Well I've lived here all my life," Mark said. "Almost 30 years. But Atlanta's not the same anymore. Still a good city, but just not the same Atlanta I grew up in."

"What's changed, Mark?"

"Well for one thing, a lot more people are living here. Over a million now, I think. Traffic has gotten horrible. Heck, I can remember when I was a teenager, it'd only take 15 minutes to drive from Buckhead to Five Points using Peachtree Road. Today that same trip would take over an hour if it's anywhere near rush hour."

"You guys down here don't know much about mass transportation ... I mean like subways, trains, and buses," Zack said, responding to Mark's complaint about Atlanta's traffic.

"I agree, Zack. It's a shame the MARTA system and the I-285 perimeter highway are about 20 years behind the population. I guess I can put up with the traffic jams, but there are other changes in Atlanta that I don't like. They worry me even more."

"Like what?"

"Well, like the crime rate. Just look at what we see here at Grady. Over 200 gunshot wounds a month come through our ER alone. Granted, some of them aren't serious and don't have to be admitted. But when you and I started out, we didn't see that many GSWs, did we? Mostly stabbing, wasn't it?"

Zack scratched his chin, then rubbed his head pensively. "Well, yeah. It was mostly stab wounds—or joogin'—as the Rooters say. Why do you think shootin' is now a lot more common than joogin'?"

"Don't know, Zack. But a while back I read in the *Atlanta Journal* that about 80 percent of Medicaid checks are cashed in liquor stores. Medicaid started here in '65, I think. So cash equals money to buy booze ... and guns. That's why I think Atlanta now has the dubious distinction of being the homicide capital of the United States."

"Well, if I could be in charge of Medicaid, or whatever the welfare thing is called, I could fix a few things," Zack said, seemingly serious.

Mark simply couldn't imagine Zack being in charge of Medicaid, or any type of welfare system, but out of courtesy to his bull session partner, he responded with a question. "Just exactly what would you do, Zack ... to fix the system?"

"Well first thing, I'd want to see that all the poor people got good nutrition. I'd go to Ralston Purina, or whatever the checkerboard animal food company is and say, 'Hey! I want you guys to formulate a good *People-Chow'* ... one that has all known nutritional requirements for humans. I'd have 'em supply it in 50-pound bags. All you gotta do is add water."

"Get serious, Zack! You really don't think people are going to eat *dog food* do you?"

"Hell no! It'd be *people food.* They'll eat it if they get hungry enough, and be glad to have it ... and it'd be better for ya than some of that fast-food shit we eat! But first, ya see, you don't give them the *money* ... that's the point. You simply give 'em the food instead. Then second—for housing, clothes, and medical care—you give them a list of vendors that are willin' to supply basic needs. Nothin' fancy, just basic. The vendors would bill the welfare program directly. So they'd have their basic needs filled, but still they ain't got no money to buy booze, bullets, drugs, and guns."

"Zack, just how long have you been thinking about this?"

"Several minutes I guess. Just since we been talkin' about what's right and wrong with Atlanta."

Even though Mark didn't feel Zack's welfare plan would work in the real world, he couldn't help but be amazed at the way solutions to fairly complex problems just seemed to rapidly find their way into Zack's head. Other problems, such as a cue ball stuck in a patient's mouth, or a light bulb up a guy's butt, were no real challenge for Zack; such trivial problems were solved at the speed of light.

"Zack, some guns are going to get into the wrong hands anyway. Even if your no-cash-to-spend welfare system works. How would you deal with that?"

"First, you're right. Some welfare people are going to get guns anyways. And drugs, too. But that's another issue. But as far as guns go, I think I've got a solution to that problem, too."

"Like what?"

"Well first, everybody on welfare—and of legal age—would have a gun issued to them *by* the welfare system ... along with a permit to carry."

"What would that accomplish?" Mark asked, having serious doubts.

"The welfare system could require that they own a *real gun*, like that .357 Max the ER cop carries. Just *give* a .357 to them ... *after* they've attended a police academy course in marksmanship. Don't give 'em a gun and permit till they know how to shoot."

"Sounds to me like you're arming the poor, Zack."

"Absolutely right. They're armed anyways, with popguns, and Saturday-night specials. Cheap guns. They can't shoot worth a shit. They're just not effective at killing one another. But they are expert at *maiming* one another ... and that's what causes the injured a bunch of suffering, and the taxpayers a bunch of expense."

"I don't know, Zack. I think that could shift the whole balance. You could end up with the welfare folks armed even better than our law enforcement."

"If that happens, you require law enforcement to get better weapons. In the meantime you could even solve some of our military problems in Southeast Asia."

"Military problems?" Mark asked, feeling Zack was way off track.

"Yeah, like Vietnam," Zack said.

"*Vietnam?*" Mark asked, more puzzled than ever by his freethinking roommate.

"Yeah! You know it's sorta like a welfare war over there anyways. We're over there fightin' with one freakin' hand tied behind our back. We're fightin' with the bare essentials. Our own government won't even let us use some small nukes!"

"So?"

"So we send a bunch of the welfare people over there ... the folks who have .357s and know how to shoot 'em."

"And?" Mark prompted, no longer taking Zack seriously.

"And then we identify a problem area in the 'Nam conflict. Next we get a bunch of them big-ass Huey helicopters and we fill 'em with .357-qualified welfare troops. Do it on a Saturday night ... right after they've chugged a fifth of Army-issue Wild Turkey. Give 'em a handful of extra bullets for the .357's, then parachute 'em out of the Huey choppers right over the hot spot. I bet they'd kill themselves, and everything else in the hot spot ... maybe even before they hit the ground. Man, they'd be sorta like a living A-bomb! Know what I mean?"

"You're something else, Zack," Mark replied laughing, but knew their bull session had now degenerated into a full-blown fantasy session.

Looking out their 14th-floor window, Mark saw dusk rapidly approaching. Atlanta's lights were beginning to bloom. His stomach growled, and he was contemplating his evening meal in the cafeteria. Then the phone rang.

"Paslaski here," Zack answered. Listening to the caller, his face became increasingly somber. "No shit! When? Where?" Zack listened another moment or so, then said "Thanks for lettin' us know, but I really ain't one of his fans." Zack hung up, and blankly stared out the window as darkness fell on the fourth day of April, 1968.

"Well?" Mark asked, fearing it must be bad news about someone Zack knew.

"Well, I hate to tell you this, but some fucker just shot and *killed* Martin Luther King!"

"You're kidding me, Zack! Martin Luther King, Junior?"

"Yeah, at some motel in Memphis, Tennessee. The Lorraine Motel, the operator said. She also said that none of the hospital staff can leave the hospital until further notice. And there's going to be a meeting of the entire hospital staff in the auditorium this evening. They'll announce the time later, she said."

Mark's mind was in overdrive. He really hadn't given Martin Luther King, Jr. much thought lately. He knew that King was Atlanta-based, and seemed instrumental in keeping integration in Atlanta nonviolent. Mark searched his brain for what he knew about the man. He remembered King getting arrested during a 1960 sit-in at Rich's. Shortly before he came to Grady for internship, Mark recalled seeing King's face on the cover of *Time Magazine*, as Man of the Year. Then there was something about King's winning the Nobel Peace Prize. Reruns of his *I Have a Dream* speech still occasionally aired in Atlanta; he'd seen portions of King's *I've Been to the Mountaintop* speech on Atlanta TV last night. That was the extent of his limited knowledge regarding the fallen civil-rights leader.

"Zack, you mean even the doctors can't leave?"

"You got wax in your ears, like old Professor Cromwell? *Nobody leaves till further notice,* the operator said."

"No, I don't have a problem with earwax. I'd just planned to spend the night with Anne at her apartment. Her roommate is out of town, and that's really the only private time we get at her place."

"Well just take a cold shower, and cool your tool, buddy ... before the auditorium meeting."

"If you had a girlfriend like Anne, you'd be a little more sympathetic, Zack."

"Well anyways, I saw Anne in the OR earlier today. She was working the seven-to-three shift, and they're running way over with a bad GSW. I bet she's still in the building and can't leave either."

Mark was beginning to realize how serious the situation could be. There may be riots in Atlanta. He'd previously considered riots something that only happened in *other* cities—Northern cities—and just couldn't happen in Atlanta. Dr. Mark Telfair was now worried about his hometown, sorry he'd just spouted-off about its decline, sorry that some crackpot killed MLK.

"Hey Mark, I'm really sorry the guy got killed, OK? Harlem just let Atlanta down, that's all."

"Harlem did what?" Mark asked, still in a daze.

"Let you guys in Atlanta down," Zack answered.

"I don't follow you, Zack. Explain."

"Well, NYC didn't let you down, though—they got old Malcolm X. But in '58, when I was in college, your Martin Luther was nearly killed in Harlem, stabbed during a speakin' tour there. Then in '64 he was stoned by a buncha Black Muslims in Harlem, but he survived. I know that musta busted his pride. So Harlem tried, but failed. And now, you guys down here in this nice City of Atlanta are goin' to get the fallout from what some asshole in Tennessee did."

"Did the operator say if the shooter was black or white?"

"Nah, only that King was shot dead!"

"Well if it had to happen, I hope the shooter's black." *Otherwise it's going to be hell to pay in Atlanta. My Atlanta,* a now very concerned Mark Telfair thought.

Mark's thoughts were interrupted by the muted sound of the PA system in the hallway. He opened their room's thick door to better hear the PA's calmly spoken announcement:

"Attention: All visitors will now leave the hospital immediately. All physicians and nursing staff not directly involved in a patient's care at this time shall report to the hospital auditorium immediately. All interior security officers, maintenance personnel, laboratory personnel, and X-ray personnel are to report to the hospital auditorium immediately. I repeat, all visitors ..."

Mark and Zack debated on whether to use the stairs or the elevators.

Since it was the peak of normal visiting hours, they elected to use the stairs, figuring the elevators would be jammed full. They talked as they began walking down 14 flights of stairs.

"What you think this meeting is all about, Zack?"

"I think they're expecting some real bad stuff to go down."

"Like what? Riots? Fires?" Mark asked.

"Living in Harlem you soon learn there's always a riot waitin' to happen. Seems folks are just lookin' for any excuse they can find to riot, loot, and burn. I been through a lot of riots up there. I just hope Atlanta's ready, Mark."

"Me, too. But the worst Atlanta disaster I can remember was a big hotel fire downtown when I was a kid about eight years old—the Winecoff Hotel fire. Dad said it was 'Atlanta's *Titanic*.' More than 100 people died. Pop told me people were even jumping out windows, and Atlanta's hospitals were totally swamped with burn and smoke-inhalation patients."

The pair went down the last six flights more slowly. Apparently most of the house staff had chosen stairs over elevators, and the closer they got to ground level the heavier the stairwell traffic got. *Like cattle in a chute,* Mark thought. When they finally entered the ground-floor auditorium, a sea of white clothing greeted them. Skin colors varied from pale white to dark black. This "sea" of white clothing was punctuated with widely scattered other colors: dark blue uniforms of the cops; gray for the maintenance folks; tan for the security guards; green for those who'd come in scrubs. Mark wondered: *Who's looking after the patients?*

The piercing squeal of the microphone's feedback silenced the large room's chattering audience. Dressed in a three-piece business suit, a balding middle-aged portly man stood before them. He adjusted an amplifier adjacent to the podium, and the PA's penetrating squeal ceased. Most of those present did not recognize Mr. Ben Borgman. He was Chairman of the Fulton-DeKalb Hospital Authority, essentially making him the CEO of Grady Hospital. Borgman calmly adjusted the mike for his short stature, and cleared his throat before speaking.

"Can everyone hear me OK?" The crowd replied "yes" in unison.

As Borgman introduced himself, Max Bollinger, the ER cop, moved to Borgman's right side; Mr. George Timkin, the Senior Hospital Administrator, moved to Borgman's left. With only a single microphone present, Mark felt each of the three men would probably speak in turn.

Borgman began: "First, I want to thank all you fine people for coming to this meeting on such short notice. Second, I want everyone to remain calm. To avoid panic among patients and visitors, the exact reason for this meeting was intentionally not given over the PA system. The operators made many phone calls to those of you that were in-house, and they explained the reason for this meeting. But for those among you who don't already know, I regret I must tell you Martin Luther King, Jr. has been assassinated in Memphis, Tennessee. It happened about two hours ago."

The response to Borgman's statement indicated many did not already know. Many, especially the black staff, were having difficulty containing their emotions. Borgman allowed an appropriate interval for his somber message to sink in.

After the initial shock subsided, Borgman continued: "I know this is terrible news for nonviolent social change. Bad news for the entire United States, and terrible news for Atlanta, Dr. King's home base. The Hospital Authority fully recognizes the gravity of this tragedy, and we've already had an emergency meeting. The Hospital Authority also feels that Grady—and other Atlanta hospitals—will face a potential civil emergency of unprecedented proportions. I do want to emphasize *potential emergency.* I'm sure you staff members might have some questions, but I'd appreciate it if you'd allow these other two gentlemen to speak before I answer any remaining questions."

Borgman introduced Senior Hospital Administrator George Timkin. His words simply mirrored what Borgman had already said. Zack was sitting next to Mark. Zack whispered, "That Timkin fella ain't sayin' jackshit, nothin' new. He should just shut up and let Max talk."

"Agreed," Mark whispered back.

Fortunately, Timkin wasn't long-winded. Authority Chairman Borgman stepped back to the mike after Timkin finished. "I now want to introduce a gentleman who is relatively new here at Grady. It is my pleasure to introduce Lieutenant Max Bollinger from the Atlanta Police Department. He was assigned to the Grady Surgical Emergency Room in July of 1965, and continues to work in the Surgical ER when on regular duty. Because Lieutenant Bollinger has expertise in certain areas— specifically with civil crisis—he has been designated as APD's Watch Commander here at Grady. He will be in constant communication with other APD units throughout Atlanta. Grady's regular security guards will be under the direction of Lieutenant Bollinger. So will the entire hospital staff. Please listen carefully to what Lieutenant Bollinger has to say."

"Lieutenant?" Mark whispered to Zack. *I've never asked Max about his rank. Max doesn't wear any rank on his uniform. He doesn't give a hoot about rank,* Mark thought.

Zack whispered back, "Up where I come from, the lieutenants are Watch Commanders full time. How'd we rate a lieutenant as an ER cop?"

Mark started to whisper something back, but didn't because Max was about to speak. It took Max a moment to adjust the mike to his own height; he was a foot taller than Borgman. Max still kept his head shaved and wore no rank, yet still projected a confident image in his spiffy APD uniform. Satisfied with the mike's position, Max began speaking:

"I know everyone here is wondering if we are overreacting to the possibility of civil unrest here in Atlanta. Please remain calm. We do not have any civil unrest in Atlanta, as of ten minutes ago," Max said, checking his watch. He next removed a neatly folded white paper from his uniform's breast pocket. After he unfolded it, he continued:

"So that we are all clear on our duties and responsibilities, and to give everyone here the rules we must follow, please listen closely.

"Number one: A Command Center has been established on the 15th floor of this building. We have set up radio communication capability with all APD units, all state police units, and all Grady security folks as well. We also have the capability of speaking directly with the Governor, the Georgia National Guard, and federal troops as needed. I will be at the 15th-floor Command Center at all times, and I'll will remain there as long as necessary. House staff may communicate with the Command Center by dialing the hospital operator; just ask her to connect you to Command Center. As we speak, hospital maintenance is making multiple phone lines available at the center. So please call if you even *think* a problem is developing. To avoid panic, the hospital's PA system will be used as little as possible by Command Center. Command will give the 'all clear' over the PA using a code-statement. When the hospital's PA announces *Doctor Red, return to X-ray,* you'll know the threat has passed."

As murmurs rippled through the crowd, Zack leaned to whisper to Mark. "He's talkin' some serious shit here." Mark was too stunned to reply. *Here goes Atlanta ... down the tubes,* he thought.

Max continued: "And number two, is our mission statement. Our primary mission is to provide emergency medical care in the event of mass casualties caused by civil unrest, should that occur. I do emphasize, *should that occur.* But for Grady to remain effective as a potential mass-casualty unit, we must fully protect occupants of this building—its patients, doctors, nurses, and other personnel. At the same time, we must protect the integrity of this very building itself, and its functional capability of providing the equipment needed for treatment of those who may be injured during civil unrest. To protect the integrity of the building, only a single rear service entrance, and the ER entrance, will remain open. Those two entryways will be secured by heavily armed guards from APD's SWAT team. All other entrances will be locked and under surveillance by armed guards. To retain our full functional capabilities, each and every one of you in this room could be essential. That is why I must tell you ... *no one is to leave this building.*"

Murmurs around the room gradually grew into full-blown raucous conversations, making the auditorium sound like a convention of Ginsu Knife salesmen all talking at once. Max waited about half a minute, and when it became apparent the staff members were not going to settle down on their own, he blew a traffic cop's whistle directly into the mike. The startled crowd fell silent.

"OK, ladies and gentlemen—listen up! Let me tell you like it is. The Governor of this state has ordered the Hospital Authority to require that all on-site personnel remain on site until ordered otherwise. The Governor has further ordered that all off-site personnel be returned to Grady. As we speak, APD is rounding up off-site folks and escorting them back to this hospital. Any questions thus far?"

A number of hands went up. Max pointed to the raised hands and fielded the questions. A medical resident in the crowd asked the first question: "I'm off call and supposed to start my vacation tomorrow. I've made plans ... even bought plane tickets. Surely this doesn't apply to me!"

"Sir, you are on site and a member of Grady's staff. After this meeting, I'll put you in touch with the governor's office. If the Governor says you can leave, you may leave, sir," Max said without emotion.

Mark noted many of the raised hands were now being slowly lowered. Only a nurse, Zack, and a few others still had their hands up. Max pointed to the nurse.

"What if we have a family emergency?" the nurse asked. "Could we leave then?"

Max quickly answered her. "If such a family emergency arises, contact the Command Center. They will relay the nature of the emergency to the governor's office. Command Center has already been given a list of emergencies that would possibly permit some of you folks to leave before we make the PA announcement, *Doctor Red, return to X-ray.* Final permission to leave, however, must come directly from the governor's office."

Max answered several other questions before he finally got to Zack, who'd changed the arm he'd raised after waiting so long. Max finally pointed. "Dr. Paslaski, if I remember your name correctly from the Surgical ER—what is your question, sir?"

Zack stood to ask his question. "Are we, uh ... like under house arrest here?"

"Doctor, I'm not a lawyer, but I do know the laws of the State of Georgia grant the Governor certain emergency powers, and I presume the

Governor is exercising his authority within the framework of the very laws he has sworn to uphold."

"Just wanted to be sure I don't have no arrest record!" Zack excitedly replied. The room burst out in laughter. "Hey everybody," Zack yelled loudly, in his arrogant accent, "let's just pretend we're living down on the coast ... and have one heck of a *hurricane party!*" The crowd again laughed and started clapping, releasing tension. Max was smiling too, as he got his whistle out to again silence the meeting room.

"Dr. Paslaski, that's the spirit I want to see in this group! But I'm in charge of this meeting ... so stand down, sir. We've got several other points to cover, and I don't want to spend all night doing it." A large round of applause erupted. It was difficult to tell for whom: Zack or Max? Max again reached for his whistle. He didn't have to blow it; the applause immediately stopped.

"OK guys," Max said with less formality, "the third area I want to cover concerns several miscellaneous items." Max rechecked his list. "The cafeteria is prepared to work around the clock, as are laundry and housekeeping. At the state's expense, any ladies' personal items needed will be procured by the female APD officers in the Command Center. Just call and ask for a female Command Center officer, and tell her what you need ... you know what size, how many et cetera," Max said, then immediately turned crimson as he reflected upon his own words. Boisterous laughter erupted. Max used his whistle this time!

Still flushed and smiling, but well composed, Max resumed his speech: "I apologize to you ladies for my choice of words. I do not wish to embarrass you. Nor do I wish to frighten you. I'm now talking to all of you ... not just the women. Any one of us could become a hostage. Very unlikely, but if that should happen, it could threaten our entire mission, not to mention your life. Again, a hostage situation with civil unrest is very unlikely. The best approach is prevention. So the rule is this: Never work alone in the presence of strangers. APD and Grady Security will do their best to be sure no strangers, other than bona fide patients, enter this building. Time is also of the essence. So if there is a possible hostage situation, call the Command Center immediately."

Max briefly consulted his notes again before resuming. "As a possibly redundant precaution, each shift's department head is going to be instructed in the use of a new electronic device, one that only recently became available to APD. It's called a stun-gun, or Taser. Basically it's a small hand-held device that shoots a pair of electrodes up to 15 feet. It does not kill. It delivers an electric charge, called Taser waves, or T-waves, and I'm sure you doctors know more about T-waves than I do. All I know is they cause a person to fall to the ground ... totally unable to perform any coordinated action for quite a while. Each hospital department will be issued one Taser. The person in charge of the current departmental shift will be called up to the Command Center. There, department heads will receive instruction regarding the Taser's use; they, in turn, will pass instruction to their own staff and to the next shift's department head."

Max again rechecked his notes, then spoke. "And one final thing. Everyone in this room is an adult in the eyes of the law. There are plenty of beds, bathrooms, and showers here. Administration has agreed to relax the hospital's normal sleeping and living arrangement rules during this potential crisis ... they simply ask that you be discreet," Max said, blushing again. "And these relaxed rules apply *only* until you hear the all clear code on the PA. Administration has also said that all off-duty house staff may use the 16th floor—the floor above Command Center—as a lounge area during this period. If there are no additional questions, meeting adjourned."

There were no further questions. Hospital Administrator Timkin, Authority Chairman Borgman, and especially Lieutenant Max Bollinger received a standing ovation from a now fully supportive house staff.

As the staff rapidly exited the auditorium, and despite the solemn news about MLK, everyone appeared in improved spirits and resigned to their house arrest. Mark looked around, hoping to spot Anne. He did not see her anywhere.

Mark turned to Zack and spoke. "I think APD had a very special reason for sending Max to Grady, one even more special than simply replacing an inadequate ER cop."

"Could be," Zack said. "I think admin and APD have been expecting that King fella would get nailed, sooner or later. And planned for it. And since he's Atlanta-based, they've anticipated the reaction here would the worst. Bet you five bucks Atlanta has one helluva riot!"

Mark paused in thought a moment before speaking. "Zack, I thought you told me you don't gamble. Awhile back, remember?"

"Hey Man, it ain't no gamble. It's a sure thing," Zack immediately replied.

"Well I'll just up the ante. In fact, I'll make that ten. Ten bucks that we *don't* have a riot here!" Mark said trying to appear totally confident. In reality, Mark knew Zack was almost certainly right. But just for once, he'd love to win a bet ... and see Zack dead wrong about something. Anything!

"OK, you're on for ten bucks ... sucker!" Zack said, accepting Mark's wager with a handshake and a confident grin Mark found absolutely alarming.

Mark and Zack made their way to the cafeteria to eat supper. Mark could already see the effect of the potential crisis. The cafeteria was filled almost to capacity. Though Grady Hospital had been desegregated for quite some time, the more common spontaneous natural seating patterns—nurses with nurses, doctors with doctors, black with black, white with white—seemed to have suddenly vanished. In terms of both color and profession, each table now had mixed groups ... all actively talking to one another, all discussing exactly the same thing. *Crisis binds,* Mark thought.

A couple of hours after the auditorium meeting, the house staff had almost finished creating its own "command center." Actually, it was a "Party Center," or PC, as it was quickly dubbed. The PC was set up on the 16th floor, one floor above the official APD Command Center that Max had mentioned during the meeting. Grady's 16th floor was rarely used. The architects, in their wisdom, had apparently designed the floor for receptions, celebrations, and parties. It had a central enclosed area with hardwood floors about the size of a basketball court. An abundance of folding chairs and tables made it a meeting room; removing chairs and tables made it a dance floor. The wooden-floored space was completely enclosed by glass walls. Just outside the glass there was an open perimeter colonnade that permitted an excellent view of Atlanta's skyline and many of its major streets. Mark knew nurses sometimes brought wheelchair-bound patients to the 16th-floor colonnade for fresh air, and a change of scenery. But for now, the area was being totally commandeered by Grady's captive house staff.

At 10:30 p.m. Mark and Zack arrived at the PC. The sound of mellow slow dance music already filled the air. More subdued background sounds from multiple radio and TV newscasts competed with, but did not overpower, the soothing music.

"Been up here before?" Zack asked.

"Only a couple of times," Mark replied. "Guess we don't have enough spare time to explore the entire hospital, but I'm glad admin has no objection to us being up here now. At least they should make some concession for our being under house arrest."

Since the last time Mark had been on 16, there had been a miraculous transformation. All of it was being quickly improvised by house staff, who'd been working on it for a couple of hours. Card tables were now in one corner of the enclosed area. Another corner had been designated as the "dance floor." Several resident physicians—those who could afford the luxury—had brought their TV sets and stereo systems to the PC.

Numerous transistor radios were scattered throughout. One resident physician, an amateur radio operator, had even brought a police scanner radio from his 14th-floor room. They would have all the amenities during their period of incarceration, save one ... no booze. But that didn't matter to the great majority there, and for the others there were well known ways of "borrowing" ample quantities of 200-proof grain alcohol from the in-house pharmacy.

Midnight was approaching, and Mark had growing concerns regarding the whereabouts of Anne. Amidst the crush of off-duty personnel in the PC, Mark finally spotted her.

"Honey, where have you been?" Mark asked, as he gave her a tight hug. "I've been worried silly about you. No answer at your apartment. They wouldn't let me use the PA to page you. I even called the OR and they said you weren't there."

"Well, I don't know who you talked to in the OR, but they obviously didn't look hard enough! I was there, in scrub. Way back in room 14. And we ran over my shift. *Way* over. We just finished a laparotomy on a GSW about 15 minutes ago. A real mess. Colon, liver, aorta, cava, and left kidney. Twelve-hour procedure, but we think the patient's going to be OK."

Mark and Anne finally broke their embrace because others were beginning to stare at them. "So, Anne, I guess you missed the meeting in the auditorium with Max Bollinger?"

"Yes I did. But I've been pretty much filled in by the Grady grapevine. So why don't we go watch the news on one of these TVs, and see what's going on now."

Holding hands and walking toward one of the TVs, they passed Mark's "non-gambling" roommate. Zach had strayed to one of the card tables, and was fully engrossed in the cards he held. Mark and Anne didn't even speak to Zack as they passed him on their way to folding chairs in front of one of the TV sets. Coverage was live, and almost continuous. Riots were occurring in 125 US cities. Federal troops had already been called into Washington, Baltimore, and Chicago. Some 15,000 rioters had already been arrested in those cities. An Atlanta Channel 5 TV reporter concluded: "Locally we have nothing to report. Hopefully, Atlanta will set an example regarding nonviolence. That's what Martin Luther King, Jr. was all about. Stay tuned." A commercial for Maxwell House Coffee quickly filled the TV screen.

"I've had about enough of this already," Anne said. "I'm really beat, honey."

"Me too," Mark said. "Let me go tell Zack we're leaving. He's still playing cards."

Mark found Zack, and whispered in his ear: "I'm goin' to call it a night. If you don't have any problem with it, I'm going to let Anne sleep in your bed. OK?"

Zack looked up from a winning poker hand. "Yeah, OK." Two seconds later Zack motioned that Mark should come closer. Zack whispered in Mark's ear, "On second thought, why don't you both sleep in *your* bed. I don't want her perfume or your pecker tracks in *mine!*"

"You're gross Zack! But knock before entering ... OK?"

"Sure thing, Mark. Hey full house you guys, aces over kings!" Zack said as he raked in the pot of chips, and added them to the large neat piles stacked before him. *Zack's rules don't last very long. He doesn't always color within the lines ... even if he drew the lines,* Mark thought.

Anne and Mark left the PC using the stairs. They entered the 14th-floor room Mark shared with Zack. Anne had never been there before—strictly off limits by normal hospital policy. Upon viewing her surroundings she said, "Pretty Spartan in here, but I could care less. I'm sorry our planned evening in my apartment was spoiled ... and even more sorry we've lost a great leader for nonviolence."

They both got undressed, used scrub shirts as pajamas, then quickly got into Mark's narrow bed. Due to the limited space, they reclined on their sides.

"Let's just snuggle and crash ... and remember I love you, Little Man," Anne said, using her favorite pet name for him.

Mark knew she was utterly exhausted from her long day in the OR. "Snuggling's just fine with me too," Mark replied, realizing how emotionally exhausted he was from worrying about the fate of Atlanta ... *his* Atlanta. "We'll get through all this somehow, Anne. I love you too. Good night."

In their reclining posture, Mark tenderly kissed the back of her neck. Only a stopwatch could have determined which of the exhausted pair crashed first.

At 5:00 a.m., both were rudely shaken from deep sleep by a loud banging on the room's door. Mark finally got out of bed. He opened the door, to be greeted by his roommate. Zack had Alisia Petroski, an attractive X-Ray technician, in tow. "Won her in the final poker game!" Zack explained. "Clear the room in five minutes. It's our turn to 'rest' now!"

During the next six days, all off-duty staff could be found either on the 16th floor at the PC, or on the 14th floor in bed alone, or with a partner. By the third day of their house arrest, Mark knew there probably wasn't a single virgin of either sex left at Grady. When hanging on the door knob of any 14th-floor room, lingerie, usually a bra, became their standard "do not disturb sign." It wasn't uncommon to see multiple "do not disturb signs," and even two or three bras hanging from the *same* knob! *Guess Grady has more than one Hot Body, Mark thought.*

When not responding to their hormones, they were at the PC listening to the frightening news being presented by TVs and radios. Over 130 US cities now involved in riot ... some 20,000 now arrested. Tensions heightened as people listened to Ralph Abernathy conduct the April ninth funeral service at Atlanta's Ebenezer Baptist Church. TV described the funeral as an international event, being attended by civil-rights leaders, black entertainers, and athletes. Even four presidential candidates were reported to be present: Robert Kennedy, Eugene McCarthy, Hubert Humphrey, and Richard Nixon. Over 60,000 listened to the service over outside loudspeakers at Ebenezer Baptist Church; TV and radio reporters indicated over 300,000 joined in the funeral procession as King's casket was carried through Atlanta's streets in a mule-drawn farm cart.

Immediately following the graveside service and interment at Atlanta's South View Cemetery, the Party Center's police scanner became very lively. Though many of the scanner's messages were static-filled, garbled, and clipped, Mark heard one very clear APD transmission. It was the familiar voice of Max Bollinger, obviously being strongly transmitted from Grady's 15th floor: "Grady Command Center to all APD units: It's now or never. Repeat, now or never!"

Mark figured "now or never" was probably some code phrase, but whatever it meant, apparently *now* never came. The PC's scanner fell largely silent through the long night. At 6:00 a.m., the resident's police radio in the PC became active again, and repeatedly announced: "All units 10-99 ... repeat that's a 10-99." The voice was again that of Lieutenant Max Bollinger. As the message was being repeated, the resident who owned the scanner explained that it was a "ten code" message which literally translated: "Mission completed. All Units Secure." Some of Atlanta's regular radio and TV reporters seemed a little disappointed that they didn't have a disaster to cover, but appropriately thanked those who had remained nonviolent in honor of slain civil-rights leader, Dr. Martin Luther King, Jr.

An hour after the scanner's 10-99 message, the crisis was officially over for Grady as well. Precisely at 7:00 a.m. on the tenth day of April, 1968, the Grady PA operator's voice proudly—and repeatedly—announced: *"Dr. Red, return to X-ray."* In terms of emergency room visits, the last six days had been the quietest ever in Grady's entire history ... the 14th and 16th floors, however, had been the most frolicsome in anyone's recollection!

Mark and Zack were both at the PC when the long-awaited hospital PA announcement came. "Where's my ten bucks, Zack?" Mark said, then held out his hand to accept the crisp ten-dollar bill Zack would be removing from his wallet stuffed with poker winnings. Though Mark smiled as he accepted Zack's money, he had a single overpowering thought: *God bless Atlanta ... and Dr. Martin Luther King, Jr.*

22

GOING TO THE DOGS

"Can I go up to the lab and see where you guys do your surgical research?" the attractive blond WAC had asked Dr. Mark Telfair while he made his rounds at Atlanta's VA Hospital. Mark would soon wish he'd never offered the Women's Army Corp surgical patient a chance to view the excellent surgical research facility located at the VA.

He even found himself wishing his first rotation as Chief Surgical Resident hadn't taken him away from Grady at all. When the Emory-VA program and the Grady program combined their originally separate surgical residencies into a single larger one, the VA had become an unavoidable part of it, even for the Grady doctors. If only his scheduled VA rotation had been timed a little differently, Mark knew he would not have gotten in the middle of a public relations dilemma involving the VA research lab. Nonetheless, even before he'd officially become Chief Resident, his fate had already been chiseled in stone.

Two months earlier, administration had told him exactly how he'd spend the entire year as Chief: The first four months would all be spent at VA—two months in the VA research lab, followed by two more in clinical surgery there.

The Atlanta Veteran's Administration Hospital was a modern eight-floor structure on Northeast Atlanta's Clairmont Road. It was a mere stone's throw away from Emory University Hospital, where Mark would spend another four months following his VA rotation. His final four months as Chief Resident would take him back one final time to Grady Hospital. Following his final Grady rotation, administrators of the surgical training program would release their iron grip upon his life. His course would then be charted by a totally different master: The United States Air Force.

The 13-mile rush-hour commute between Grady and the VA was getting old. Fortunately, about a week earlier, Anne's roommate had announced she was engaged, and would be moving out to live with her future husband. After Anne's roommate had moved out, Mark gladly accepted Anne's invitation to move into her apartment. Anne's Northeast Atlanta apartment was not only convenient for their relationship, it was also convenient to both VA and Emory Hospitals, each being located only a mile or so away.

Though living with Anne made Mark's life a lot happier, what would soon happen at the VA would make him the most miserable he'd been during his training years, even worse than when he'd been stabbed by the mojo witch during his internship at Grady. Mark's thoughts returned to the recent circumstances leading up to his problems at the VA.

"Nice Dogger ... Nice Dogger, you're doing great, gal!" Mark said, as he reached through the partially open sleeping quarter door. He affectionately scratched the tan and black dog's head between her soft floppy ears. The 35-pound tail-wagging female mongrel obviously adored Mark. Nice Dogger was technically test animal VA-32-C-68. That is, she was the VA's 32nd canine test animal obtained by their surgical research lab during calendar year 1968.

Ten days ago, Mark, and Dr. Morris Schumaker, the lab's internationally known elderly research surgeon, had implanted a new highly experimental cardiac pacemaker inside Nice Dogger's chest. This unique device "read" carbon dioxide levels in her blood, and was supposed to increase her heart rate as her activity increased, and her blood carbon dioxide increased, then slow down artificial pacing when she rested and carbon dioxide levels fell. In that way, it mimicked what would happen naturally in a healthy heart during varying levels of physical activity. If the pacemaker worked in dogs, it would almost surely work in humans. Such a device would improve the quality of life for pacemaker-dependent humans, or at least for the ones who wanted a lifestyle with a wider range of physical activity than present pacemakers allowed.

Going back two more weeks, before the pacemaker surgery, Mark Telfair remembered Nice Dogger had been a guest at the Atlanta Dog Pound. The pound was the source of all their canine experimental animals. Because Nice Dogger wasn't very attractive, no one had been willing to adopt her. The dog pound had had to schedule her for euthanasia on the very day she'd been picked up by the VA courier who'd transported her to the VA lab. Four additional mongrels of similar fate had accompanied Nice Dogger on her ride to the lab that day. When Nice Dogger and her four companions arrived, they had been treated like royalty: They'd been logged in, weighed, bathed, wormed, immunized, fed, and petted. Each had their own spacious quarters for sleeping and eating. The quarters were inside the lab, therefore climate-controlled.

Their diets were scientifically balanced—smelled gourmet, Mark thought—and far better than the food average dog owners fed their prized pets.

One of the lab's doors opened directly onto the expansive eighth-floor roof of the VA Hospital. This permitted access to a number of 100-foot-long concrete-floored dog runs located on the hospital's flat roof. The run floors were always impeccably clean, thanks to a clock-activated automatic wash-down system. Wastewater from the cleaning process entered special drains connecting to the municipal sewer system that served the hospital. Arched green canvas awnings provided adequate shade over the entire length of the chain-link fencing that formed the sides of each run. Each dog was exercised in their run several times daily, in an attempt to bring each animal to optimal canine health, both before and after their experimental surgery.

Inside the lab, Mark petted Nice Dogger's head and ears a few moments longer, then fully opened her sleeping pen door. She bounded out to return the affection by giving Mark's hands a few gentle licks. When she had settled down, Mark placed a special collar around her neck. Only slightly thicker than an ordinary dog collar, it bore a pack of electronic sensors which monitored her heart rate transmitted from the implanted pacemaker's telemetry circuit.

Mark snapped a leash onto the special collar. "Come on girl. Time to walk!" he said, taking Nice Dogger out on the roof to her run. He slowly walked her the first six down-and-back laps. Removing the restraining leash, he then allowed her to choose her own level of activity. She'd elected to run as fast as she could down the 100-foot track and return to Mark to give him a few licks ... then take off again and repeat the process.

After 15 minutes of this rambunctious activity, Mark decided it was time to take her back inside the lab. He removed her collar, and put her back in her quarters. She immediately slurped water, then ate about half of her food.

"Hey, Dr. Schumaker!" Mark yelled, after connecting the dog's recording collar to a computer the size of a small refrigerator. "I think you're going to like this!" Dr. Schumaker removed himself from the low-power microscope he was using to examine an experimental ventricular electrode used in a previous pacing experiment—one that had failed miserably.

"Well, what did she do?" Schumaker asked, referring to Mark's canine charge.

"She ran like a rabbit, after I let her loose from six warm-up laps. The warm-ups are the first four minutes of the telemetry record; the last 15 minutes you see here are her own spontaneous activity, mostly running."

"By God!" Morris exclaimed, looking at the data printout. "This one worked! Must be the platinum in that new electrode. I want you to do the same thing with VA-32-C-68 every day you have left on your lab rotation."

"Glad to, but let's call her Nice Dogger, sir. That's what I've named her, and she responds to that name. I've only got four weeks left before I go to my clinical surgery rotation here at the VA. I'll have to leave her then."

"Think you could steal a little time from your clinical surgery schedule ... to come back up here and check on your Good Dogger now and then?" Schumaker asked.

"Yes sir," Mark replied. "But her name is *Nice* Dogger, sir."

"Whatever ... but I'd be so pleased if you'd come back up to the lab to check on her. That dog's a paper, son! If her variable-rate pacer keeps working, I'll publish it in several scientific journals, and your name will be right next to mine. Though my brain still seems to work fairly well, I know I'm getting old. My hands are shaky now, my eyesight beginning to fail. I couldn't have done it without your help, especially the part where we ablated her heart's own intrinsic nerve supply to induce pacemaker-dependency. And the actual electrode implantation itself? *Impossible,* without your help."

"After my rotation here is done, I'll come back up when I can, sir. But I know you've already figured it out ... I'm just not cut out to be a research surgeon. I do OK with my hands, but my brain and heart just aren't into basic research. I just like to take advantage of what you research folk feed us clinical people."

"Mark ... you don't mind if I'm informal, do you?"

"Well, no sir. Not at all. I mean Mark *is* my name."

Dr. Schumaker smiled warmly in a fatherly way. "Mark, from your second day in this lab I knew you'd never become a research surgeon.You get too attached to the animal patients. But my job here would be totally meaningless without clinically oriented surgeons, such as yourself. What good would it do to have brilliant research discoveries, yet have no one who'll utilize those discoveries in the clinical setting? How good would that be?"

"Not good at all, sir. I agree. It takes both kinds of surgeons," Mark replied. He couldn't help but recall the last true nerd he'd encountered: Dr. Thomas E. Wellington III, the Chief Medical Resident he had met during his Grady internship over four years ago. Simply put, Wellington was a bad nerd; Dr. Schumaker was a great nerd, the type he hoped he himself would be, if so inclined.

The final weeks of Mark's research lab rotation were passing rapidly. Mark assisted Dr. Schumaker with the implantation of a number of experimental insulin pumps and vascular grafts placed in other canine test animals. A little to Mark's surprise, his first canine surgical patient, Nice Dogger, continued to have her heart rate appropriately controlled by the experimental variable-rate pacemaker. Even on Mark's last official day in the lab, well over a month following Nice Dogger's surgery, the pacemaker continued to function flawlessly. During the daily exercise sessions he supervised, her heart rate frequently reached the 150s during exercise, then appropriately returned to the low 60s when she was sleeping or resting in her quarters. *God, I hope her pacemaker keeps on working,* Mark thought on the day he sadly left his canine friend.

Mark had now been out of the VA research lab about a month, but enjoyed checking on his favorite dog when he could. He was also enjoying his clinical surgery rotation—until a female VA patient came under his care. She would prove to be the source of his brief but intense frustration.

She was one Major Debra Tanner, a 29-year-old WAC, with natural blond hair and intense blue eyes. As a member of the Women's Army Corps, she was entitled to treatment at VA, though female patents were a rarity there. Debra Tanner was an insulin-dependent diabetic. She kept her diabetes well controlled by diet and self-administered insulin injections twice daily. Her diabetes had been diagnosed at Fort Stewart only two years earlier. But she was not at the Atlanta VA because of her diabetes; she was at VA because of an invasive cancer of her cervix. The malignancy had been diagnosed at Fort Stewart less than a week before. She had been sent to the Atlanta VA simply because Stewart temporally did not have a surgical oncologist, and wouldn't have one posted there for over a month.

Having a perfect figure for her five-foot-five frame, Debra Tanner was indeed a "looker." She was obviously well educated. She worked as a linguist, spoke 11 languages, and did translations on the foreign language communication intercepts received at Fort Stewart.

"Good morning, Major," Mark said, approaching her bedside for the first time. "I'm Dr. Mark Telfair, Chief Surgical Resident."

"Glad to meet you Doctor. Just call me Debbie," the female major said extending her soft warm hand.

"Well, Debbie," Mark replied, "I've reviewed the records they sent up from Stewart. I think we're in good shape. I want to review your records with the Chairman of the Department of Surgery here at VA. If he agrees, I think all you need is a simple hysterectomy."

"*Simple* hysterectomy?"

"Yes. By simple, I mean we'll remove only your uterus, cervix, and your fallopian tubes. We may not have to remove your ovaries and all the lymph nodes in the pelvic area ... which would make it an extended hysterectomy."

"What about my vagina? That'll still be there ... won't it?"

"Yes, Debbie. We do have to remove a little bit of the upper end of the vagina, but functionally that shouldn't make any difference that you can tell," Mark explained.

"Well just as long as I can keep the *playpen* ... I really don't care about the nursery part anyway!"

"Well, as I said, I want to review your records with the department chairman here at VA. We'll also arrange to have one of the Emory GYN oncology professors assist during your surgery."

"May I call you Mark?" Debbie asked in a seductive voice with matching smile.

Mark closely studied his provocative center-fold-material patient for a few moments. Her nipple erections were quite apparent through her thin non-issue hospital gown. The pupils in her sky-blue eyes were widely dilated. As she shifted position in her hospital bed, she casually allowed her gown to rise to a revealing level. Because she'd made the rank of major at the young age of 29, Mark now wondered if she had used what was located between her ears ... or was it between her legs?

"Major, I think it's best that you call me Doctor ... and I call you Major. OK?"

"As you like," the WAC curtly said as she pulled her gown down below her knees. She was obviously pissed. *Off to a bad start,* Mark thought.

Two days later, Mark and a GYN oncology professor from Emory did her simple hysterectomy. Normally it would have been a quick one-hour procedure. Because of the invasive nature of her cervical cancer, numerous frozen-section biopsies of surrounding tissues had been done during the course of her surgery. It took over two and a half hours—over twice the normal time. Fortunately, all the biopsies of lymph nodes, ovaries, and other surrounding tissues were negative. Mark knew, in the field of medicine and surgery, there is never a never ... and never an always. But this WAC was almost certainly cured of her cervical malignancy.

Major Debbie Tanner's recovery went smoothly. During Mark's rounds on her fifth postoperative day, she asked if she could go outside to get some fresh air.

"I'll ask your nurse to take you out on the cafeteria deck today," Mark said.

"Cafeteria deck?" she questioned.

"Yes. The cafeteria is on the third floor, but it opens directly onto a deck where folks can eat al fresco, if the weather's OK. They've even got tables with umbrellas ... our taxpayer dollars at work!" Mark added.

"Will you be out there?" Major Debbie Tanner asked. "I'd love to eat with you ... get to know you a little better," she said, suggestively licking her lips.

"I doubt it. I'll probably be in surgery the rest of the day," Mark added, showing no visible emotion.

"Aren't you going to check my bandage?" she said through her slight Demerol haze.

Before Mark could stop her, she had pulled her gown well above her ample breasts. Debra Tanner's full frontal nudity greeted him. Her tan-lines made it quite clear that she wore bikinis, very small ones at that. Fortunately, her bikini-cut hysterectomy incision fell in the white zone, but just barely. A little five-day growth of blond fuzz indicated where her natural pubic hairline had been prior to its being shaved off for surgery. If the heat Mark felt in his face was any indication of its color, he knew Debra Tanner had succeeded in acquiring his nonprofessional attention.

Mark demurely pulled her bed sheet up. "Everything looks OK, Major," Mark said, sans sensitivity.

"Just OK?" she curtly asked. "I thought you'd say it looks great. Most fellas would."

Mark thought a moment: *Need to have a female nurse with me next time I see her.* "Uh ... Major. I'll have the nurse come in and remove your dressing. She may place some small strips of tape across your incision. You don't have any stitches that show. In fact, all your stitches are buried beneath the skin, or they're located inside your body. All your stitches will dissolve on their own. You can take a brief shower if you like. I'll return tomorrow and go over your final pathology report, but I'm not expecting any problems."

Mark made a swift exit to the chart room where he wrote appropriate orders. The nurse was to remove the patient's wound dressing and reinforce the incision with new Steri-Strips. After reviewing her vitals and current labs, he advanced her diet to a standard diabetic diet at appropriate caloric level. He also wrote orders permitting her to be taken out on the cafeteria's al fresco deck. In the doctors' progress notes, he started to make an entry about her provocative exhibitionism, but didn't. He somehow felt the written words may come back to haunt him.

The next morning Mark entered her room with a seasoned female nurse in tow. A changed Debbie Tanner greeted them. She had applied makeup tastefully and brushed her stylish short blond hair. Mark noted she had the sheets pulled up to her chin. After handing Mark the chart, the nurse accompanying him stood silently by with her arms folded over her chest.

"Major, looks like we have some very good news," Mark said while checking the pathologist's detailed report. "Your path report indicates we had a clean resection. Permanent sections of all adjacent tissues are all negative for tumor. The stage of invasion was actually a little less than we'd anticipated from your cervical biopsies done at Stewart. I feel very confident in saying you are cured."

"Great news, Doctor! But when can I have sex again?"

"Six weeks," Mark replied, not knowing where the conversation would lead. He paused in thought: *The question is a logical one. Perhaps I've been too quick to judge ... and her blatant flirting and exhibitionism are all due to emotional stress, or pain drugs.* "Any other questions, Major?"

"Yes. But before I forget to tell you, let me say I appreciate your letting me go out on the cafeteria deck yesterday. The fresh air and sunshine were really a nice treat, but while I was out there, I'm sure I heard dogs barking. It sounded like they were up in the air somewhere. Hearing them made me miss Boo and Tasha, my dogs at home. So, Doctor, exactly where are those dogs I heard barking?"

Mark risked a warm smile. "They are up on the roof of the hospital. Up on the eighth floor. We have a surgical research facility up there."

"Sounds very impressive, Doctor. Can I go up and see where you guys do your surgical research?"

"I don't know of any restrictions that would prohibit it." Mark paused a moment. "Tell you what ... when I get out of surgery this morning, I'll check with Dr. Schumaker. He's the director of the lab, and if he has no objection, I'll take you up there on my lunch break. I've got a favorite dog in the lab I'd like to check on anyway."

Mark and the mid-50s female nurse left Debbie's bedside, and they began walking back to the nurses' station. Suddenly the nurse stopped in the hall, turning to speak. "Doctor, that woman is trouble."

"How so?" Mark replied.

"Trust me. I can see it in her eyes. That WAC really has the hots for your bod. Better be careful, fella!"

"Well, I appreciate the advice ... but I think you're just stroking my ego. And I think her earlier actions, the ones I told you about, were due to stress and the pain meds," Mark replied.

"No way, Doctor. Think what you like. A *woman* knows another woman. Now I'm certainly not a lesbian, never have been, never will be

Going to the Gradies

... if that's what you're thinking. A woman, even a fully heterosexual one, just *knows*. Far better than men do ... and you can take that to the bank. I've been around a long time, Doc. That hot little bitch could really be a pile of trouble for you, so don't turn your back on her." The nurse paused, giving Mark a sincere stare that eased into a knowing smile.

Without words, Mark smiled back, shaking his head as he turned heading for the elevator to take him down to surgery. *God, what a paranoid old nurse,* he thought.

At 11:00 a.m. Mark had just finished helping a VA surgical intern struggle through his first hernia repair. Following surgery he called the dog lab and spoke to Dr. Schumaker, who seemed thrilled: "I hope to be here all day. I'm planning on having lunch up here in the lab. I'm doing an inventory of our pacemakers, valves, and telemetry devices ... and recovering what I can from the euthanized lot of dogs we have in the freezer. So please bring her up. Any time is fine. You know, it's really nice to have a *patient* interested in what we do up here!" Schumaker said excitedly.

Clad in his unbuttoned white jacket casually draped over full scrubs, Mark rolled an empty wheelchair into Debbie Tanner's room. "Your taxi to the dog lab is here, Major," Mark said, risking his second warm smile to the woman.

"Is that really necessary, Doctor? I can walk just fine."

"I'm afraid so, Major. Hospital policy. Let me help you get in."

As Mark assisted her into the chair, she brushed her breasts against his upper arm, and one of her knees lightly grazed his crotch. *Unintentional ... probably just an accidental touch,* Mark thought.

He escorted her to the elevator, then up to the eighth floor. While pushing her chair he explained the lab's operation: He told her that Dr. Schumaker was internationally known, and among other things, was currently working on an implantable insulin pump to be located just beneath a diabetic's skin. If successful, it would free diabetics from the drudgery and pain of daily self-injections. They'd merely have to inject insulin through their skin, and into the pump's reservoir, about once a month. The pump would then painlessly release small preset amounts of insulin from its reservoir, at times determined by a tiny clock built into the pump itself. He briefly mentioned pacemakers, artificial heart valves, artificial joints, and synthetic vascular grafts, all of which were being studied in dogs prior to human trials.

In the hall approaching the lab's main door, Mark explained how the animals were procured; how they were given anesthetics just as she had received for her own surgery; how they were humanely treated, and even given pain shots following their surgery. Without making any obvious overtures, Debbie Tanner listened intently to all Mark's comments regarding the dog lab and its mission.

Upon entering the lab, Mark immediately spied Dr. Morris Schumaker hunched over a thawing dog carcass resting on a stainless-steel table. Miss Tanner saw it as well. Morris had the animal's chest widely open, and was in the process of removing an experimental mechanical heart valve, one that would probably be modified, then tried again in another test animal. When the elderly doctor realized he had company, he discreetly tried to cover the dead dog's body with a small towel, and quickly snapped his rubber gloves off.

Schumaker extended his hand to Mark. "Good to see you Dr. Telfair. Nice Dogger will be glad to see you too." Schumaker's eyes quickly met those of the attractive patient. "And just who is this absolutely gorgeous creature you've brought up here with you?"

"Sir, this is Miss Debbie Tanner. She's the patient I called you about earlier, the one who said she would like to see the lab. She's a major in the WACs, and recovering nicely from a TAH for cervical CA (hysterectomy for cervical cancer). Miss Tanner is also an insulin-dependent diabetic, and she's doing well in that regard too."

Upon hearing Mark's voice, Nice Dogger violently started wagging her tail in her quarters. Her tail banged on her pen's metal mesh with a loud ringing thump.

"Quite a place!" Debbie said to Mark, scanning the complex equipment in the lab. "So *this* is where you mad scientists work! But what's that racket I hear?"

"Oh that's just Nice Dogger banging her tail against her quarters," Mark answered. He then turned to address Dr. Schumaker. "Can I let her out, sir?"

"Sure. Let the pretty lady see Nice Dogger," Schumaker replied with a warm smile.

Mark let Nice Dogger out. The dog immediately started licking Mark's hands. She was so excited to see Mark she peed on the floor. Mark stepped over the small puddle, and went over to Debbie, expecting Nice Dogger to follow. The dog wouldn't budge in Debbie's direction. Instead Nice Dogger went to a lab door—the door that opened to the roof—and barked. She wanted Mark to take her outside to the run.

"Can I take her outside and let Major Tanner see her run?"

"Sure," Dr. Schumaker said. "If you don't mind, just put Nice Dogger's collar on and collect some data while you're at it. Also, and I hope you two won't think me rude, I've just discovered I need to scoot down to the pathology lab to check some tissue slides under one of their more powerful microscopes. Shouldn't take me but a half hour. So, Doctor, I'd appreciate it if you'd conduct the Major's lab tour in my stead ... just show this beautiful lady what it is we do up here."

Debbie Tanner blushed at Schumaker's compliment, though she'd obviously heard it many times before, from many men.

"No problem. Glad to, sir," Mark responded. Schumaker promptly left the lab carrying a box of glass microscopic slides.

Mark put on Nice Dogger's collar. Major Debbie Tanner quickly got out of her wheelchair unassisted, and continued actively scanning every detail in the lab. She followed Mark and the dog out onto the roof. Mark, Debbie, and Nice Dogger entered the run. Nice Dogger did her usual routine ... running to the end of the run, returning to lick Mark's hands, only to take off again and repeat the process. On the return runs the dog always came back to Mark. Nice Dogger still flatly refused to have anything to do with Major Tanner despite Mark's best efforts at encouraging their interaction. After 15 minutes of running, Mark took the dog back inside, removed her collar, and Nice Dogger bounded into her quarters on her own. Mark closed the pen's door, cleaned up the small puddle of urine, then washed and dried his hands with a paper towel.

As Mark turned away from her to throw the crumpled towel into a trash can, he felt Debbie's hands slip beneath his white jacket and encircle his scrub-clad waist from behind. He was initially startled by her move, but remained immobile, not uttering a sound. Mark held his breath and slowly rotated to face her, as her hands loosened their grip enough to allow his subtle movement.

He felt his pulse quicken and a feeling like an electric charge tingled from his finger tips to his groin. He sensed it was the same for her, as she tilted her chin slightly upward to meet his gaze. Their lips sought each other's and touched, their arms tightening. Mark's fingers grazed a breast, as he felt the tingling sensations intensify. Closer their bodies and lips pressed as his groin processed the message that his brain was sending there.

He was dimly aware of the hint of jasmine and the soft roundness of her breasts as they pressed more and more eagerly into his chest. He felt himself being swept away towards a pleasurable place of no return.

He abruptly pulled away, breaking the soft seal their lips had formed while the tips of their tongues had sought one another's.

Reason returned to his addled brain. *Damn!* he thought.

"What's the matter with you?" Debbie asked, puzzled.

He paused.

"I can't."

"Can't what?"

"Go any further."

"Why not?" her voice becoming louder and more shrill.

Mark felt his heart rate diminish, the flush fading from his face. For a full moment, he felt unable to answer her demanding questions. Frustrated, he decided to proceed as though nothing had happened.

"Well Major, I'm sorry Nice Dogger wouldn't take a liking to you. You want to take a look at the pacemaker data her collar just picked up?"

"No! Not unless you've changed you mind about *us!*" Debbie shrieked, suddenly hostile.

Fully composed now, he spoke to Debbie. "Major, I think we need to step outside and talk. Dr. Schumaker could return to the lab at any moment now."

She quickly followed him back out to the roof. There, they stood about four feet apart, each tightly folding their arms over their own chests. Mark knew his words had to be well chosen; the textbook sections that mentioned doctor-patient attractions didn't tell him what to do or say in this situation. They stared at each other for a beat or two while Mark searched for appropriate words. *She's undeniably a beautiful woman,* Mark thought. Finally, words found his lips.

"Debbie you are a stunning woman," Mark began. "I'd have to be blind not to notice. Thanks to modern medicine and surgery you have a very reasonable life span ahead of you. You'll have plenty of good years left, and you'll have no problem finding the right one. Just as there is no way I can make a laboratory dog respond to you, or like you, there is no way you can make me fall in love with you, or have an affair with you. I've had a steady girlfriend for several years. We love each other very much. I think she's all the woman I'll ever need or want."

"You bastard! You'll never know what you've missed. I can put it on you like you've never had it before. You'll soon regret this!" Debbie hissed, then turned away.

She abruptly sashayed back inside the lab and plopped down in her wheelchair, totally pissed, her arms still tightly wrapping her torso. Mark followed, too befuddled to reply to her last remark. He quickly wheeled Major Debbie Tanner out of the lab. Not a word was uttered between them during transit. Arriving at her bedside, Mark finally spoke curtly: "Unless something changes Major, you will be discharged in about 48 hours. I'll arrange for Fort Stewart to do your follow-up care, and you can hand-carry your records when you return." He quickly left her room, not offering her any chance for rebuttal.

Her unspoken response showed up big time ... the next morning. The *Atlanta Journal's* three-column quarter-page article in the letters to the editor section was titled: *WAC Says VA Whacks Dogs!* Mark had been unaware of the article when he arrived for work at seven. He heard his name paged the moment he walked inside the VA building, and promptly answered using the nearest phone. It was the hospital administrator. He demanded that Mark come to his office immediately. Thirty seconds later, Mark walked into the administrator's office. "What can I do for you, sir?" Mark innocently asked the elderly physician administrator, a fellow who was well-respected by the entire hospital staff.

"You care to explain this, Dr. Telfair?" the administrator said, thrusting the newspaper article toward Mark.

Mark read in silence. The more he read the angrier he got. When he finished the article he looked up, now fuming, hands shaking. "That heinous nympho bitch must have written this and called the newspaper immediately after she left the lab! How did I know she was some charter member of the SPCA. Sir, her letter is an outright lie! Her reference to 'filthy lab conditions' must be the small puddle of dog pee I cleaned up. And the part about Dr. Schumaker's 'ripping apart dogs without anesthesia' must refer to his removal of implants from a *frozen* dog euthanized several months ago!"

"Lie or not, Dr. Telfair, this article gives us some very bad press! Your name appears seven times in the article. The VA's name 11 times. Since we are affiliated with Emory, and now Grady too, it puts them in a bad light also. All in a very blasphemous light. And even Dr. Schumaker is mentioned twice in a negative way. I've been getting phone calls from Emory, Grady, and the TV stations. The SPCA has even planned a demonstration in front of this very hospital tomorrow morning!"

"Sir," Mark said, fully appreciating the wrath of the scorned, "please allow me to explain what I think is behind her letter ... what I think motivated it."

"By all means, do! A lot of butts are in hot water, Doctor ... yours, mine, and Schumaker's to name a few."

Mark felt he was pretty good at bullshit, but this wasn't the time for it. He went through a ten-minute explanation, telling the fatherly administrator *everything*. After he finally quit explaining himself he asked, "How can I fix it, sir?"

"A front-page retraction on her part would be extremely helpful. Is she still an inpatient?"

"Yes sir," Mark replied. "She's due for discharge tomorrow."

"Then I'd say you've got your work cut out for you. I want a front-page retraction in tomorrow morning's paper."

"Sir, I can't promise she'll even write a retraction, much less front page, but I'll do my best. If you've got any pull with the paper, that might help."

"Doctor, you'd better somehow get a draft of her retraction on my desk before the sun goes down. I'll see it makes front page!" The administrator paused, his face softening a bit as he added a final note spoken with sympathetic understanding. "Believe it or not, I was once young myself, discovered my own imperfections, and did impulsive things. I appreciate the guts your complete candor with me required ... and I still think you are a damn good surgeon. Good luck, son."

As Mark left the administrator's office his knees were shaky, and he felt a tight bubble in the pit of his belly. *God, what have I done to deserve this? What made me risk blowing it all when I'm almost through?* Mark thought. Panic soon subsided, reason prevailed. He knew he had his work laid out for him. Fortunately, he was in a position to enlist others at the hospital to fill in for him. He'd ponder the problem in the solitude of the Emory library before he confronted the enemy: Major Debbie Tanner.

In the tomb-like silence of Emory's medical library, Mark searched his brain. Call Mose? He always seemed to have the answers to emotionally loaded problems at Grady. Maybe call Anne? Probably not a good move, considering the "other woman" overtones, and Debbie Tanner's *Playboy* centerfold potential. What about Zack? He always seems to think on his feet, always five or six moves ahead of the pack. Maybe even call Ms. Costellanos, the drillmaster RN in Grady's GAC? Without warning, a thought suddenly struck him: *Hit the WAC where it hurts! Just tell her where she'd be if animal research never existed ... where she'd be if products derived from animals were not available to her.*

By noon he had half a legal pad full of notes. Over a quick lunch at the Emory cafeteria, he formulated and memorized his approach. He quickly drove back to the VA, located less than five minutes away. Major Tanner was not in her room, nor the indoor part of the cafeteria. He felt tinges of panic, but finally located her. She was sitting alone at an umbrella-shaded table on the al fresco deck. Mark approached her table.

"Mind if I sit down, Major?"

"Mark, I knew you'd change your mind," she said with a sexy smile, fiddling with her bathrobe just enough to expose her ample cleavage, the viewing of which could be used as a cardiac fitness test. It was obvious she was going to make another attempt at seduction.

Mark pretended not to notice, then spoke. "Major, I'm here to change *your* mind. I'm wanting you to write a retraction regarding that article in the newspaper. See that it gets to the hospital administrator's office before dark today. But first, I want you to answer some questions for me. OK?"

"I'm not in the mood to write anything. As for your questions, it depends on what they are. But ask anyway," she responded coyly.

"Major, what would happen to you if you had no insulin? It hadn't been discovered yet?"

"Well I'd be *dead*, that's what!"

"Exactly. Do you know where your insulin comes from?"

"Eli Lilly and Company, that's all I need to know," she added, leaning forward to give Mark an even better view of her breasts.

"Well let me tell you where Lilly, and other companies, get their insulin from—or at least the type you use. It comes from the pancreas of cattle. In the slaughterhouse, cows go down a chute which ends in a stunning box. The cattle are given no anesthesia or sedation. In the box, they're hit in the head with a captive-bolt stunner. The stunner is a handheld pneumatic device that blows an iron rod through their skulls. They have seizures as they fall over, with no control over their bowels or urine. They fall out one side of the death box where their guts are quickly ripped out. The animal's pancreas is immediately removed and preserved. Your insulin is extracted from that pancreas!"

Her facial expression reflected shock. "Just why the hell would you think I'd know about all that stuff!"

"I didn't think you would know, and that's exactly why I'm telling you now. I'll also bet you didn't know insulin was first discovered in a canine lab. Yep, some mad scientist in the late 1800s found that if you cut out a live dog's pancreas, they'd instantly become diabetic ... and soon die! Then, in 1921, a surgeon named Frederick Banting, and his assistant Charles Best, figured out how to extract precious insulin from a dead dog's pancreas. By injecting that extract obtained from the dead dog's pancreas into live dogs that had *no* pancreas, they were then able to keep them alive and healthy!"

She blankly stared toward the roof of the VA. Mark continued: "And all those dissolving catgut sutures buried in your belly came from animal tissue. They cause fewer complications in your type of GYN surgery than other types of sutures, like nylon, cotton, or silk. Your gut sutures didn't come from cats, as most folks think, but rather from the intestines of cute little lambs. Those cute little lambs are killed the same way as the cows ... with a captive-bolt stunner that punches a big hole in their precious little lamb heads. Then their bowels are removed, and the sutures that ended up in your body were made from the collagen obtained from their little lamb guts."

Mark could see she was stunned. Tears began forming in her eyes. "Why are you telling me all this? It's all about that article I wrote, isn't it?"

"Partly," Mark answered, "but the point I want to make, Major, is this: If you truly believe what you've written in that letter to the editor, you should allow us to go back inside your belly and take all your gut stitches out, and replace them with man-made or plant materials. After we get your animal-product sutures out, then you can refuse to take your animal-product insulin for a few days ... and then you can *die* with a totally clear conscience!"

She continued to stare at the roof. The faint barking of Nice Dogger indicated Dr. Schumaker had her outside the lab in the run. Tears now started running down Debbie's face. She retrieved a tissue from her bathrobe pocket and dabbed her eyes. *Mark felt like the bastard she had called him yesterday.* There was a part of him that wanted to dry her tears, or give her a hug. He somewhat reluctantly turned, then briskly walked away. He delegated her VA discharge to another resident, and never saw or heard from her again.

Exactly how it had all happened remained a mystery to Mark, but the next day's morning paper ran a front-page article, complete with a very flattering photo of Major Debbie Tanner: *WAC Retracts All.* The article was well written. Her retraction statement contained some of the information Mark had given her about insulin and gut sutures. It praised the humane way VA lab animals were handled, and contained personal apologies to the Atlanta VA, Dr. Mark Telfair, Dr. Morris Schumaker, Emory University School of Medicine, and Emory's Department of Surgery. The last line of her retraction statement summed it up best: "*My own selfish emotions and ignorance temporarily blinded me, but thanks to Dr. Mark Telfair, my sight is now 20/20, my foolish emotions now contained, and my appreciation regarding the true value of animal products and research has been greatly enhanced.*"

23

GOING TO *POSSUM TROT*

As Mark's VA hospital rotation in clinical surgery drew to a close, no new Debbie Tanners appeared to make his life miserable. The bad press about the VA dog lab had been completely squelched by the WAC's retraction in the newspaper. The SPCA demonstration had been canceled, and Dr. Mark Telfair's name had been cleared. Though they didn't communicate often, even Mark's widowed mom had called him: "Son, I'm so glad to read the blight on the Telfair name has been removed," she'd said. But even more important to him, Anne had sympathetically accepted his entrapment by the scorned sexy WAC.

Mark sat at his office desk, daydreaming about Anne. It was his last day at the VA. The loud ring of his desk phone dispersed his daydream.

"Telfair speaking," Mark flatly replied. An expansive smile quickly spread across his face as he immediately recognized the voice of a man he hadn't seen in three years. The caller was his friend, Dr. Jerry Bacon, phoning from his private practice office in Gainesville, Georgia.

"Man it's good to hear your voice, Jer! Haven't seen you since your Chief Resident rotations at the Gradies. So what's happening, good buddy?"

Jer Bacon had called to invite Mark and friends to his Gainesville home for a couple of days, "... just for loving, hunting, fishing, reminiscing, and drinking," Jer had put it. Mark's last day at the VA would be followed by a couple of free days in his schedule, so Mark had instantly replied, "Hey man, count me in!"

During the lengthy conversation that followed, Jer explained that he had plenty of room at his house, but so far only Dr. Adrian Brevard and Dr. Zack Paslski had schedules that would allow them to leave their hospital duties for a full two days. Both Adrian and Zack would be bringing significant others with them. "Bring your girlfriend too," Bacon had offered. Jer said he'd even phoned the Grady ER and invited Mose Mallone. The orderly had apologetically indicated he couldn't get away, but deeply appreciated the invitation anyway. *Mose probably didn't want to miss a single night of keeping his gym boys out of trouble,* Mark thought upon learning this news.

During their conversation Mark had written down detailed directions to Bacon's home, located about 25 miles north of Gainesville, GA. While Jer talked, Mark sketched a map complete with labels for landmarks and roads, though the labels were largely unreadable by anyone—except Mark Telfair.

After Jer's phone call, the rest of Mark's last VA day crept by like a sedated snail. Mark had no surgery scheduled. He forced himself to keep busy with nonessential last-day paperwork. He said a personal goodbye to his favorite hospital patients and surgical personnel. With a red face he specifically thanked the surgical nurse who had warned him about Debbie Tanner, then endured the five minutes of the "I told you so" he knew he had coming. He retrieved his possessions from his desk drawers and OR locker, then packed them into the trunk of his ancient Volvo. He even made a trip to the dog lab to say a sad goodbye to a tail-wagging Nice Dogger and the lab's chief, Dr. Morris Schumaker. Morris congratulated Mark for the way he'd handled the sexy WAC, then proudly went over the voluminous pacemaker data gleaned from Nice Dogger's electronic collar. With a big smile, and a paternalistic hand on Mark's shoulder, Schumaker told Mark his name would be listed as co-author of the resultant scientific journal article; it had already been accepted for publication in *Circulation,* a widely known international scientific journal. Other equally prestigious journals were also reviewing submitted drafts. The news brightened Mark's day. He knew "being published" would look good on his curriculum vitae, but as much as he admired Dr. Schumaker, he still couldn't bring himself to consider surgical research as a career.

I just get too attached to the test animals, he thought, smiling on his way out of the lab. Mark smiled not because he was happy about learning he was published; it was because Schumaker had solemnly promised to fulfill Mark's simple parting request: "Sir, please don't put Nice Dogger down when her work here is done. Just keep her here as a pampered lab mascot. That way you can fix her up when she needs a new pacemaker battery."

After leaving the dog lab, all Mark could think about was getting to Anne's apartment to tell her about Jer's invitation. Mark left the VA at five in the afternoon; ten minutes later he entered Anne's apartment. No Anne. He looked out the apartment window to check the parking lot—her car was not there either. Mark felt a tinge of panic but soon found her note on the kitchen counter: "Called back to Grady to fill in for a sick nurse. Stuff in fridge for supper. See you a little after 11:00 for your dessert!

Love, A."

Mark watched some uninteresting TV, had a beer, made a sandwich, and suddenly realized how completely empty and lonely the apartment felt without Anne's being there. Bored, he stretched out on the couch and fell asleep.

A few hours later, he was gently awakened by a soft kiss. He didn't even open his eyes; he knew Anne's touch and fragrance. Even after years of exclusive dating, her touches and subdued perfumes still remained exciting. He slowly opened his eyes to find Anne already in one of her revealing nightgowns. She spoke softly and pointed: "Here?" indicating the sofa, "Or there?" pointing at the bedroom door with a naughty grin. *I've got to be the luckiest man alive,* Mark thought, as he pointed at the bedroom.

Following their lovemaking, Mark found himself so mentally and physically content he'd completely forgotten Jer's phone call. Just as his breathing and heart rate returned to normal, Jer's call flashed in his brain. "Hey Anne! I almost forgot. Guess who called today? It was Jer Bacon! He wants us to come up to Gainesville and visit for a couple of days ... tomorrow and the next day, then come back here on Sunday. Adrian Brevard is taking his new girlfriend, and Zack is taking his fiancée. Wanna go?"

Anne didn't immediately respond. *Has she not heard me?* Mark's mind questioned. After a moment, Mark gingerly asked again, "Anne, do you want to go?"

"Mark, we need to talk about *us.* Tonight is not the right time. Yes I'd love to go to Jer's with you. My schedule is OK for that, but I'd have to be back at Grady by seven on Sunday morning. Maybe while we're at Jer's we can find some private time for a long-overdue talk. About our future together ... or not together ... or whatever our relationship is going to be."

Mark could see moisture forming in Anne's troubled hazel eyes, but the tears he'd anticipated did not materialize. Though he desperately tried, he could read no meaning there, but sensed she had some deep emotion she didn't want to share at the moment. Suddenly he felt frightened ... frightened that he may no longer be the only luckiest man alive. Could Anne be seeing someone else? Had she really been called back to work at the hospital? Could she be pregnant, despite the reliable precautions they took? He knew a talk about their future was long overdue. It was something they both had avoided simply because the present seemed to be working so well. It worked well despite their often-conflicting work schedules, which lately seemed determined to afford them little time together.

He also knew in less than eight months he'd be going on active duty with the U.S. Air Force. Where would the Air Force send him? How far away would it be? If his few remaining months in Atlanta went as fast as the rest of his surgical training, he knew they had to talk soon. Very soon. If they didn't, their wonderful present would fall apart ... and they might never be able to put it back together again ... never build a future together.

They agreed to somehow find a way to be alone for a long talk about their future while at Jer's. They then settled in each other's arms in complete relaxation. Peaceful sleep quickly came to them both.

The next morning Mark and Anne woke up in festive moods. Because his vehicle was the largest car in the group, Anne suggested that Mark should offer to drive his Volvo to Gainesville, though it really didn't have comfortable room for six. Those in the back would have to sit in one another's laps. But at least it would only be a two-hour trip, and the large trunk should have enough space for their luggage. Besides, Zack—the car's exclusive mechanic for the last four years—had recently pronounced the Volvo ready to roll despite her quarter-million miles. After a few phone calls, the Grady guys and gals all agreed to ride together in Mark's car. It took less than an hour to gather everyone and their luggage. By 10:00 a.m. The Bomb was rolling north up the Buford Highway, heading for Jer Bacon's home near Gainesville, Georgia.

The chatter in the car sounded like a group of sugar-high preteens during a pajama party. Mark found it hard to concentrate on his driving, but managed to do so, despite all the interesting chatter.

"Woman! You could talk the tits off a boar hog!" the familiar voice of Zack Paslaski boomed over the din. Zack was addressing his fiancée, Alisia Petroski, who was sitting on his lap. Alisia was the X-ray technician Zack had "won" in an all-night poker game during their house arrest at Grady. She was a brunette with sky-blue eyes and perfect snow-white skin. A little under five feet tall, and weighing less than 100 pounds, she still had an appealing figure. Though the obvious initial attraction between her and Zack had been physical, they were now very much in love. Neither made any attempt to hide the fact. Alisia proudly wore an engagement ring Zack had bought her with his poker winnings. Zack called Alisia "Mighty Mouse," or usually just "Mouse" ... a term of endearment, according to Zack. Alisia loved it, and lived it. Mighty Mouse could talk just as rough as Zack, and with a few words uttered, or with a special look, could immediately bring Zack in bounds, should he step across the line. Mark was happy to know Mouse was capable of such feats, especially since Zack had loaded four cases of beer along with his meager luggage.

As they left Northeast Atlanta, the traffic thinned and the chatter slowed. Adrian Brevard's recently acquired girlfriend, Betty Britt, was the most soft-spoken of the group. Her voice could finally be heard as she talked while sitting on Adrian's lap in the Volvo's back seat. Despite her demeanor, she seemed completely at ease with her more boisterous companions. Betty was a widowed full-time pediatric nurse at Grady, and had a three-year-old son whose father had been killed in Vietnam two years earlier. Betty was the only woman Adrian had dated following the abrupt end of his childless marriage. Physically, Betty strongly resembled Adrian's deceased wife: petite, with short brown hair, creamy complexion, and absolutely gorgeous large brown eyes. As the miles passed, Mark could not help but wonder: Was Adrian attracted to Betty because of her strong resemblance to his deceased wife? ... or was it because they shared a natural bond created by mutually losing mates to tragedy?

As the Volvo approached the Gainesville city limits, Mark vigorously started feeling and patting all the various pockets of his plaid shirt and khaki pants. He was searching for the map he'd made regarding the location of Jer's home. *He couldn't find it!* Anne, riding in the front passenger's seat, observed Mark's odd behavior a few moments before speaking. "Did you lose something, Mark? Or are you just fondling yourself, or what?"

Mark didn't answer Anne's specific questions but replied anyway. "When I talked to Jer on the phone, he gave me directions to his house. I made a map and notes. I'm sure I've go it ... *somewhere.*"

"Sure?" Anne asked.

"Yeah, positive. Absolutely positive!" Mark replied, irritated with himself.

"What did it look like, Mark?"

"It was just a piece of white paper folded into a square. Had some of my scratching on it. You know, the stuff you claim you can't read anyway."

"Sorta like this?" Anne asked, as she removed the folded map from her pocketbook.

Mark flushed. "Where the heck did you find it?"

"You left it on the kitchen counter. I got it as we left the apartment to pick everyone up."

"OK, Wonder Woman! Could you please unfold it and at least try to read it to me?" Mark asked, with forced humility.

"Wonder Woman? Read what?" Mouse chimed in after catching the last of the front-seat conversation. Mouse was seated directly behind Mark, sitting on Zack's lap.

Anne looked at Mark's hopeless scratching, quickly gave up, and passed the unfolded note back to Mouse. Mouse briefly studied it, then spoke. "Damn! This scratching looks just like some of that chickenshit writing we get on the X-ray requisition forms from the Grady doctors," Mouse proclaimed. "But I'm quite familiar with this particular doctor's handwriting, so I can actually read this one ... *Doctor Telfair!*"

Mark patiently waited for the group's laughter to subside, then replied, "Well it looks like Wonder Woman here has just passed off to Mighty Mouse ... so Mouse, you're now the official navigator. OK?"

"With pleasure, Doctor. We need US 23 out of Gainesville. About 12 miles out we'll pick up State Road 52, a right turn off 23. Just holler when you get on 52, because after that it gets kinda complicated by a bunch of turns, lookin' for mailboxes and stuff," Mouse replied, then promptly resumed chitchatting with the rest of the group.

North of Gainesville, the countryside became more rural. The rolling hills, green fields of winter rye, grazing farm animals, and the early hint of North Georgia's colorful autumn foliage were a pleasant contrast to the congestion of the bland metropolitan Atlanta landscape. Mark was using this serene setting to formulate his words and thoughts ... exactly what he'd say to Anne when they had their talk about the future. Their future. Mark knew bachelors—once past a certain age—didn't seem able to make a *commitment*. He kept coming down to another troublesome word: *confinement*. Mark's thoughts, desperately trying to decide how he would temper the two troublesome words, were suddenly jarred by the high-pitched voice of Mighty Mouse.

"Hey Dr. Dingbat! I think you went past State Road 52!"

"Mouse, you sure?" Mark asked, wearing an embarrassed look.

"Well I just saw a sign that said Toccoa 7, South Carolina 24, and I thought we were going somewhere in Gainesville, or just a little north of Gainesville. But hey, I'm just a dumb-broad navigator reading this chicken-scratch note I inherited from Wonder Woman!"

Mark didn't lose his cool as he made a U-turn at the first convenient spot, and backtracked the 22 miles to his missed turnoff for State Road 52. Anne grinned, but politely remained silent. Once on 52, Mouse hung over the back of Mark's seat studying both odometer and the hand-drawn map like a hawk. In the process, she gave Mark the most explicit backseat-driving experience he'd ever encountered.

The only encouraging words Mark heard from the rear were from his old Grady roommate, Zack. "Hey Mouse, cut Markie some slack, will ya? We ain't got no train to catch! No freakin' fire to put out!"

After driving well over two hours, and seemingly countless turns, the group finally arrived at Dr. Jerry Bacon's rural gravel driveway. It was marked only by a black mailbox, with BACON sloppily hand painted in large white block letters. No box numbers or initials were apparent. Jer's driveway turned out to be some four miles long. The Volvo passed a sizable Black Angus herd, multiple pastures, three cattle guards, and several multiacre ponds. It crossed two wooden bridges over creeks. Finally a massive three-story Georgian-style mansion came into view atop a hill. The house had a slate roof sprouting many chimneys. A tasteful red brick exterior, six three-story white fluted columns, and rocking chairs on the front porch completed a picture you'd expect on the cover of *Southern Living* magazine. *Only the slaves and cotton fields are missing,* Mark thought.

Those who'd arrived by ancient Volvo were indeed awestricken as the car stopped at the mansion's front door. All passengers had some off the wall comment: "Holy shit!" popped out of Zack's mouth. "This had got to be where they filmed *Gone With the Wind*," the Mouse commented. Adrian and Betty simply said "Nice," in unison. Anne said, "And he's been in private practice only what now ... *one year?* Come on guys, let's get real." Mark was last to meekly comment: "Well at least I—or rather Mouse—managed to find farmer Bacon's little ramshackle sharecropper's shack!"

Two chocolate Labs approached the car, wagging their tails while barking effusively. Jer Bacon sprang out of the mansion's ornate leaded-glass front door and hushed his dogs. He was wearing well-worn bib overalls, blue denim shirt, brogans, and white socks. He'd put on a few pounds and was a little more waistline challenged than when at Grady, but hadn't quite reached the Pillsbury Doughboy stage yet. His bald spot was much bigger, but his ear-to-ear smile remained totally unchanged; genuine Jer Bacon ... *Bacon to the bone,* Mark's mind said.

Jer quickly approached the car. "God, it's sure good to see y'all! Welcome to *Possum Trot* ... that's what me and Sylvia call this place. Y'all come on in! I'll get Lem to bring your stuff in."

A round of hugging, handshaking, and backslapping ensued while Lem, a sturdy but ancient white-haired servant, unloaded Mark's car. Zack couldn't resist helping Lem carry the beer inside. The four cases of Coors were deposited in a walk-in refrigerator larger than the room Zack and Mark had shared at Grady. Still amazed, Zack uttered another "holy shit" as he sized up the giant refrigerator ... and began trying to determine where the mechanical guts were that made the thing work.

As the group assembled in the massive foyer, Sylvia, Jer's wife—the former Sylvia Banks, Grady Nursing School grad—descended the spiral stairs with some precious cargo. Sylvia was clad in blue jeans, white sneakers, and a red University of Georgia sweatshirt that did little to conceal her figure—one admired by every male, and envied by every female at Grady. Sylvia was still as beautiful as ever, but obviously maternally intent regarding the small bundle she was carrying proudly.

"Well everybody, or those of you that I don't already know, I'm Sylvia, and this is our baby JJ. Stands for Jerry Junior. And welcome to *Possum Trot*. Let me take JJ back up to his nanny, and I'll be right back down to fix you guys some lunch."

Lem escorted each couple separately and carried their luggage to their upstairs quarters. He delighted in showing them the impressive amenities of their spacious rooms. After Mark and Anne's skimpy luggage had been deposited, Lem left and closed the door behind him. Mark turned to Anne and commented, "I really feel like I should have tipped that nice old fella."

"Honey, don't spend money we don't have yet," Anne whispered, as she playfully planted a substantial kiss on Mark's surprised lips. The kiss lingered a little longer than either anticipated.

Mark forced himself to stop their embrace. "I think we'd better go down and join the others for lunch ... before they have to come looking for us!"

The three Grady couples soon assembled in the large walnut-paneled dining room. Jer and Sylvia appeared with trays of pimento cheese sandwiches, potato salad, sweet pickles, salads of sliced pineapple on lettuce beds, and iced tea. The hastily prepared lunch seemed to clash with the opulence of the room—as well as the fine silver, gold-rimmed china, and linen at each place setting. Jer's overalls and brogans, and Sylvia's sweatshirt and jeans, looked equally out of place. Everyone served their own plates from a long sideboard, and seated themselves as a group at one end of the long table ... the table which Zack loudly and proudly pronounced to be "... longer than any freakin' bowling lane in Harlem!"

After everyone was seated, Jer tapped on his tea glass—actually a crystal wine goblet—to garner attention. He proposed a toast to his Grady friends: "Here's to the Gradies, and her finest men and women!" A round of applause and glass clinking ensued.

Mark stood up, studied the iced tea in his crystal wine goblet a moment, then spoke. "Here's to Jer ... and his extremely obvious success in private practice!" More applause and glass clinking.

Jer's face turned red as he stood to address his Grady friends. "Fellas and gals, let me set the record straight right up front. My practice *is* doing well, but still getting off the ground. Ain't no way Jer Bacon could afford this 27-room mansion and the 1,900 acres it's situated on. This place belongs to the estate of my recently deceased bachelor uncle. Uncle

Edgar's will gave me the right to live here expense free for five years after I finished my surgical training. My uncle did that because when I was a kid, I use to spend my summers up here fishin', huntin', ridin' horses, and just gladly putting up with the eccentric old coot. No one else in the family could stand him. He was really a neat guy, just misunderstood by most folks. He's the one that encouraged me to become a doctor, and helped with my medical school expenses. He taught me a lot about huntin', fishin', cattle raisin', and horse ridin'. But living here permanently ... well that just ain't my style, and I think you guys know it. Sylvia and me are saving up for our own little place we plan to build a lot closer to town. But for right now, it's ours to use and enjoy—so let's get down and boogie!" Applause, laughter, and relieved looks filled the room. *At least Dr. Jerry Bacon is still the same ole totally honest Grady-Jer,* Mark thought.

As lunch progressed, Jer explained that no particular activities had been planned—except for the evening meal tomorrow at seven. Then they'd all be treated to some of Lem's famous barbecue pork ribs, "The *sine qua non* of a Southern man's culinary skill," Jer had put it, murdering the Latin in the process. They could hunt, fish, ride Jeeps or horses, sit and talk, or use their hormones as they saw fit. "And if any of y'all get a possum, a coon, squirrel, fish, or something with feathers, just give it to Lem. I tell you no lie ... if it walks, crawls, runs, swims, or flies, Lem can cook it!" Jer proudly announced.

While they were eating, Jer continued. They'd been given full run of the entire estate. Any hunting or fishing gear needed would be provided. "Just be careful and don't shoot none of the estate's expensive Angus. And don't you worry about a fishing license or hunting license, 'cause the Game Warden himself is a close friend of mine and my deceased uncle. He won't bother you guys. I promise. Heck, the Warden himself shoots over our baited dove fields all the time," Jer informed. "At *Possum Trot,* me and Sylvia learned quick that so-called Guest Hunting Rights and Warden's Rights are just a couple of the fine points regarding North Georgia Game Law."

After lunch, Zack and Mouse opted to go to a dove field and hunt somewhere on the very back of the property. Adrian and Betty chose a "nap," followed by a trip to one of the several fishing ponds. Mark and Anne asked for the keys to the red Jeep they'd seen parked at the side of the house; they planned to drive around and locate a suitable private spot to discuss their future.

Mark had studied a framed plat of the estate displayed on one of the lavish drawing room walls, and soon had the layout of the property in his head. Jer smiled when he'd tossed Mark the Jeep's keys. Five minutes later, a quarter-mile behind the house, Mark steered the Jeep onto a well maintained firebreak road. They rode in silence, until Anne finally spoke. "This couldn't have worked out better for us could it? For our talk, I mean."

"Well, I guess not, Anne. So let's find a nice spot where we can get out and talk. Sure couldn't ask for a better warm fall day, could we?" Mark asked, making small talk until an appropriate spot was selected.

After Mark had driven several miles, Anne spoke. "How about right over there?" She pointed to a huge oak tree that shaded a secluded clearing on one side of the dirt road.

Mark stopped the Jeep and they got out. Holding hands, both walked 25 yards to the huge tree. They tried to hug the massive trunk; their combined arm lengths would not come close to encircling its impressive girth. The only larger diameter oak Mark Telfair had ever seen had been of a different species, a live oak, located in Coastal Georgia. *Anne really knows how to pick a good spot ... just hope I can pick the right words,* Mark thought. As if to welcome North Georgia's fall, the tree was beginning to shed its leaves when teased by the light warm breeze. Each falling leaf was tinted in various shades of red and gold. They agreed on a spot beneath the tree's massive branches, then sat upon the colorful leaf-covered ground Indian-style, facing each other.

"Well, who's going to start?" Mark finally said, anxious to get rid of the apprehension they mutually shared.

After a pause Anne said, "I'm deeply in love with you Mark, and I hope you know it."

"I do know it, Anne. I think you know I'm equally in love with you too ... and that's what scares me. Sometimes I'm frightened when I think about how much I love you. I'm completely petrified when I think about what I should say right now. Sometimes, I feel like I'm on solid ground, then on a greased slope. The word commitment—then the word confinement—keep popping into my head. I'm not sure we're both fully ready. How do we ever really know? How do I, or *we,* deal with that problem, Anne?"

"I share all your concerns about commitment and confinement. But I've got an even bigger problem. Mark, you're the first and *only* man I've ever had sex with." This was a revelation that caught Mark totally off guard. His emotions quickly stirred to a point where he felt he might cry. He avoided her beautiful eyes, knowing that if he looked there now, he would surely lose it.

Anne continued: "Sure I've done some heavy petting with previous boyfriends, but you're the only one I've ever gone all the way with. I think our sex is terrific, but I really don't have any personal basis for comparison, only what other women have told me about that part of their relationships with their men. And I know you've had other women, even lived with a girlfriend for several years. So how do I compare with them?"

"Anne, there just is no comparison. With you, it just seems so perfect, so right, so absolutely natural and fantastic. I just don't see any end in sight. Four years ago, when we first started dating, I fully expected the physical side of our relationship to begin cooling down, but it hasn't. I know the day will eventually come when our libidos back off to a more reasonable level. And I know we presently both act like we're still totally awash in puberty, but hopefully we can decline together. If we didn't make each other so damn horny, maybe we could think a lot straighter right now.

"All I know is I love you dearly, I don't want to lose you, and I want both of us fully comfortable with any commitment we make. I just don't want commitment to feel like confinement ... for either one of us. Maybe we could have some kind of compromise, something short of a formal commitment."

"A compromise? Like what?" Anne asked, her face a blend of anxiety, confusion, and suspicion.

"Well, I'll be going into the Air Force in eight months ... right?"

"Seven months and three weeks, to be exact," Anne said. She was looking down, tumbling a large colorful oak leaf in her hands.

"Well why don't we just live with and enjoy the status quo until I have to leave? After I go, date some other guys if you want. Even have sex with them if you are comfortable with them. I trust you ... and your judgment. Just don't you dare let me know any specifics—even if I ask for them. I honestly don't think I could handle the jealousy. Can you promise me that much?"

"Yes," Anne replied. "But we still wouldn't have any commitment, would we?"

Mark swallowed, and felt his pulse quicken. *Now or never,* he thought. "Anne ... will you marry me after I've been in the Air Force six months, provided some tall, dark, and handsome fella doesn't bump me out of your life while I'm away?"

Anne raised her eyes to meet Mark's gaze. She paused for what seemed like an eternity. She finally smiled, then spoke: "Yes ... yes, yes! You absolutely crazy little son of a bitch!" she exclaimed, her smile rapidly becoming covered in a flood of tears. "I thought you'd never ask, you ... you ... Dr. Dingbat! And, Little Man, don't you *dare* let some bimbo Air Force nurse like that hot-pants WAC Debbie Tanner bump me out of your life ... and don't you *dare* tell me any details about the ones that try!"

For a long while they sat and silently hugged, rocking back and forth slowly, enjoying the secure feeling they created in each other. Mark finally broke their embrace and felt compelled to speak.

"As a form of commitment, before I leave for the Air Force, I'll give you an engagement ring to keep in its box. I want you to help me pick it out. While I'm away, we'll talk on the phone often. Anytime after six months, just let me know when you're ready for me to fly home and put that ring on your finger."

"Mark I really don't need a ring to hold on to. Just your *asking* me to marry you is all the commitment I'll really need." They embraced again, cried, then laughed *and* cried, as they made passionate love beneath the oak tree on a blanket of colorful leaves.

The great oak had dropped countless acorns in its day, even witnessed a Civil War battle or two ... but it had never witnessed such carrying on as presently displayed beneath its branches ... not in 125 years of life!

Relieved, sated, relaxed, and composed, Anne and Mark slowly made their way back to the mansion in the Jeep.

"Mark, do I look like I've been crying?" Anne asked.

"Do I?" Mark replied.

"Well so what if we do!" Anne said. "If anybody notices, we'll just tell them we had one of our tickling matches, and we tickled each other until we cried."

"Anne, you usually pee in your pants when we do that, but maybe nobody will check that closely." The statement earned Mark one of Anne's playful slaps.

After parking the Jeep, they walked slowly back toward the house. Mark suddenly felt Anne touch his low back at the belt line. She inserted her fingers between his shirt and slacks, then extracted a large half-hidden telltale white oak leaf in its fall color—trapped there when Mark put his slacks back on following their "talk" beneath the tree. Anne showed the leaf to Mark. "Some women save roses given them by a lover ... but I'll be happy with just this leaf." *You are still the luckiest man in the world,* Mark's mind told his muddled brain.

Mark and Anne turned as they heard the crunch of gravel from a vehicle directly behind them. It was Zack and Mouse returning from a dove field. Zack bounded out the pickup's cab and yelled to Mark. "Hey Telfair, when Anne gets through playing with your butt, or whatever she's doin', come take a look. You just ain't going to believe this shit! Come over here and look in the back of this freakin' truck!"

Somewhat embarrassed that Zack and Mouse had probably seen Anne's leaf removal, Mark and Anne approached the pickup. Its bed was carpeted with dead dove—maybe 50 or 60 in all. A rabbit, two squirrels, and five or six quail were also in the mix.

"Looks like you guys did great!" Mark said.

"*Guys* hell!" Zack replied. "Mouse shot every damn one of 'em! If we hadn't run out of shells, she'd have filled up the whole freakin' truck. She don't miss. Boy are we gonna eat good tonight!"

Zack was obviously more proud of Mouse than a redneck father on the occasion of a newborn son ... the son who'd be hunting with a shotgun well before his sixth birthday. Zach effortlessly lifted little Mouse up off the ground, swung her around in a circle, giving her a big kiss while she was still airborne. Zack put Mouse down then spoke. "Mark I want you to be the best man at our wedding, and Mouse told me she wants Anne to be maid of honor. You guys do it?"

"Sure," Mark and Anne replied almost in unison. Then Mark dropped a hint: "We may ask you guys to reciprocate sooner than you think."

Anne quickly punched Mark in the side with an elbow, then whispered in his ear. "Let's keep our talk and decisions a secret until it's official ... OK?"

"You're right. I guess I'm so happy we made at least some decision I just had to blab," Mark whispered back.

Fortunately Mark's casual comment didn't register with either Mouse and Zack. As an additional distraction, Betty and Adrian were now walking up from one of the ponds at the rear or the house. The last rays of sunset were kissing the colorful fall horizon when Adrian appeared. He was dragging a long stringer of assorted fish; Betty was following, carrying two fishing rods and a small tackle box. For some reason the friendly Labs started barking, possibly at the stringer of fish. Lem came out of the house to investigate the barking, and was greeted by the most abundant assortment of local game he'd seen in quite some time.

Surveying the bounty, Lem shook his snow-white head and said, "Lawd you mister doctors and miss nurses sho know how to do it. We goin' to be a fixin' some fine eatin' tonight!"

Everyone pitched in and helped Lem with the skinning, scaling, plucking, and gutting. Zack had retrieved a case of Coors from the giant refrigerator and kept everyone, including Lem, fully supplied during the game supper preparation. It was a sight to behold. Zack had Mouse watch Lem's every move, especially when it came to the pan-fried gravy-smothered quail and dove.

Mark and Anne were on their third beers when they suddenly realized

Jer and Sylvia were nowhere to be seen.

"Lem!" Mark said. "Where is Doctor Jerry and Miss Sylvia ... and the baby!"

"Oh, I almost forgets. They's done all gone to Gainesville. One of Doctor Jerry's patients at the hospital ain't a doin' too good, and the doctor what was takin' the call for Doctor Jerry, he ax him to come. Doctor Jerry say he be back soon as he can, and y'all s'pose to drink, boogie, and then eats when it's ready. But don't you fret none. We goin' to have us a good supper anyway, and it'll be a plenty leff over for 'em when dey gets back."

Lem suddenly became the head of the mansion household. He had six willing house staff that helped him prepare a game meal befitting a king. When all was finally prepared, and everyone seated at the long table, Lem refused to sit at the table's head.

Zack put his twelve-beers-down mind into action. "Hey Lem, the head of the table is only a place to put one of the many chairs we've got here. Right?"

Lem thought a moment, then replied, "Well dat do make some kinda sense to me, Dr. Zack."

"Lem, would you sit in *my* chair?" Zack asked.

"Well I sho would, Doctor Zack."

"Well good, Lem, 'cause I'm movin' my chair to the head of the table. Just put your butt in it when I get it moved there. OK?" Lem could not resist Zack's logic, and sat down at the head of the table after Zack swapped the chairs.

They ate until it seemed they could hold no more. After Zack's four cases of Coors vanished, Lem went to the wine cellar, returning with enough shine and wine to numb the entire City of Gainesville. Lem placed several wine bottles and Mason jars on the table, then reseated himself at the table's head. It soon became obvious: Lem's ancient GI tract was apparently not accustomed to such abundance. As he adjusted his chair's position, a very loud uncontrolled passage of voluminous flatus exited his anal sphincter. Though his skin tone concealed the blush that was surely there, Lem was deeply embarrassed. "I's sho sorry 'bout dat, but I jes' couldn't hep it folks," Lem said with sincere apology while wearing the most remorseful look Mark Telfair had ever seen on any face.

Since Zack had succeeded in placing Lem at the head of the table, he felt obligated to come to Lem's rescue. "Hey Lem, my man! Don't apologize for somethin' that's natural and normal. We Grady doctors sometimes pray for our patients to fart after their belly surgery ... lets us know their guts have started workin' right again. We've even classified farts our patients let after surgery. Goes somethin' like this: peeps, freeps, fraps, single-reverberators, double-reverberators, flutter-blast, fuggie-farts, blue-darters, ass-rippers, wet-bennies, church-creepers, fog-of-death, and the max is what we call a green-holocaustic-fog-of-death ... with a linger-factor of five! But Lem, I'd say that one you just let was a lowly single-reverberator ... so it *could* have been a whole lot worse!"

Lem quickly took a sip of clear liquid from a Mason jar, one that Mark knew contained local moonshine. Setting the jar back down, Lem spoke. "Dr. Zack, you sho makes me feel a heap better 'bout dat. I think I done a few of dem church-creepers only dis las' Sunday," Lem said, chuckling. "Lawdy, you doctors be somethin' else ... the way you fellas go 'round classifyin' everything, you know."

After the laughter stopped, everyone was intently listening to Lem and Zack's dialogue. "Well Lem, that's what doctors do—classify stuff. We do that so we can better describe things when we talk among ourselves. Heck, Lem, we've even classified the nurses at Grady Hospital."

Lem pondered a moment, then said, "Sho nuff? Lack they be good nurses, bad nurses, black, white, fat, skinny, short, tall... somethin' lack dat?"

"Uh ... no. Not exactly, Lem," Zack said, then briefly whispered something in Lem's ear.

Lem burst out laughing. After he recovered his composure he said, "Well Dr. Zack, I ain't never heard of classifyin' how good a woman can shake de bed covers, if you get my meaning. Lawd dat is somethin' else now. How do it go?"

Zack surveyed the table occupants. Mouse was not giving him one of her special looks. Everyone else was eagerly waiting for Zack to deliver the Grady docs' classification of nurses to Lem. The Grady men all knew what was coming, but wondered if Zack was sober enough to get it right.

"Well Lem," Zack finally decided to say, "I'll probably be in trouble for tellin' you this, but the latest Grady classification of nurses goes somethin' like this: ice bags, hunchers, humpers, moaners, groaners, squealers, screamers, slow-rotators, fast-rotators, zizz-wheels, and the very best we doctors call ball-bearing multidirectional random-orbit hyper-zizz-wheels!"

Lem erupted in an infectious laughter, which rapidly spread to the entire group. Even Adrian's demure Betty Britt was laughing to the point of tears.

"I sho didn't know doctorin' was so complicated," Lem allowed, then took another sip from his Mason jar.

After the laughter subsided, Mouse, blitzed as she was, loudly chimed in. "Hey you guys! You docs don't have the classification market cornered. And by the way, Zack, you left out the Black-and-Decker-pecker-wreckers! But anyways, we classify you guys too, you know. Now I won't go into all the various class levels, but our guy-classification goes from needle-dicked bug-fuckers all the way up to to salami-rockets. And we ladies all know which of you guys are lefties and which are righties, and who wears boxer and who wears tightie-whitie or Jockey. We also know who the Award Fairy is ... that doctor who goes around putting those engraved plaques at our desks ... the ones that say BITCH OF THE MONTH, MISS PMS OF THE MONTH, and MS. POSTMENOPAUSE OF THE YEAR, and shit like that. But hey! We gals don't go around making such a big deal out of it. And we are all zizz-wheel or better, and you guys damn well know it!"

The girls gave Mouse a standing ovation. Lem laughed till he cried. The Grady guys politely clapped with forced smiles. *God! Zack's going to have his hands full,* Mark thought, now accepting it as an absolute fact.

Mark was definitely feeling the beer and wine, and even considered expounding on the several breast-size classifications the Grady doctors had devised: the DHF or double-handful scale; the CMF or cubic-mouthful scale; and the FS or fruit scale that ranged from olives to pumpkins. But barking dogs signaled someone's arrival, so Mark, prudently, remained silent.

Sylvia (definite four-plus pumpkin), carrying a sleeping JJ, entered the dining room through the kitchen. Jer wasn't far behind. Lem almost fell over trying to get out of his chair at the head of the table, and quickly explained, "I's just keepin' this chair warm for you, Dr. Jerry, and I been a learnin' some doctor and nurse classificatin' stuff."

Jer laughed as he sat down in Lem's vacated chair. "Well I see you guys still know how to get down and boogie! Looks like I got some catching up to do. Sorry I had to leave you guys, but my patient, our preacher, is going to be fine. He went into DTs five days after I did his gallbladder and common bile duct exploration. He jerked his T-tube out ... so we had to reoperate to replace it. Mark, maybe you can mail me one of your Telfair DTs test cards ... you know the one with the big tarantula? Anyway, I got him on some IV alcohol and Valium, and he was just a preachin' fire and brimstone to the nurses in the recovery room when I left!"

The group's laughter had just subsided when Lem returned from the kitchen with Jer's late super: a liter of white wine, a plate of birds, cornbread, lima beans, plus a squirrel, a rabbit thigh, and a fish or two on the side. After putting JJ in the nursery, Sylvia joined them, eating the same as Jer in smaller portions. Everyone had to replay their day for Jer and Sylvia. Mark and Anne were last to do so, explaining they'd just driven around in the Jeep, talked at length, ate and drank way too much, but it had been the best day they'd ever had together. It was close to midnight when Jer finally said, "Don't know about you guys, but I've got to call it a day. I didn't even get back home from the hospital till around five this morning ... a few hours before you guys got here today. Maybe I can really boogie with y'all tomorrow."

As if on cue, everyone stood up and thanked Jer, Sylvia, and Lem for their great day. Like pairs of animals boarding the *Ark,* the guests ascended the stairs with their partners. As Mark and Anne went up, they heard the faint clink of china and silver as Lem began cleaning up the dining room and kitchen ... while softly singing *Amazing Grace.* To himself!

"Well Doctor?" Anne said, once in their room, the room she felt was spinning.

"Well what, Wonder Woman?" Mark replied with a slur he noted in his own voice.

"Well am I a zizz-wheel ... or what?"

"Absolutely, and I hope I'm a salami-rocket, or whatever... but I don't think we should even attempt to operate such complicated machinery while we're both shitfaced drunk!"

"Agreed," Anne said with a hiccup as she retrieved the colorful white oak leaf from her purse, and placed it on their bedside table ... a reminder of how truly special their day had been.

The following morning the mansion's atmosphere was far more subdued. Everyone except Jer and Sylvia nursed hangovers till noon. Though the daylight was painful to the eye, each visiting couple managed to go out to check on Lem at the barbecue pit from time to time. His famous slow-cooked ribs were already absorbing hickory smoke and Lem's secret sauce. Zack had refused to take Mouse hunting again; he knew his hangover headache would go ballistic if he heard a shotgun's blast. So he had Mouse writing down details of Lem's cooking technique, while he personally tried to pry the barbecue sauce recipe out of Lem's head. A smiling Lem just kept shaking his snow-white head and telling Zack, "It ain't been classified yet—jus' an old slave recipe!" In truth, the sauce was a commercial one marketed by Johnny Harris, a famous barbecue restaurateur in Savannah, Georgia. But Lem slightly modified the commercial sauce by diluting it with an undisclosed amount of moonshine, then aged each batch in Mason jars for several months.

Anne and Mark found time to sneak away from the barbecue pit and assorted bull sessions at the house. They went back to the great white oak where Mark had made his spontaneous marriage proposal the day before. Despite the ambiance of the spot, they immediately decided against additional outdoor sex beneath the great tree. Unfortunately, they both had acquired a massive case of chiggers from yesterday's romp on the leaf-covered ground. Sitting on the hood of the Jeep, and scratching their posteriors, they were satisfied with just talking. They discussed their desires regarding having children; further pursuit of professional careers; where in Atlanta they might want to live and practice; what kind of house they might want to build; their six year age difference, and just about everything else they had neglected to discuss in depth during the last fast-paced four years.

While Anne and Mark were continuing their talk in the woods, the other couples remained at the house or on its nearby grounds. Zack and Mouse relentlessly pestered Lem for more recipe details, and wrote down any secrets he let slip out. Adrian and Betty had ridden horses nearby, then played with JJ on the mansion's great room floor for several hours. JJ's nanny was off on Saturdays, and with JJ thus occupied, Jer and Sylvia could be even more gracious hosts; they continually circulated among the visiting couples, barbecue pit, and various bull sessions. Mark and Anne were barely missed.

Once Anne and Mark returned from the oak tree, they went straight to the barbecue pit where Lem had remained in almost constant attendance. They found him adjusting the coals to his liking. Inhaling the smoky aroma of ribs, Anne whispered into Mark's ear a line stolen from a beer commercial: "It just doesn't get any better than this."

Mark whispered back, "I'll tell you after we taste these ribs, but it's going to take a culinary nuke to top yesterday's activity under that oak tree!" The remark cost him another playful slap from Anne, one that Lem witnessed.

"Lawd, all you folks makes me want to be young and playful again. I's had such a good time fixin' fo' y'all, and funnin' wit' y'all. And 'specially learnin' dat classificatin' stuff from Dr. Zack and dat Miss Mouse—Lawd she somethin' else! I sho hates to see you folks gotta leave in de mornin', but rat now my ribs is jus' axin' to be took up, and we goin' to let everybody know they's ready ... and we gonna do what Doctor Jerry call, *de boogie!*"

And boogie they did. They ate, drank, laughed, lied, and rehashed the Gradies till about 1:00 a.m. Jer and Sylvia had insisted that a reluctant Lem again sit at the head of the table ... to "properly honor" the rib feast he'd masterfully prepared. From the head of the table, despite his 82 years, Lem hung in there with Grady's best, just telling stories, and, most assuredly, a few white lies about his own life and childhood.

The next morning at five, the Grady group left *Possum Trot*. Some, including Anne, had to be back at work by seven. On the ride back to Atlanta, everyone in the Volvo was soundly asleep ... except its *two* drivers: Mark in the front seat, Mouse in the back.

24

TUFFSTUFF

Three months had passed since Mark and Anne had returned from their weekend at *Possum Trot*. Anne continued her work at Grady where she'd recently been promoted to the position of Night Operating Room Supervisor. Mark served as the General Surgery Chief Resident at Emory, and worked almost exclusively in the daytime. Their schedules now seemed even more out of sync, preventing another carefree weekend away together. But when their work schedules placed them in the apartment at the same time, they openly discussed a date of their foremost concern: the first day of July, 1969. Following that date, Mark's whereabouts would be totally dictated by the United States Air Force. The promises they'd made beneath the great oak tree at *Possum Trot* became even more important to them both. Those promises— unceremonious as they were—seemed to diminish the intimidation of their upcoming separation, now only five months away.

Mark's exposure to Emory Hospital and its associated clinics provided an excellent academic environment. He polished the basic skills he'd learned at Grady, and further refined his knowledge regarding state-of-the-art surgical oncology. Comfortable at Emory, he somehow missed Grady's frenzied pace. The vast majority of Emory's admissions were elective or scheduled. Unlike Grady, Emory Hospital really did not have an extensive emergency room; it had more of an "urgent care" receiving room, and severe trauma was rarely seen there.

The most Grady-like thing Mark experienced at Emory had been a fluke: a boy who'd been run over by a train. On a freezing December day, the eight-year-old had been walking across a Southern Railroad trestle spanning a creek near the Emory campus. He'd apparently misjudged the train's speed. Less than ten minutes following the accident, the youngster had been taken to Emory Hospital. He'd been considered dead by the ambulance attendants who'd retrieved his body parts from the cold shallow creek beneath the trestle.

Mark, and Chief Residents representing other specialties, had been summoned to the Emory Hospital's urgent care receiving area. Even his Grady experiences did not prepare him for the shock of what he saw: The young white male had been *cut completely in half!*

The upper part consisted of everything located above his navel, the bottom part his lowermost abdomen and legs. Surprisingly, both "halves" were not severely damaged. There was no blood. All of it apparently had been lost in the chilly waters of the creek. Mark's mind speedily questioned: *What part of the train could be so sharp, making it look as though a giant surgically sharpened guillotine had fallen across the boy's belly at the level of his navel? Could the child have been chilled rapidly enough to freeze his metabolism, suspending oxygen demands, and perhaps spare his brain and other vital organs?*

"Hey fellas, I can feel a heartbeat! No peripheral pulse, but I definitely feel a faint heartbeat. I can feel it right through this kid's thin chest wall!" Mark yelled, lightly touching his fingers to the dead patient's cold chest. Everyone looked at Mark as though he might be insane.

One of the Emory residents loudly cleared his throat. "You're just feeling your own pulse in your fingers, or possibly the kid's faint agonal myocardial contractions. You Grady guys never know when to give up, do you?" he asked insultingly.

"Only when necessary," Mark shot back, ignoring the way the Emory residents looked down their noses at the Grady residents rotating through *their* program. "Just look, fellas," Mark said as he checked the child's pupils with a penlight. "They aren't fixed or dilated yet. Even respond to light. So let's give it a go!"

With reluctance on everyone else's part, two IVs were started in the little boy's arms. He was infused with IV fluid and type O-negative blood. Large vascular surgical clamps were placed across the major thumb-sized vessels (aorta and vena cava) clearly exposed at the lower end of the kid's upper half. An endotracheal tube was placed in his windpipe, and he was artificially ventilated by Emory's Chief Anesthesia Resident who continually monitored vital signs, but with little enthusiasm. Twenty minutes later the child had an acceptable blood pressure, and his pupil signs still indicated that he possibly had not sustained irreversible brain damage.

Following a condescending sigh, the sarcastic Emory resident who'd made the comment about the Grady guys never giving up spoke to Mark again. "What do you suggest we do next, Mr. Grady Doctor ... now that we have a blood pressure and pulse pushing blood through a brain that's deader than a doornail? Think we should call all the king's horses and men ... and see if they can put him back together again?"

"Not exactly," Mark said, ignoring the resident's sick humor. "But with all that's available here at Emory, we should at least try to save the upper half!"

And save it they did. Professors and residents from multiple specialties pitched in at various times during the six-hour procedure. At the end of the surgery the patient had a small round "bottom" which resembled a half-basketball. It had two openings: The ureter from each kidney had been internally joined to form a "Y," and the lower single limb of that "Y" brought to the skin surface as a solitary urinary drainage opening; the second opening was a colostomy, to permit bowel movements.

The child's recovery was not entirely uneventful, yet smoother than anyone had anticipated. Thankfully, due to effective pain killers, the boy experienced only the usual postoperative pain. The single most important observation came about 48 hours following surgery: *The child's brain functioned perfectly.* So did his other vital organs and arms. Two weeks later, the young patient actually reveled in the media attention, and turned out to be a quite a ham when interviewed. Psychiatrists at Emory weren't sure what the long-term psychological effects would be, but were surprised at how the tough little fellow seemed to take his fate in stride. All the doctors would soon be equally amazed at his innovative physical adaptations as well.

Though the boy's physical recovery seemed a success thus far, Mark found himself concerned about the kid's future. Not a single family member had visited. Except for the media, no one had even inquired about the youngster. Emory's social service workers had determined the child's father was in prison serving a life term; his mother was a drug addict who worked as a stripper, and she had not shown up for work since the accident. She was also wanted on drug charges and considered a missing person by APD.

A month following his injury, the child was transferred to Henrietta Egleston Hospital, a renowned pediatric facility located across the street from Emory. At Egleston he'd receive further rehabilitation. Famous doctors specializing in prosthetic design came from around the world. Each specialist seemed determined to design some type of a "socket" to fit his lower-end "basketball." Artificial legs, perhaps electrically powered ones, would be attached to the socket, thus allowing the youngster to walk again. *Like a robot,* Mark thought when he'd heard rumors of the plans.

Though no longer directly involved in the patient's care, Mark frequently visited the child following his transfer to Egleston. They'd already become fast friends. While still in Emory Hospital, Mark had nicknamed the child "Tuffstuff," and the kid loved being called that. On one of his later visits to Egleston, Mark found Tuffstuff's bed empty. *Maybe Social Service placed him in a foster home? Perhaps he could have suddenly died?* Mark thought, fearing the worst. He headed toward the nurses' station to inquire about his favorite young patient. Briskly walking down the hall, Mark heard a strange noise in the hallway behind him: *clap-it-ty-clap* ... *clap-it-ty-clap* ... *clap-it-ty-clap* ... echoed off the tile floor. It sounded like a pony running. Mark turned and froze. Astounded, he could not believe his own eyes: Tuffstuff was running toward him on his *hands!* His little basketball-butt jutted straight up in the air, covered by what appeared to be a giant knitted cap. The child rushed up to Mark.

"Dr. Mark!" Tuffstuff yelled. "I thought you were gonna leave without even telling me hello! And some big doctor from England is supposed to see me in my room in a few minutes!"

A moment later, the Egleston PA system softly announced: "Tuffstuff, please go to your room. Now, please. Your doctors are there to see you."

Sounding like a small round of applause, Tuffstuff tore off down the hall toward his room. He'd only gone about 50 feet, then abruptly stopped. Standing on a single hand, he silently motioned a rapid come-on to Mark with the other. He wanted Mark to be present while the doctors examined him in his room.

Mark found himself running to keep up with the child. As they entered the boy's room, several doctors in long white coats now stood around his empty bed. Finding a space between the white-clad doctors, Tuffstuff quickly did a handspring and a flip, which landed him perfectly in his bed—squarely on his basketball-bottom!

"Sorry I'm a little late, doctors," Tuffstuff said, "but I went to get some water at the cooler, and then I saw Dr. Mark here, so I had to go chase after him. It's OK if I asked him to be here, isn't it? You know he was one of the doctors that saved my life over at Emory across the street."

The astonished visiting UK prosthetics doctor broadly smiled before speaking. "That's quite all right, young man. I certainly have no objection to your Dr. Mark being here with us. But how long have you been doing that?"

"Doing *what?*" Tuffstuff replied, obviously bewildered.

"Running about on your hands as you do ... doing these handsprings to get into bed ... things such as that?"

"Oh, *that!* I've been doing it since they tried to make that first bucket-thing here at Egleston ... you know, with the legs on it. *I hated it!* I could use it OK, but it was *so* slow, and I was always afraid I'd fall and hurt myself. So, I like walking on my hands a lot better. And it's easier to take care of my pee and poop bags when that bucket's not in the way."

"Young fellow I'm sure you probably don't know it, but I design artificial limbs, special hands, even shoes, and things like that. But I must admit, I can't design anything that would work nearly as well as what you've already figured out on your own—just by fully using your own hands and arms. So it looks as if I've made a trip 'cross the ocean for nothing. Do you have any questions?"

"Yes sir. When can I go home?"

Home? My God! The poor child doesn't even have a home! Mark thought.

"Your doctors here at Egleston must decide that, my lad, but I don't see any reason for you to remain in the hospital. What they've already designed for you here at Egleston is certainly as good as I could possibly do."

"Well, can I ask you another question, sir?" Tuffstuff asked in a hopeful timid voice.

"Sure. Of course you can. So what is your question, lad?"

"You think you could make me some really good shoes for my hands ... before you go back to England? My hands get kinda cold and dirty, especially when I walk outside."

"You bet I can! But before I get started on designing your shoes, do you think you could do me a very special favor?"

"Oh, yes sir! Anything I can do I will, sir," Tuffstuff replied, hoping he'd be able to do whatever the famous visiting physician desired.

The amazed English prosthetics doctor warmly smiled at the spunky kid before speaking. "I'd very much like for you to show me just exactly how you manage to use that water cooler you mentioned ... the one that's up so high off the floor?"

"You bet, sir!" Tuffstuff beamed with confidence.

Without further words, the child did a flip out of the bed, landing with a *clap* on the palms of his hands. He went to his room's closed door and began opening it by standing on one hand, then reached up to the knob with the other. He then pulled the heavy door open with only the one hand planted on the floor for traction. Tuffstuff shot down the hall in his rapid *clap-it-ty-clap*. He stopped precisely at the cooler, and patiently waited while the bedside group caught up with him. When they'd gotten there, Tuffstuff executed a handspring and flip. He caught the lip of the cooler with both hands, chinned up, held the position with a single hand, then proudly operated the cooler's button with the other. After drinking, he simply reversed the procedure and was "standing" again in an instant.

A few days later, Mark had an opportunity to see Tuffstuff's promised shoes. They resembled leather mittens that had ribbed high-traction "soles" in their palms. About an inch of thumb and index finger tips remained exposed on both "shoes." This permitted Tuffstuff to fasten buttons, turn book pages, and do other tasks requiring fine motor skills ... without taking his "shoes" off.

After three months of hospitalization, and the completion of his "shoes," Tuffstuff was moved from Egleston to foster care.

Mark dismissed himself from Emory the following day; he had completed his scheduled four-month rotation there, and would next go back to Grady. Mark still detested Atlanta's rush-hour traffic. Feeling certain it was frozen in gridlock, he'd waited until 11:00 p.m. to leave Emory. He continued thinking about the tough little kid as he parked his Volvo in the familiar Grady parking lot, but while walking toward the hospital another thought came:

This is the last four months of my formal surgical training.

25

SAFE HARBOR

Though he'd stopped at Kmart, actual driving time from Emory to Grady had been only 20 minutes. Inside Grady's massive foyer, Mark Telfair felt like he was passing into a safe harbor upon return from a long voyage. *Perhaps I've survived that storm I first entered here five years ago. I first entered it exactly at this same spot ... exactly where I am right now,* he thought while passing the reception desk which was unstaffed at night. He recalled the ancient receptionist who'd embarrassed him on his first day of internship by pointing out his name tag was on the wrong side of his jacket. *How could my jacket's name tag have been so vitally important as an intern, and seem so utterly trivial now?* his mind questioned. As he continued walking, many comforting familiar sights, sounds, and faces surrounded him. He had made it back to the Gradies. He was safely home. *This is the home I'd become so frightened of ... and had almost abandoned as an intern,* he thought.

He confidently boarded the elevator to the 14th floor, and went to the room he'd shared with Zack. Mark hadn't slept a single night in his Grady room in the last eight months; he'd spent his nights at Anne's apartment while away at VA and Emory. In his familiar room at Grady, he discovered Zack was not there, apparently working somewhere in the hospital. Nothing had changed in the room except for a very flattering framed photo-portrait of Mouse, Zack's fiancée. It was the sole item on Zack's bedside table.

Mark unloaded a small bag of toiletries he'd picked up at Kmart, duplicates of the things he kept at Anne's. As he removed the six items from the bag, he was still a little pissed at the village-idiot cashier at Kmart. It had taken her only 30 minutes, and six tries, to correctly total the six items he'd purchased. Mark rarely forgot a face. Names, yes. But rarely a face ... especially the eyes. He'd recognized the Kmart clerk immediately. About eight months ago that same Kmart clerk had worked for the U.S. Postal Service, and had helped him with his mailing address change when he'd moved in with Anne. It had taken a mere two months to straighten out the mess she'd created, and since he was expecting his orders from the Air Force, he was now glad he had kept his mailing address at Anne's. He'd still be spending most nights there anyway. He simply wanted the option of staying at Grady the nights he'd be on call during the final four months of his residency.

He picked up the phone and dialed the three-digit extension for the OR supervisor's office.

"Anne Hunt, Night Supervisor speaking. How may I help you?"

"Wanna go shopping for an engagement ring?" Mark whispered.

"You crazy nut! I love you, but I told you that wasn't necessary. That oak leaf I've been carrying around in my purse is beginning to break up and it's making a mess ... but I can live with that. I can't leave the OR now anyway. We've got four rooms running right now. So why don't you come down to my office and have a cup of coffee with me?"

"Be there in a few minutes," Mark said and hung up.

At Anne's glass-walled office on the third floor, Mark felt a twinge of jealousy when he saw a good-looking resident sitting on her desk. From the side and back, he looked very much like Hot Body, the Orthopedic Chief Resident who had left Grady several years ago. The resident hadn't seen Mark's approach, and continued to madly flirt with Anne. *Be cool*, Mark thought, still fighting jealousy. Mark opened Anne's door, and loudly cleared his throat while poking his head inside to speak: "Uh, Honey ... did I get any mail at *our* apartment today?"

"Oops!" the resident said as he flushed. "But hey man ... you can't blame me for trying. She's a knockout!"

"I know!" Mark said to the resident, rapidly departing Anne's office.

"You little devil," Anne smiled. "If these walls weren't glass I'd give you a proper welcome!"

"Seriously Anne, did any mail come for me today? I'm expecting my orders any day now. Some of the deferred-entry guys already have theirs."

"Yeah. I think that may be what it is. It's a big thick brown envelope with USAF and some Denver return address," Anne said. "Let's open it together tomorrow evening before I have to go to work."

And they did exactly that. Mark's orders were for Ramey AFB in Puerto Rico. In terms of geographical area, an assignment to Hawaii would have been the only better one possible. Both were elated about the place, but not so elated about the distance that would soon separate them—or so they thought. Two weeks later Mark got new orders. He had been reassigned to Wurtsmith AFB in Oscoda, Michigan—a small SAC base which he knew would have long winters with abundant snow.

According to an explanatory letter sent with his revised orders, a fully trained surgeon, a native of Puerto Rico, was currently serving at Wurtsmith. He had requested a hardship transfer to his native land, where his father had suddenly died and his mother was terminally ill. He had no brothers or sisters and needed to be closer to his mother and the family's construction business to keep all from being lost. Mark hated to admit it, but he felt the hardship transfer had been justified, even though it meant he had lost the posh Puerto Rico assignment.

Mark mostly regretted the financial hardship caused by his reassignment to the Strategic Air Command base in Michigan. He had impulsively gone into debt. He bought a 20-foot boat, assorted SCUBA and underwater photography equipment, and had already shipped everything to Ramey AFB in Puerto Rico. Undoing the screwup took weeks, and cost him dearly in shipping fees before all was settled. Anne had not been critical; she had even been optimistic. She'd said, "Look at it this way, Little Man. At least we'll be closer together, phone calls won't cost as much, and we could even drive the distance to see each other." *I've got to be the luckiest man alive. She makes me feel so good ... even when I make a serious blunder,* Mark had thought.

Comfortable with the familiar Grady environment, the last four months of his Chief Resident year flew by, but there were no more *Possum Trot* weekends. The inner-city hospital still had its steady flow of trauma patients, but there were no new mojo witches, no new Cowboys, no shots fired in the ER, and no cue balls or light bulbs hiding where they didn't belong.

As his time to depart closed in, Mark went to plan "B": He sold the Volvo to Zack for next to nothing, then went into additional debt by purchasing a new Chevy pickup truck with a bed-mounted camper. He planned to use the camper to haul his limited possessions to Michigan, and if he didn't like living on base, he'd just live in the camper off the base, or so he reasoned.

On their last Atlanta night together, Mark and Anne went to the House of the Rising Sun, a local supper club. There they ate, drank, and danced until the wee hours; later, at Anne's apartment, they made love in a tender whirl of pleasure and tears that lasted until way past dawn, each behaving as though it might be their first and last time.

26

OFF TO THE WILD BLUE YONDER

Midmorning, on the first of July, 1969, Anne helped Mark load his possessions from her apartment into the new camper. Then Anne said, "Don't kiss me. I know I'll cry ... again."

Upon starting his truck Mark simply said, "Ditto." He promised to call her the following afternoon to let her know where he was.

As Mark pulled out of the apartment parking lot, his tears came again. He tried to suppress a thought but it came anyway: *God, I sure hope I'm doing the right thing by sticking to our plans made at Possum Trot ... just hope it won't be a case of too little, too late. Should have bought her a ring, instead of this damn truck and camper.*

Mark stopped for the night at a truck stop on I-75 just south of Lexington, Kentucky. He knew he'd promised Anne he would call the next afternoon, but couldn't wait. He dropped coins into the truck stop pay phone, dialed Grady, and asked for the Night Operating Room Supervisor. Despite the pocketful of quarters he'd used, Anne's "I miss and love you too" were the only six words of their conversation he remembered. Utterly exhausted, he returned to his camper in the parking lot, where an unrelenting army of large diesel truck engines snorted around his camper through the night. Finally, he found restless sleep.

The next morning at four he ate a hearty trucker's breakfast, then got back on the road, heading north on I-75, consulting his new *Rand McNally Road Atlas.* Glancing at the map, a twinge of panic soon began to develop; there was no Oscoda anywhere on the Michigan map! He'd found it a month or so ago, using an older map, one he had since discarded—but Oscoda wasn't on his new *Rand McNally!* In full panic, he pulled over to the emergency lane and stopped to recheck his USAF orders and verify the town's spelling. *Finally,* he located the minuscule Oscoda, 200 miles north of Detroit, on the coast of Lake Huron near the mouth of the *Au Sable* River ... and such a tiny town, it was almost completely obscured by a staple in the new atlas. *Really in the boondocks*, Mark thought, but he was relieved he'd finally found it again.

He crossed the state of Ohio and kept wishing he had his old Volvo back. The pickup with camper was top-heavy, and didn't drive nearly as well as the 14-year-old car he'd sold to Zack. *Zack is definitely both crazy and brilliant, but no fool,* Mark thought, as he headed north to Flint, Michigan, using US 23 to avoid Detroit's traffic. Ten hours later Mark rolled into Oscoda, a small postcard-perfect resort town. All impressed him: the vast gray-blue expanses of Lake Huron, fir and birch trees, marshes, placid marinas. *Boondocks are not so bad after all,* he had to admit.

Wurtsmith AFB was obviously the dominant nontourist industry in the small town. As he approached its impressive main gate, Mark was surprised to find stone-faced guards bearing guns. They insisted on seeing his orders and driver's license. After they thoroughly inspected the contents of his camper, Mark was finally permitted to pass after receiving explicit directions to the base site where he'd be "in-processed," one of the gate guards said gruffly .

He found the initial processing site without difficulty, but ended up going to several different buildings before his full processing was over. He'd been re-fingerprinted; issued a military photo-ID card; given a gate pass decal for his vehicle; fitted with summer and winter uniforms; given keys to his quarters, and had acquired a stack of base regulations over two inches thick. Several hours later, he finally plopped down on the bed in his BOQ room. The Bachelor Officers' Quarters reminded him of his room at Grady—functional basics only. Mark was startled when the phone promptly rang on the table at his bedside. *So soon? Maybe Anne?* he thought.

"Dr. Mark Telfair speaking."

"Well hello there!" the excited male caller said. "I know you probably don't recognize my voice, but I'm Dr. Bill Lebowitz. The Lebowitz from Grady. You know, the short little Jew guy that did med school at Harvard? Remember me?"

Mark drew a momentary blank, but a second later it hit: "I sure do, Bill! You were one of my interns when I was the JAR in the Grady ER. That's been about four years ago. You were the intern who had that patient with a light bulb stuck up his butt. But where the heck are you right now, Bill?"

"I'm at the base hospital. I was just going over the roster of new folks we're getting, and I couldn't believe it—your name was on it!" Lebowitz said. "So I got your BOQ room and telephone numbers from the base operator."

"What a small world, Bill. How in the heck did you end up here at

Wurtsmith?"

"Long story, and I gotta be in the OR for an appendectomy in just a few minutes. But how about I pick you up, say eight o'clock, and you have dinner with me and the wife at my house tonight?"

"That'll be great! See you at eight," Mark said, immediately feeling less isolated.

Mark showered, shaved, and dressed in fresh clothes. He stretched out on his bed hoping to catch a quick nap, still not really believing another Grady doctor had somehow ended up at the same end of nowhere. He fell into a light sleep, soon to be awakened by a knock on his door. Mark sprang out of bed and opened it. There stood five-foot-four Lebowitz, wearing his USAF uniform and a large smile. Mark gave him an Italian-style hug, a traditional greeting among Grady guys.

It took only a few minutes for Lebowitz to drive Mark to the married officers' housing area. Through deep dusk, Mark could see all the homes appeared outwardly identical—each freshly painted a light gray with white trim; impeccable lawns cut to exactly one and one-half inches; identical mailboxes, and minimal landscaping. *Functional* and *boring* were the two words that came to Mark's mind.

Dr. Lebowitz parked his year-old red Corvette in his drive and was soon introducing his cute equally Jewish wife, Imelda, whom he called Mel. He then quickly disappeared to change into his civvies, as he called his regular clothes. Soon steaks were on the backyard grill, beers were being downed, and salads tossed while potatoes baked. Reminiscing about Grady shifted into high gear around the dinner table. Mel laughed till she cried, then apologized that she had to leave for an art class immediately following dinner.

After Mel left, Lebowitz explained how he'd ended up at Wurtsmith. Bill Lebowitz had not signed up for the deferred active duty plan—the so-called Berry Plan—which allowed a physician in training to sign up in advance for a service branch of his choice. In exchange, Uncle Sam would guarantee that the doctor would not be drafted during his specialty training years. As a form of payback for that guarantee, upon completing their specialty training, a physician would immediately do a two-year active-duty hitch with their chosen service branch.

Lebowitz had elected to gamble on the draft truly being random and based upon the country's needs. He'd been unlucky, and drafted by the Air Force in the middle of his first-year surgical residency at Grady. He'd now been at Wurtsmith—he called it *Worthless*—AFB for about three and a half years, taking Air Force re-enlistments a year at a time, just waiting for a residency slot at the appropriate level to open at Grady.

Over Kahlúa and creams, Lebowitz explained details he'd learned about the SAC base: Nuke-loaded B-52s, KC-135 refueling tankers, F-4 fighter jets, and assorted less impressive aircraft made up the bulk of the hardware. "They don't tell us doctors much about the military aspects of the base ... we just hear things, little bits and pieces here and there. Mostly we learn from the NCOs. And believe me it's the noncommissioned officers that make this place work," Lebowitz explained.

"Bill, you mean we don't get some kind of official orientation ... some indoctrination or explanation of basic military etiquette?"

"Hell no! At least none of the docs here did. Heck, I didn't even know how—or even whom—to salute when I first got here. I even saluted a mailman one day, because his uniform looked kinda like the Air Force winter uniform, and his hat had a bunch of silver braid, so I figured he must be an Air Force general or something!"

Mark couldn't resist laughing. "Well I'm sure glad you're here to show me the ropes. Now that I've gotten all the uniforms, rank insignias, and name tags, I must confess I haven't the foggiest idea where all that pin-on stuff goes."

"Well it's all supposed to be in that thick wad of papers you accumulated earlier today," Lebowitz replied, "but I don't think any of the doctors ever read that stuff. It's mostly bullshit, and almost impossible to read anyway. There are only a few things you really need to sweat. Just obey the base speed limits and pay attention to the restricted-area signs. And be sure to carry your ID card at all times. I'll show you around the hospital and the rest of the base sometime tomorrow, and tonight, when we get back to the BOQ, I'll show you how to pin all that crap on your uniform."

"Thanks, Bill," Mark yawned. "And thank Imelda too, when she gets back from her class. I hate to eat and run, man, but I've really got to call it a day. I'm beat. I feel like I just pulled 36 straight on orthopedics at Grady! And I'd really like to call my girlfriend in Atlanta before I crash."

Lebowitz drove Mark back to the BOQ, where he fixed Mark's summer USAF uniform. Recalling his own exhausting first day on base, Lebowitz left the BOQ to allow Mark to rest up for the disappointments yet to come.

In the BOQ, Mark approached sleep somewhat frustrated; he couldn't get a call through to Anne ... seems Grady Hospital didn't accept collect calls, from *Major* Mark Telfair or anybody else. If a pay phone was on the base he had no idea where it might be. *I'll call her tomorrow afternoon at the apartment,* he thought while drifting off to an uneasy sleep.

The next morning his BOQ phone rang at eight. It was Bill Lebowitz. He had no surgery scheduled and his morning was free. "Want the 25-cent tour of Worthless Air Force Base?" he asked. Five minutes later, Lebowitz picked Mark up at the BOQ and drove him to the hospital. The pair started the tour with a free breakfast in the hospital's small cafeteria: coffee, orange juice, eggs, bacon, and toast (but no grits!).

Mark felt disappointed. They'd said they didn't even know what grits were. Tongue in cheek, and wearing his new uniform, Major Mark Telfair quickly explained to an NCO staffing the serving line: "Grits are a Southern crop, Sergeant. They're very difficult to raise, and even more difficult to pick, but well worth the effort!"

Regarding grits, Mark finally extracted a promise from one of the NCO cooks: "Major, you get 'em here, we'll cook 'em for ya." Anne would later arrange to send him grits via mail. While the hospital kitchen gladly prepared grits for him, there was a small price to pay: The cooks insisted on calling the hot mush "Georgia ice cream," and they quickly hung Mark with his Air Force nickname: "Major Grits."

After breakfast, Mark got the full hospital tour and had soon met 13 other doctors. All seemed to be OK guys, but as the tour continued, Mark became less and less impressed with the hospital itself. The tiny 50-bed facility seemed to be a mere first-aid station compared to Atlanta's Grady, Emory, and the VA. Nonetheless, the hospital's nurses and corpsmen were an impressive professional lot. The two ORs looked fairly good, but certainly weren't what he'd been accustomed to. After visiting them, Lebowitz read the obvious disappointment in Mark's face.

Comfortably seated at the Officers' Club for lunch, Lebowitz began explaining his personal Air Force survival plan.

"Look Mark, I know this is a big step down from where you and I were in Atlanta. At first I was disappointed too. Now that you're on board, we can do more major procedures in the OR again ... within the limits of the equipment we have here, of course. The instruments. That's the biggest factor."

"Bill, any chance we could get them to upgrade some of the instruments in the OR?" Mark asked, skepticism apparent in his voice.

"Chances of us improving our instruments here, beyond what we've already got, are slim and none ... unless we work through the NCOs. Seems they have 'procurement capabilities' unknown to the doctors or anyone else in this outfit. Don't worry, we'll get what we need," Lebowitz replied wearing a smile.

"How'd the fully trained surgeon I replaced deal with the instrument problem?" Mark asked.

"He didn't. Didn't seem to care. Dr. Garcia was the fully trained guy we had here before you arrived. But his main interest was getting a hardship transfer back to Ramey in Puerto Rico. So, I've been the only surgeon here since he left three months ago. And Garcia didn't get a chance to teach me much anyway. About half the time he was on emergency leave dealing with family health problems in San Juan. In the meantime, I've had to air-evac a lot of major surgical cases down to Wright-Patterson in Ohio. I had to do that because I didn't have but half the first-year's surgical residency under my belt when I got drafted. And I don't feel comfortable enough to do some of the more major stuff I probably could do, even if we had better equipment. It's just that I'm afraid to do it with made-in-Taiwan instruments, and only a corpsman assisting."

"Couldn't the other doctors assist you in the OR?"

"Mark, you've met the other docs we've got here, and they're all great guys in their own areas. But psychiatrists, pediatricians, internists, radiologists, rheumatologists, allergists, anesthesiologists, and opthalmologists just don't cut it when it comes to general surgery. Only the two OB-GYN fellas you met earlier today are of any use in the OR ... and once you get them away from the pelvic area, they're totally lost. They might as well be somewhere in East Bumfuck without a map!"

"Damn! Bill, I didn't realize it was this bad," Mark replied despondently.

Lebowtiz continued: "I guess it could be worse, but I'm gonna look at the bright side."

"Bright side?" Mark questioned, his spirits still low.

"Yeah, think positively," Lebowitz smiled. "We'll get the NCOs to get us the instruments we need. We can do bigger stuff in the OR. You can teach me a lot and you'll find me a darn good assistant."

Mark felt his spirits lifting as Lebowitz continued. "We're *both* stuck here now. You need to accept that fact; I already have. So let's just make the best of it and the time will go faster. You need to resign yourself to enjoying the perks offered by the Base Recreation Department, the PX, Aero Club, and this Officers' Club ... and for God's sake, use all your 30-day paid leave to preserve your sanity. Just go see the world, get away during the long winters here, or go back home to see your girlfriend. Bottom line: *Go with the system!* It'll all be over before we both know it."

Sage advice, Mark thought, and he took it. With the help of Lebowitz, other doctors, and the hospital's NCOs, Mark learned to manipulate the system. At the end of his first week on base, one of the NCOs had located an off-base apartment for Mark only 50 feet from the shoreline of Lake Huron. His liberal housing allowance covered most of the rent. With free meals, medical care, uniforms, PX privileges, and a major's annual pay,

Mark Telfair was—for the first time in his life—a rich man. His frequent phone calls to Anne would prove to be his single largest monthly expense.

Mark immersed himself in local life, both on the base and off. He bought a yellow Honda trail bike at a motorcycle and snowmobile shop in Oscoda. Off the base he toured the miles of dirt trails in the Huron National Forest that surrounded both Oscoda and the Air Force base; on the base, he explored all sections that did not have the garish yellow signs with black letters: RESTRICTED AREA.

Off duty, dressed in civvies and riding his new Honda on base, Mark carefully obeyed all posted base speed limits. A bargain-priced Nikon bought at the PX hung from a bright red strap around his neck. Mark Telfair was on a mission: taking pictures of the base to send Anne. Still on his mission, and Honda, Mark had followed a small wooded trail into an undeveloped area within the base perimeter; it led to a runway. Several impressive-looking jet fighters (F-4s) were parked nearby. Since no signs were present, Mark eased the Honda onto the runway, then pulled under a wing of one of the jets. He dismounted, and started shooting aircraft pictures from all angles. *These should really impress Anne,* he thought.

Flashing blue lights atop a speeding dark blue Econoline van approached. Mark wore a friendly smile as he casually waved at the rapidly approaching vehicle. It screeched to a stop a few feet away. Two armed guards immediately burst out.

"On the ground ... spread eagle ... face down! NOW!" one of the men yelled.

When Mark did not immediately do as commanded, the two men simultaneously shouldered their weapons, then aimed directly at the center of his chest. Holding his now-shaking hands up, Mark said, "Hey look fellas, I think there's some mistake here. All I'm doing is taking pictures—"

"Of aircraft in a *restricted* area!" one of the guards curtly finished. They removed the camera from Mark's neck, but still kept him covered with their carbines.

"You got ID ?" one of the guards barked.

Mark slowly lowered his hands. Even more slowly he reached for his wallet, not wanting to encourage itchy trigger fingers. Cautiously, he removed the photo ID he'd been issued. One of the guards stepped forward and snatched the card from his hand, then stepped back to examine it with his partner. Both guards carefully studied the plastic-encased card. They slowly started smiling, lowered their guns, and burst out in uncontrolled laughter.

One of the guards—Hansen, his name tag said—was finally able to speak. "Major Mark M. Telfair, 853rd *Medical Group*," Hansen said, as he read the card aloud. "Damn! You must be that Major Grits the hospital cook told us about at the NCO Club coupla nights ago. We shudda known! Shit, Major, we're really sorry about this ... but how the fuck did you get out here anyway?"

"Came through a small trail in those woods right over there ... on that Honda," Mark said, pointing first to the woods, then the motorcycle. "And there are *no* signs anywhere that say that trail is a restricted area, and I don't see any signs at the edge of this runway either!"

Hansen became quite humble, then spoke. "Well we need to work out some kinda deal here, Major Grits ... or would you rather I call you Doctor?"

"After college, it took me nine years to become a specialized doctor ... and only *one* day to go from civilian to a major in this United States Air Force," Mark boldly replied, feeling in control of the situation. "So why don't you guys just call me Doctor."

Hansen continued: "Doc, me and my partner here ... well let's just say we'd both be in very deep shit if the Wing Commander ever finds out we let you get this far ... *alive!*" Hansen pointed across the runway, lowering his voice to a whisper before speaking. "Doc, we got nuke-loaded BUFFs just a 100 yards from here—just the other side of them grass-covered dirt mounds you see over there. So how about we first take that film out of your camera, and then you just completely forget you was ever out here. OK? And Doc ... we'll arrange for you to get a nice ride in one of them F-4s, or anything else we got on this base that'll fly. Deal?"

"You bet!" Mark exclaimed, smiling with relief. "But what the hell is a *BUFF*? The thing with the nukes?"

"Ah shit, Doc! Shudda known. You ain't been around here long enough to find out yet. BUFF is simply B-U-F-F. Stands for Big Ugly Fat Fucker. That's what us regulars call the B-52s, OK?"

"OK with me. Call 'em whatever you like," Mark said, then smiled as he resisted a strong urge to laugh in the faces of the guards armed with carbines. *Not a good move,* he thought as he politely retrieved his empty camera and ID card, then zipped back through the woods on his Honda. *Big Ugly Fat Fucker* still rolled in his mind, but he didn't laugh till he was well out of their sight. When his laughter did come, he nearly wrecked the motorcycle.

About a week later, Mark noted a prominent RESTRICTED AREA sign posted at the trail's entrance. He was sure similar signs were now all along the trail, and at the runway's edge too. A few days after that, a Sergeant Hansen made a call to the hospital asking for Doctor Major Grits. Mark got his promised ride in an F-4. He was permitted to do some legal photos of selected planes and certain areas of the flight line. In fact, he was permitted to shoot a number of aerial photos from the F-4's cockpit, but only when the jet was nowhere near the SAC base. Upon getting back to base, climbing out of the F-4, and wiggling out of his G-suit, Mark's mind made a quick mental note: *If an F-4 should be female, I'd definitely have to give her the Grady classification of zizz-wheel ... or better!*

Mark continued to follow Lebowitz's survival advice: "Go with the system." He no longer worried about the few remaining equipment limitations that kept him from doing all he was trained to do in an OR. He enjoyed teaching Lebowitz and the medical corpsmen, all of whom were so eager to learn.

He enjoyed activities with the group of base doctors, but they and their families socialized more or less as an autonomous group in isolation from the lifer and enlisted rank and file. Though Mark had been readily accepted by the entire medical group, he stuck out like the pregnant bride at a shotgun wedding: He was the *only* single doctor on base. Many NCOs quietly offered to fix him up with female companionship, which he politely declined. Basically monogamous, Mark found times that tried his soul; he had not been entirely successful at being celibate. His occasional lapses were discreetly self-arranged, with no strings attached. They were all with normal women, who, like himself, felt already committed to another, yet occasionally yielded to the sexual frustration of being separated from their true loves.

By December five feet of snow blanketed the ground. Tire chains, snowmobiles, and snow shovels just weren't in his Southern blood. The hot grits he'd get at the hospital every morning helped, but that only went so far. The Honda was in storage for the winter. Snow skis clashed with his water ski skills, and cutting through several feet of ice just to go fishing— well that was just plain stupid! Even the beautiful vista of Lake Huron afforded by his apartment's balcony had completely vanished; he now saw only a bleak glaring sheet of ice which stretched to the horizon, and the wind that blew across it chilled him each time he ventured outdoors. Medical group social activities had dwindled to zilch. Mark frequently got cabin fever, being confined to his apartment when not on duty. Nightly phone calls to Anne just weren't enough. He had to see her, hold her. *I need to use some of that leave time,* he thought.

Three days before Christmas, the Northwest Airlines turboprop he'd taken out of Michigan's civilian Tri-City Airport touched down at Hartsfield in Atlanta. When he exited the aircraft, the 65-degree air felt like silk, a warm breath of heaven. Spotting Anne waiting there for him ...

well, that *was* heaven.

After their initial kisses and embrace, Anne extended her left hand to him, its ring finger bare. "Mark, I know it's a bit over the six months we agreed upon at *Possum Trot*, but after a little comparison shopping, I now know you're the salami-rocket that makes me a zizz-wheel. I'm now ready. Is the offer still good? Will you marry me?"

"I thought you'd never ask," Mark said, fighting jealousy, yet accurately recalling Anne's exact words to him following his proposal to her at *Possum Trot*. As they stood frozen in mutual embrace, focused only on the emotion of the moment, both remained totally oblivious to the gawking Hartsfield terminal crowd rapidly moving around them.

Several minutes later, walking toward baggage claim, Mark spotted a discarded cigar band on the floor. He quickly scooped it up, took her left hand and slid it onto her ring finger. "Think that will do until we make it to a jewelry store?" Mark asked.

"You know it will ... *King Edward!* And that oak leaf is about shot anyway," Anne said. Ignoring curious stares from passers-by, she dumped a handful of brown oak leaf fragments from her purse into the nearest ashtray. Both were laughing while she did it, acting drugged, drunk, or both. Like scavengers at a Dumpster, a couple of young stoned hippies quickly moved to the ash tray, and were thoroughly checking Anne's recent discard. Mark Telfair knew he was still the luckiest man alive.

After an amorous and rambunctious reunion at Anne's apartment, they headed to Lennox Square, a large shopping mall in Northeast Atlanta near Mark's mom's home. The jewelry stores were so crowded with Christmas shoppers, they decided to wait until later, and come back when the crowds thinned. In the meantime, Mark wanted to take Anne to his mother's home to introduce his mom to her future daughter-in-law. Mom had absolutely no knowledge of their four-year relationship. Mark had intentionally kept it that way.

While driving Anne's car to his mom's house, Mark felt a little uneasy, but finally spoke. "Anne, I know we haven't discussed my mother at length, but please, for God's sake, don't tell her we've been living together. She hasn't accepted the morality of the '60s, and probably never will. She really got bent out of shape about my old girlfriend, the one I've told you about who lived with me when I was out in my Brookhaven apartment."

"Mark, don't worry about it. I know I'm very lucky with my own mother. She's one who moves with the times, and she knows we've been living together. 'Try it before you buy it,' she told me on the phone. That was shortly before I asked you to move into my apartment. It's my devoutly Catholic father who has the same problems as your mom, and *he* certainly doesn't know we've lived together. If he did, it would break his heart. But I love him anyway. You can be assured my mother hasn't told my dad anything about our living arrangement, and I certainly won't say a word about it to your mom. So, relax!"

Anne and Mark's mom immediately hit it off, possibly because their first names were identical—both "Anne" with an "e" at the end. His mom seemed delighted when Mark told her he and Anne were going to get married. Possibly it was because Mark's Anne was an RN, a title of distinction, one that deserved to marry her little-boy doctor son. In any event, Mark's mother immediately decided she should be called "Mom" by Mark's Anne. After the third round of hot toddies, lunch, and a quick catchup regarding very carefully censored details of their Grady courtship, Mom casually spoke. "Anne, would you be offended if I offered Mark a family ring? One that he could give to you as your engagement ring?"

"I'd be honored, Mom, if that's all right with Mark." *I've got to be the luckiest man alive,* Mark thought again, wondering when his seemingly endless luck would run out.

Mom scurried up the stairs, and returned a few minutes later with the very expensive replacement engagement ring Mark's father had given her on their 25th wedding anniversary—an upgrade from the inexpensive original they could barely afford during the depression years when they'd become engaged.

Amid tears and smiles—from both Anne and Queen Mom Anne— Mark removed the King Edward cigar band, and slid the ring onto Anne's finger.

"It's beautiful!" Anne said as she studied the large diamond in the light.

"What's that thing?" Mom asked, looking at the cigar band Mark was trying to conceal in his hand.

Mark handed the paper band to Mom, who was obviously still feeling her toddies. She studied it a moment, then exclaimed, "God Almighty, Anne! I swear I didn't raise that boy that way. I think you've got your hands full, young lady. I hope you'll be more successful than I've been at making him socially aware!"

"Well Mom, the cigar band beat the heck out of the oak leaf I had *before* that." Mark's Anne laughed, still feeling her toddies too.

Mom shook her head in mock disgust, then laughed. Mark and Anne fabricated a socially acceptable story about the oak leaf. They continued talking nonstop until it was time for the supper jointly prepared by Anne and Mom. By the time they finished their meal, a May date had been set for their wedding. *When a dam breaks—it really breaks!* Mark thought, feeling his bachelorhood definitely on the ebb.

Promising to visit Mom each day of Mark's Atlanta visit, the couple returned to Anne's apartment. In the interest of social propriety befitting Queen Mom Anne, Mark allegedly would be staying with some of his old Grady buddies during his Atlanta visit. From Anne's apartment, they first called her family in Orlando, then a number of Atlanta friends, to let them know they had chosen May 2nd as the date, and McCoy Air Force Base Chapel in Orlando as the place. Before the May wedding, both decided it would be a good idea for Anne to secretly fly to Oscoda in February and check out the off-base apartment which would become her new home following their wedding.

At nine in the evening, about two months later, in late February, Anne's plane touched down at Tri-City in Michigan. Mark was there to eagerly greet her. She'd been the only passenger on that leg of the Northwest Airlines commuter flight ... and they had managed to lose her luggage during a plane change in Detroit. With hormones raging, they spent most of the cold night in the little airport terminal. They considered a quick trip to the camper in the frozen parking lot, but didn't go, feeling they'd probably manage to lose her bags again if they even briefly left the terminal. At sunrise, her luggage finally caught up with them at Tri-City. The two-hour drive north to Oscoda seemed to take forever, but they finally arrived at Mark's apartment on frozen Lake Huron.

"This is really a cozy place, but I've never seen this much snow and ice in my life," Anne remarked, teeth chattering, as she studied the frozen expanse of Lake Huron through the balcony's sliding-glass door.

"Well, we'll make enough heat to melt it all," Mark said, his serum testosterone level dangerously high.

And they did. Or at least tried. Maybe they didn't actually melt anything in the physical sense, but psychologically the cold seemed to disappear. Mark could finally see some real beauty in the winter landscape. Anne's being there made the difference.

But it was only after Anne left Oscoda to return to Atlanta that Mark fully realized how much difference her presence made in his life. Now over all doubts about relinquishing his bachelorhood, he found himself eagerly anticipating the trip south to Orlando for their wedding. He only wished he could make the time go faster.

27

COMMITMENT AND CONFINEMENT

During Anne's absence, Mark continued following Lebowitz's advice, just going with the system, just marking time until it passed. Finally, it did. Speeding things along, he'd even been lucky enough to find a free hop to Orlando aboard one of Wurtsmith's KC-135s, headed to McCoy AFB for some type of special retrofitting. That plane ride alone had eliminated the only remaining objection to going south to marry Anne: the long drive from Oscoda to Orlando.

After their May 2nd wedding in Orlando, with Zack as best man, Mouse as maid of honor, and Adrian and Jer as ushers, they had a brief honeymoon at Cocoa Beach, Florida. For both Mark and Anne Telfair, the events surrounding their wedding would always remain an obscure blur, a simple technical event, one of social convention, a mere legal formality, an occasion primarily designed to keep both Anne's proper Catholic dad, and Mark's Queen Anne Presbyterian mother happy.

As for themselves, they'd always feel they had actually become married beneath the branches of a giant oak tree located in North Georgia ... at *Possum Trot.* Beneath that tree Mark and Anne had struggled with strong emotions, and powerful words like *commitment* and *confinement.* But those words had quickly become nonissues for them both. After *Possum Trot,* they'd rapidly realized their minds were already inseparably joined. Any further ceremony would simply be anticlimactic, and wouldn't improve the union that already existed naturally. For Mark Telfair, that union began the fateful day his scrubs fell down in the Grady OR ... and he saw her beautiful, totally unforgettable hazel eyes; for Anne Telfair, God only knows why she was attracted to him, especially since he'd so rudely called her a "dumb broad" upon their very first meeting.

Less than a week following the honeymoon, Mark used additional leave time and a small U-Haul truck to move themselves and Anne's possessions from Atlanta to Oscoda. Anne sold her four-year-old Dodge Dart to a friend before the move. Placing her furniture and other possessions in the sparsely appointed Oscoda apartment converted it into a home. She instantly fit in, not only with the medical group, but with Mark's friends off the base as well. Anne became a civilian nurse at the base hospital. Spring melted into summer. SCUBA lessons at the base, motorcycle rides in the forest, canoe trips on the beautiful *Au Sable* River, fishing for salmon in Lake Huron, short trips to Canada, all filled their abundant free time.

One pleasantly warm Sunday afternoon found them both off duty and sitting on their second-floor apartment balcony. Sipping freshly made martinis, they were absorbing Lake Huron's late afternoon summer beauty. Anne was obviously in very deep thought.

"Little Man, I've been thinking about something," she said, wearing a dreamy wistful look, her gaze fixed at some point far out in the placid lake.

"What's on your beautiful mind?" Mark said, feeling totally relaxed.

"Well, I'm thinking about how my mind seems to be changing."

"Changing? About what?" Mark replied, feeling a little insecure about what Anne meant by *changing*.

"Well, I've been thinking about small towns ... how nice the folks are, about not having a bunch of traffic lights, and how it's always easy to find a place to park. I've been thinking about how everybody knows their neighbors, and you never see a stranger in the grocery store. Everybody seems to really *care* about everyone else. Have you noticed that, Little Man?"

Relieved, Mark paused a beat before speaking. "Uh ... yeah, sure. I've been having exactly those same thoughts. I guess I've been a little hesitant to tell you, but my mind seems to be changing too. When we talked at *Possum Trot*, we both thought we'd probably want to end up in Atlanta. We both felt we had that pretty well settled. Remember?"

"Sure, I remember that too. I also remember how I felt after I'd finished my first year at nursing school. I'd promised myself I'd never let myself do two things: First, I'd never marry a doctor! They're all stuck-up, all too conceited, I thought. Second, especially after seeing Atlanta, I swore I'd never again live in a small town, like Orlando used to be ... before Disney came in and screwed it up. So, Doctor, I've already broken the first of my promises by marrying you. And in the short time I've been in this small town, my mind seems to want to break my second promise too."

"Anne, as pretty and as friendly as Oscoda is, and even having as much fun as we have here, I just couldn't live here permanently ... because of the winters. I gotta have more than two months a year without snow. And I certainly don't want to get my grits by mail order the rest of my life!"

"Little Man, I'm not talking about Oscoda. I'm talking about some *other* small town, one that has mild winters and a fine little hospital. Maybe somewhere in the South. Perhaps in Georgia, Florida, Alabama, Mississippi ... somewhere like that."

Mark was relieved ... relieved at how their minds always seemed to join, then rejoin if they'd somehow briefly separated. "Well, we've still got plenty of leave time left, and less than a year to go in the Air Force. It's certainly not too early for us to start looking at small towns."

Anne promptly gave him a warm kiss that lingered. "And I been thinking about something else too, Little Man."

"Such as?" Mark asked, feeling certain starting a family was next on her agenda.

"Well, with all that's happened to us at Grady, to me at nursing school, to you at Emory and the VA—just all those crazy times we've had, the stories and friends we both know—all that stuff should be written down in a book for the less fortunate to enjoy."

"Anne, get serious. Just when would I—or *we*—ever find the time to do that?"

"Maybe when we retire. Maybe when we get too old for sex. You know, if we'd spent as much of our free time writing as we presently do in bed, we'd probably be on page one zillion by now."

"You complaining?" Mark asked, chuckling.

"Not one bit! We'll just get to it when it's *time* to get to it."

"I suppose you already have a book title in mind?" Mark asked, teasingly.

"Yeah," she replied, "I think so. I'd just call it *Going to the Gradies* ... I guess we'd have to wait and see if private practice in a small town deserves its own separate book. Maybe we could call a second book *Beyond the Gradies,* or something like that."

Mark paused. "I'm gonna fix myself another martini. Could I get you another, or perhaps something else?" Mark casually asked, preparing to go back inside to refresh drinks.

"Little Man, I'd really prefer something else." Anne seductively smiled, as she stood to follow him inside.

They both grinned as he opened the balcony's sliding-glass door. *At this rate, we'll never write the first book ... much less a second!* Mark thought.

Made in the USA
Lexington, KY
08 June 2013